£10
0089

One Island,
Two Nations?

GEOGRAPHICAL RESEARCH STUDIES SERIES—STUDIES IN POLITICAL GEOGRAPHY

Series Editor: **Dr Peter J. Perry**
Reader in Geography, University of Canterbury, New Zealand

One Island, Two Nations?

A political geographical analysis of the national conflict in Ireland

D. G. Pringle
St. Patrick's College, Maynooth, Ireland

RESEARCH STUDIES PRESS LTD.
Letchworth, Hertfordshire, England
JOHN WILEY & SONS INC.
New York · Brisbane · Chichester · Toronto · Singapore

RESEARCH STUDIES PRESS LTD.
58B Station Road, Letchworth, Herts. SG6 3BE, England

Marketing and Distribution:

Australia, New Zealand, South-east Asia:
Jacaranda-Wiley Ltd., Jacaranda Press
JOHN WILEY & SONS INC.
GPO Box 859, Brisbane, Queensland 4001, Australia

Canada:
JOHN WILEY & SONS CANADA LIMITED
22 Worcester Road, Rexdale, Ontario, Canada

Europe, Africa:
JOHN WILEY & SONS LIMITED
Baffins Lane, Chichester, West Sussex, England

North and South America and the rest of the world:
JOHN WILEY & SONS INC.
605 Third Avenue, New York, NY 10158, USA

Library of Congress Cataloging in Publication Data:

Pringle, D. G. (Dennis Graham)
   One island, two nations?
   (Geographical research studies series; 5)
   Bibliography: p.
   Includes index.
   1. Ireland—Politics and government.   2. Nationalism—
Ireland—History.   3. Ireland—History—Autonomy and
independence movements.   I. Title.   II. Series.
DA938.P75   1985   941.508   85-8267
ISBN 0 86380 029 7
ISBN 0 471 90789 8 (U.S.)

British Library Cataloguing in Publication Data:

Pringle, D. G.
   One island, two nations? a political geographical
   analysis of the national conflict in Ireland.—
   (Geographical research studies series. Studies in
   political geography; 5)
   1. Nationalism—Ireland—History
   I. Title   II. Series
   320.5'4'09415   DA938

ISBN 0 86380 029 7

ISBN 0 86380 029 7 (Research Studies Press Ltd.)
ISBN 0 471 90789 9 (John Wiley & Sons Inc.)

Printed in Great Britain

This book is dedicated
to the memory of my father,
John Gavey Pringle (1923-1982).

Editor's Preface

This series comes into existence as the result of a
decade's experience of teaching political geography at the
undergraduate level. That experience has convinced me
that the scarcity of research monographs in the field, by
comparison with other branches of geography and with what
is now an abundance of textbooks and an adequacy of
research papers, is an obstacle to be overcome if this
particular branch of geography is to be well taught at any
level. I come to the series then as a teacher whose
experience has armed him with the conviction that exposure
of students to the fruits of current research activity at
an early stage of their undergraduate career is an
essential characteristic of university education. I am
equally convinced that the geographical dimension of
current affairs has too often been neglected in public
debate, at our peril and often by our default. The
missing contribution in otherwise well informed analysis
of the contemporary world in the media is almost
invariably that of the political geographer, and its
absence often serves seriously to weaken or undermine the
structures erected by the historian, economist,
sociologist and political scientist. This series
possesses then a practical as well as an academic aim and
is directed towards a readership outside as well as within
the universities. The study of political geography has
its part to play not only in the education of every
geographer but in the achievement of a 'just and lasting
peace among ourselves and with all nations'.

Peter Perry,
University of Canterbury,
Christchurch, New Zealand.

Author's Preface

This book is written as an introduction to the national
question in Ireland, both for readers overseas who have
little knowledge of the background to the present conflict
and for readers within Ireland who until now may not have
thought too much about its underlying causes. In writing
this book, I have adopted a long-term historical
perspective so as to place the present conflict within a
broader context, but the book is not intended as a
history, or even an historical geography, of Ireland. It
is not my intention to encourage further the preoccupation
which many Irish people would appear to have with the
past, resulting in it being fetishised in studies which
examine history in isolation and as an end in itself. The
past is of interest here only to the extent that it
provides a better understanding of the forces which are
unfolding at present while in the process of creating the
future.

Given that this book covers a period of almost two
thousand years in the space of only a few chapters, the
approach adopted is obviously somewhat sweeping. This, I
believe, serves the major objective in writing the book,
which is to outline as clearly as possible an alternative
perspective on the national conflict in Ireland. Although
many sections could be expanded considerably, especially
those dealing with events in the last two decades, I
believe that the approach adopted has the merit of
highlighting the major arguments (summarised as five
theses on page 25) and therefore presents them more
clearly than a more detailed work might do. Nevertheless,
the approach adopted is probably too swashbuckling for
most historians' taste. Many sections will no doubt cause
historians to suck breath in sharply through clenched
teeth, due to the way in which I have insensitively

x

disregarded ongoing debates about the finer details of
certain topics. Also, the lack of detail in some areas,
partly due to space considerations, possibly renders some
of the arguments made in the text less convincing than
they might otherwise be. These limitations, however, can
hopefully be remedied at some future date if the book
succeeds in generating a fruitful discussion about the
major theses outlined herein.

Given the broad scope of the subject matter, the list of
references could have been as long as the book itself.
References have consequently been kept to a minimum.
Apart from indicating the sources of quotations, I have
limited the works cited to those which I personally found
to be the most informative or stimulating.

Like all authors, I must acknowledge the assistance of
numerous people who have helped me in writing this book.
Several people read drafts of different sections of the
book. I would like to thank John Coakley, Paddy Duffy,
Jackie Hill, Andrew Maclaran, and Séamus Ó Síocháin in
this regard. Their comments, while maybe not fully
welcomed at the time, proved very useful in producing the
final version. Special thanks, however, must be given to
Proinnsias Breathnach - not only did he read the entire
book, but he had the dubious honour of reading the very
first draft of each chapter. The changes made as a result
of his extensive comments and spelling corrections made
life much less difficult for all subsequent readers.

I would also like to thank the following who helped in
various ways: Paul Ferguson for drawing the maps and
diagrams, in some cases at very short notice; the
Maynooth Scholastic Trust and College Executive Council
for their financial assistance towards the cost of
production; the staff in the Maynooth Computer Centre for
their advice and technical expertise; Peter Perry, the
series editor, for his patience over a very long period of
time and his reassuring comments on earlier drafts; and
Veronica Wallace in Research Studies Press for her prompt
and helpful replies to my enquiries and for not reminding

me (each year!) that I had exceeded my deadline.

Finally, and most of all, I would like to thank my wife
Rosaleen for her continuous support throughout and for
looking after the Pringlettes on the many occasions when
pressure of work forced me to keep unsociable hours.

D. G. Pringle.
16th. January, 1985.

Contents

List of Figures

List of Tables

List of Abbreviations

BICO	British And Irish Communist Organisation.
DUP	Democratic Unionist Party.
EEC	European Economic Community.
GAA	Gaelic Athletic Association.
ICO	Irish Communist Organisation.
INLA	Irish National Liberation Army.
IRA	Irish Republican Army.
IRB	Irish Republican Brotherhood.
NICRA	Northern Ireland Civil Rights Association.
NILP	Northern Ireland Labour Party.
OUP	Official Unionist Party.
RIC	Royal Irish Constabulary.
RUC	Royal Ulster Constabulary.
SDLP	Social Democratic And Labour Party.
UDA	Ulster Defence Association.
UDR	Ulster Defence Regiment.
USC	Ulster Special Constabulary.
UVF	Ulster Volunteer Force.
UWC	Ulster Workers Council.

Conventions

The terms 'Nationalist' and 'Unionist', spelt with a capital letter, refer to the political parties of that name in Northern Ireland. The terms 'nationalist' amd 'unionist', beginning with a lower case letter, generally refer to the Irish nationalist and Ulster unionist communities in the broader sense (i.e. to the Irish and Ulster nations, as defined in Chapter 2). The term 'nationalist' is sometimes used to refer to nationalists in general (i.e. to everyone who subscribes to the general nationalist ideology, irrespective of their nationality).

An attempt has been made to define the most important terms within the text.

CHAPTER 1
Introduction

Numerous events in Northern Ireland since 1968 have
attracted the attention of politicians and political
commentators throughout the world: civil rights protests;
street rioting; the introduction of the British army; IRA
bombing of business premises; internment without trial;
the abolition of Stormont and the introduction of direct
rule from Westminster; sectarian and political
assassinations; the Ulster Workers Council strike; H Block
protests and the hunger strikes; 'supergrass' trials; and
so forth. The continuing violence and political turmoil,
euphemistically referred to as the 'troubles', has
affected life for everyone in Northern Ireland. Apart
from those who have been injured or who have lost friends
or relatives, people have had to adapt to the
inconvenience of being searched at shop doorways, to live
with the risk of personal injury, and to adjust to various
other subtle changes in the whole fabric of life. Yet,
with a few notable exceptions, the 'troubles' have
attracted surprisingly little professional interest from
geographers. This book, which is an attempt to trace the
historical origins and evolution of the Irish national
question from a political geographical perspective, is
written in the conviction that geographers, working within
a broad multidisciplinary framework, have a potentially
useful contribution to make to an understanding of the
present conflict.

Like many conflicts, the 'troubles' in Northern Ireland
are complex and multifaceted. Although the problem is
largely political in nature, it would be a delusion to
believe that it is readily amenable to a political
solution. A political initiative of some sort is, of
course, an essential prerequisite, but a comprehensive
solution would need to take due cognizance of economic,
sociological and even psychological factors. For example,
it is important to remember that many of those actively
involved in paramilitary activities are not old enough to
remember the relatively peaceful times before 1968. As in
Vietnam, a whole generation has been reared in a culture
in which violence is an accepted part of normality:
memories of past aggressions are long lasting and call out
for revenge; peace is a much more difficult concept. It
must also be remembered that were it not for the
'troubles' many of those most actively involved in
violence would be confined to a degrading life on the dole
because of chronic unemployment: paramilitary activities
not only provide some with a certain type of status in
their local community, but may even provide a degree of
financial substance through protection racketeering.

Problems of this type will eventually need to be faced
if a lasting peace is to be secured. However, there is
little that can be done to tackle these problems so long
as the basic underlying problem remains. It is argued in
this book (and, I believe, generally accepted) that the
major problem is seen to be the national question. This
book represents an attempt to provide an alternative
analysis of the Irish national question from a political
geographical perspective.

There are essentially two objectives in writing this
book. The first is to provide an historical introduction
to the Irish national question for readers in other
countries. The issues involved, and the reasons for these
issues, would appear to be very poorly understood by many
people outside Ireland. For example, many overseas
observers would appear to regard the present conflict in

Northern Ireland as a straightforward struggle between the
British government and the oppressed Irish people
(represented by the IRA) who live in 'British occupied
Ireland' (i.e. Northern Ireland). This impression, which
is reinforced by Irish nationalist propaganda, is not
without some basis, but it is inadequate because it
totally ignores the fact that the majority of people
living within Northern Ireland regard themselves to be
British rather than Irish. It is the refusal of this
majority within Northern Ireland to be taken over by what
they regard as a foreign country, rather than the refusal
of the British government to grant independence to one of
its 'colonies', which forms the major barrier to the
political re-unification of Ireland.

The second objective is to encourage people in Ireland
to examine the national question from a new, non-
nationalistic, perspective. Events in Ireland are usually
interpreted from either an Irish nationalist or an Ulster
unionist perspective, but both ideologies impose a narrow
vision which results in only a partial understanding of
the overall situation. A full understanding of the Irish
national question, it is argued, requires one to transcend
the limitations imposed by nationalistic interpretations
by locating the analysis of the conflict within a
long-term historical context.

The remainder of chapter one is divided into five
sections. The major features of the national question in
Ireland are outlined in the first section. This is
followed, in the second section, by a brief review of the
principal arguments put forward from a nationalistic
perspective by each side in the conflict. Various
possible outcomes of the conflict are then examined in the
third section, but it is argued that none of these
scenarios appears to offer a feasible solution which would
satisfy the nationalistic aspirations of both sides. This
means that the conflict cannot be resolved in the
foreseeable future if both sides continue to view the
question from a nationalistic perspective. It is

therefore argued in the fourth section that, if it is to
be resolved, the conflict must be analysed from an
alternative, non-nationalistic perspective. This is the
objective of the remainder of this book. The structure of
the book is outlined in the final section.

THE NATIONAL QUESTION IN IRELAND

The national question in Ireland focuses upon the
constitutional position of Northern Ireland. Although a
relatively small island, Ireland is politically divided
between two sovereign states (Figure 1). The Republic of
Ireland, with a population of 3.5 millions in 1981, has
sovereignty over 26 counties (i.e. approximately 80 per
cent of the total area). The capital, and largest city,
is Dublin. The remaining 6 counties, with a population of
1.5 millions, comprise Northern Ireland and are part of
the United Kingdom. Between 1921 and 1972 Northern
Ireland had a regional parliament at Stormont in Belfast,
but this has been abolished and replaced by 'direct rule'
from London in more recent years.

The United Kingdom makes no claims to the territory of
the Republic of Ireland, partly because the territory of
Northern Ireland is already larger than could be justified
by reference to the national allegiance of the inhabitants
in border regions. (See the sub-section below on
'repartition' for further details). The Republic of
Ireland, however, has a territorial claim to the whole of
Northern Ireland. It is the wish of most people in the
Republic that the political unification of Ireland should
be peaceful and only with the consent of the Northern
Ireland majority, but the Constitution of the Republic of
Ireland, written in 1937, is less compromising. Article 2
of the Irish Constitution states:

> 'The national territory consists of the whole
> island of Ireland, its islands and the
> territorial seas.'

5

FIG. 1   Political Divisions.

Article 3 of the Constitution reinforces this territorial
claim:

> 'Pending the re-integration of the national
> territory, and without prejudice to the right of
> the Parliament and Government established by
> this Constitution to exercise jurisdiction over
> the whole of that territory, the laws enacted by
> that Parliament shall have the like area and
> extent of application as the laws of Saorstát
> Éireann (i.e. the Irish Free State) and the
> like extra-territorial effect.'

This implies that unification is to be achieved by the
incorporation of Northern Ireland into the Republic rather
than by a negotiated merger between the two parts.

The claim of the Republic of Ireland to the territory of
Northern Ireland is made against the wishes of about two
thirds of the people living in Northern Ireland, as
indicated by the results of every general election in
Northern Ireland since partition. Confirmation was also
provided by a referendum held in 1973. The referendum
resulted in a low percentage poll (59 per cent), mainly
because of a boycott organised by Irish nationalists.
Nevertheless, a clear majority (57.4 per cent of the total
electorate, or 98.9 per cent of those who voted) voted in
favour of the continuation of the union with Britain and
against a united Ireland. Thus, the majority in Northern
Ireland, most of whom are Protestant, are unionists who
are basically content with the present constitutional
arrangements, although some would prefer the return of a
regional parliament within the United Kingdom; whereas the
minority in Northern Ireland, most of whom are Catholic,
are Irish nationalists who favour some form of unification
with the Republic, although they would not necessarily
favour an extension of the existing Republic to the whole
of Ireland. Given that the Republic of Ireland is
nominally about 95 per cent Catholic, it follows that
national allegiances in Ireland closely follow religious
affiliations: Catholics in general favour a united

Ireland, whereas Protestants in Northern Ireland favour
the continuation of partition. (It should be noted,
however, that the small Protestant minority in the
Republic would appear to be quite content as citizens of
the Republic, and probably very few would be averse to a
united Ireland).

CLAIMS AND COUNTERCLAIMS

The reasons for the territorial claim of the Republic of
Ireland to the whole of Northern Ireland, against the
wishes of the majority of the people in Northern Ireland,
are rarely articulated, but at least three different lines
of argument may be identified. Each line of argument
frequently appears in slightly different forms, and in
some instances some forms of one argument may appear to
contradict other arguments. This, however, is not
unexpected given that there are a number of different
factions within Irish nationalism which desire a united
Ireland for different reasons and whose ideas of what form
a united Ireland should take differ considerably.
Nevertheless, it is useful to summarise the major
arguments, albeit in a somewhat generalised and simplified
form.

1a) The Natural Unit Argument. It is argued that, by
virtue of being a small island, Ireland is a natural
political and economic unit and therefore it should not be
divided between two states. It is also argued that
unification would be mutually beneficial to both parts of
Ireland. There are several variations on this theme.
Republican socialists, for example, argue that unification
would facilitate a more purposeful struggle against the
dependency of both parts of the island upon British
imperialism; whilst more conservative groups argue that
business and farming interests would benefit from cost
sharing and a larger home market. It should perhaps be
stressed that this belief in the benefits of unification

to both parts of Ireland, irrespective of whether or not
it is linked to socialism, is probably a genuine belief
for most Irish nationalists rather than merely a
propaganda exercise to legitimise what is regarded by the
Northern Ireland majority as an aggressive territorial
claim.

2a) The Historical Argument. It is argued that Ireland
was politically united in the past before the 'British'
intervened in Irish affairs. The British should therefore
withdraw and return Northern Ireland to the Irish. It is
not too clear what is to happen to the Northern Ireland
Protestant majority who regard themselves as British. The
general opinion seems to be that the Protestants will be
encouraged to remain as fellow Irishmen, but more extreme
minority variants on this theme envisage a mass
repatriation of the Protestants to Britain.

3a) The One Nation Argument. It is argued that all of
the inhabitants in both parts of Ireland form part of a
single Irish nation. The Protestant minority of this
nation do not have the right to opt out of the nation,
even if they form a majority in part of the national
territory. Following the principle of the right of
nations to self-determination, this nation has a natural
right to a state which includes all members of the nation
(i.e. a united Ireland).

Each of these arguments is countered by a corresponding
argument by Ulster unionists (i.e. the mainly Protestant
Northern Ireland majority).

1b) The Natural Unit Argument. It is argued that the
notion of a natural political or economic unit is an
extreme form of physical determinism which totally ignores
the wishes and needs of the people living in the contested
region. Political and economic units are man-made: they
are not natural units. Indeed, it is argued that, in the
case of Ireland, regional economic divergence since at
least the mid-nineteenth century is one of the major
reasons why the island does not comprise a single

political unit at present. (This argument is developed in
more detail in Chapter 7). Besides, even if it was
accepted that physical units provide natural political or
economic units, one could just as easily argue that the
British Isles form a natural political unit (similar to
Japan or New Zealand) and that the Republic of Ireland
should therefore be reintegrated into the United Kingdom.
2b) The Historical Argument. The notion that the
entire island has ever formed a united political unit is
rejected by Ulster unionists. East Ulster, it is argued,

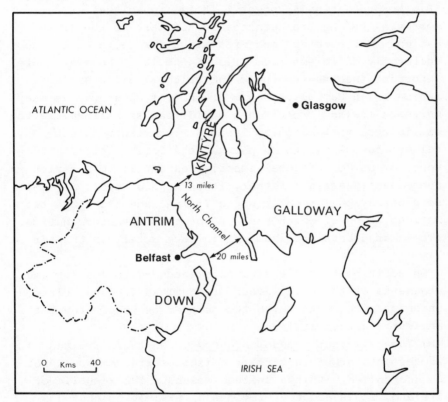

FIG. 2   The Situation Of Northern Ireland Relative To
          Scotland.

has been linked throughout history to Scotland (only 13
miles away by sea - Figure 2) rather than to the rest of

Ireland - communications over land with the rest of
Ireland were historically more difficult than those over
water to Scotland, especially before the widespread
development of roads in the eighteenth century. Political
units in history have not always recognised the sea as a
natural boundary, but have sometimes treated it as the
focus of kingdoms which straddled the North Channel (e.g.
the kingdom of Dál Riata in the 5th. to 8th. centuries,
and the lordship of the MacDonnells in the 15th. and 16th.
centuries).

3b) The One Nation Argument. It is argued that
Northern Ireland Protestants are not part of the Irish
nation. Northern Ireland Protestants are ethnically and
culturally different from Irish Catholics. However, more
important than these ethnic and cultural differences
(which Irish Catholics claim are not as clear-cut as many
Northern Ireland Protestants would like to believe) is the
simple fact that Northern Ireland Protestants do not
believe themselves to be part of the Irish nation. The
sense of common national identity essential to a nation is
consequently absent; rather, it is argued, there are two
sets of national identities in Ireland and therefore two
nations, each of which has a right to self-determination.
(These arguments are examined in more detail in Chapter
2).

In addition to these arguments intended to counter the
arguments of those in favour of a united Ireland, Ulster
unionists frequently make two further types of argument
against a united Ireland:

4b) The Religious Freedom Argument. Northern Ireland
Protestants argue that their religious freedom could not
be guaranteed within a united Ireland. The Republic of
Ireland, it is argued, provides an example of what
Northern Ireland Protestants could expect in a united
Ireland with a four to one Catholic majority. Although
the small Protestant minority in the Republic of Ireland
obtains some financial support for private schools from
the state, the bulk of the primary and secondary level

education system is controlled by the Catholic Church.
Catholic doctrine and moral values have found their way
into state legislation with little consideration given to
the civil liberties of the non-Catholic minority.
Divorce, for example, is prohibited under article 41 of
the Irish Constitution; until recently contraceptives
could only be obtained on a doctor's prescription; and
censorship, although now much more relaxed than
previously, is still quite strict, especially on material
pertaining to sexual matters. The Catholic Church also
exerts a high degree of control over the health system,
and is able to dictate in some cases the types of
operations which may or may not be performed. Although
many Northern Ireland Protestants might personally favour
the fundamentalist moral values in the Republic of
Ireland, the use of secular legislation to enforce the
beliefs of any religious group is regarded by most
unionists as a denial of civil liberties and as contrary
to Protestant beliefs in the freedom of choice governed by
personal conscience.

5b) The Economic Argument. Northern Ireland, as part
of the United Kingdom, has traditionally enjoyed a higher
standard of living than the Republic of Ireland, although
it has a lower standard of living than Britain. The
Northern Ireland majority, although conscious of their
inferior quality of life relative to the rest of the
United Kingdom, fears that a united Ireland would result
in a very real reduction in their living standards.
Although high unemployment in Northern Ireland has been
endemic since the creation of the state, the Northern
Ireland majority would point to the fact that they at
least have the full benefits of the British welfare state.
Welfare state benefits, including a national health
system, are superior to those available in the Republic
and are probably one of the major reasons why Northern
Ireland has not been as adversely affected by emigration
as the Republic. Direct and indirect taxation levels are
lower in Northern Ireland, with the result that the rate

of personal income tax and retail prices are generally
lower than in the Republic. Infrastructure (e.g. the road
and telephone systems) is also superior in Northern
Ireland and there are fears that the investment required
for esssential maintenance and improvements in Northern
Ireland would be deflected for development in what is now
the Republic in the event of a united Ireland. Space does
not permit a full inventory of the perceived economic
advantages of remaining outside a united Ireland, but it
suffices to say that the Northern Ireland majority see
few, if any, economic advantages in leaving the United
Kingdom, whereas they see numerous disadvantages in
unification (although not in economic co-operation) with
the Republic.

Needless to say, these arguments are not accepted by the
proponents of a united Ireland, resulting in two
counter-arguments from Irish nationalists:
4a) The Religious Freedom Argument. There are many in
the Republic who would accept that the Republic is in need
of major reforms to guard the civil liberties of
minorities, but it is sometimes argued that the very close
relation between church and state would not have been
possible if there had been a large non-Catholic minority
(as in a united Ireland) rather than a small non-Catholic
minority (as in the present Republic). It is also argued
that the Republic of Ireland originally became a Catholic
state in the 1920s and 1930s largely as a reaction to the
development of Northern Ireland as a Protestant state (see
Chapter 8): if Northern Ireland had not existed, the
Republic would not have been diverted from its development
into a secular republic. It is widely accepted within the
Republic (although the implications have probably not been
thought through) that a united Ireland would have to be
either a secular state or a pluralist state with realistic
safeguards for the freedom of minorities; a more pertinent
issue is whether these reforms should be implemented
within the existing Republic or whether they should be

deferred until a united Ireland is achieved (and thereby be offered as a concession to the Northern Ireland Protestants). It is also pointed out that, although the legislation of the Republic may enshrine Catholic values, there is very little, if any, active discrimination against non-Catholic minorities within the Republic; in Northern Ireland, on the other hand, although there is very little, if any, anti-Catholic legislation, there has been anti-Catholic discrimination in the activities of the state, especially in the spheres of employment and housing (although there have been major reforms since the late 1960s). One of the major emotive appeals for a united Ireland, in fact, is the appeal to Catholics in the Republic to liberate their oppressed co-religionists in Northern Ireland from Protestant oppression.

5a) The Economic Argument. Although it would be generally accepted within the Republic that Northern Ireland has traditionally had a higher standard of living, it is pointed out that the gap in living standards has closed rapidly during the past decade. Since 1958 the Republic has pursued a very active and successful policy of industrialisation by offering concessions to foreign industrialists. This has resulted in a very rapid growth in the industrial workforce, whereas Northern Ireland in the same period has seen a continual decline in its older and less competitive traditional industries. Entry into the E.E.C. has also provided a major boost for the Republic's very large agricultural sector, especially for beef and dairy farmers. The overall growth in the economy has been reflected in a fairly rapid expansion of the social welfare system; whereas in Northern Ireland, as in the rest of the United Kingdom, the trend would appear to be towards reducing the role of the welfare state. It would not be correct to say that disparities between the Republic and Northern Ireland have been totally eliminated (especially with respect to infrastructure), but the overall trend would at present appear to be towards convergence given the generally expansive nature of the

Republic's economy and the generally declining nature of
the Northern Ireland economy (which is not of course
helped by the continuation of the 'troubles'). It is
argued that unification, far from creating a reduction in
living standards in Northern Ireland, would create
economic growth in Northern Ireland due to the supposedly
complementary nature of the northern and southern
economies.

The arguments, as presented here, are by necessity
incomplete and many readers will no doubt feel that I have
not presented the arguments in favour of one side or the
other as fully as I should. The objective, however, is
not to argue in favour of one side or the other, but to
show that what appears to be reasonable and just to one
side is usually regarded as dogmatic or aggressive by the
other. The national question has polarised the population
of Ireland into Irish nationalist and Ulster unionist
camps, each of which regards itself to be in the right and
the other to be the source of the problem. The solution,
as seen by both sides, is for the other side to recognise
that it is being unreasonable. Unionists argue that the
Catholics in Northern Ireland should recognise that they
are better off within the United Kingdom, and should stop
challenging the existence of the Northern Ireland state;
whereas nationalists argue that Protestants should
recognise that they are being offered the hand of
friendship by their fellow Irishmen, and that the best
long-term solution for all is to agree to a united
Ireland. In other words, both sides argue that the best
solution is for the other side to give in. This, needless
to say, is at present highly unlikely.

POSSIBLE SCENARIOS

Given these arguments, it is pertinent to consider the
various possible outcomes of the conflict, even though the

evaluation must by necessity be to some extent
speculative. At least five possible territorial outcomes
may be identified.
1) A United Ireland. This would appear to be
extremely unlikely in the immediate future. The idea of a
united Ireland is totally abhorrent to the majority in
Northern Ireland for the reasons discussed in the previous
section. Given that Northern Ireland Protestants feel
that the guerrilla campaigns of the IRA and other
nationalist groups are directed at them as a community,
rather than at the agents of British imperialism as
claimed by the IRA, and given that the Republic of Ireland
is seen by the Northern Ireland majority as providing at
least tacit support for the IRA (e.g. by the retention of
articles 2 and 3 in the Irish Constitution), it is
extremely unlikely that the Protestants in Northern
Ireland will consider agreeing to the demands of those
perceived as attacking them.

A future united Ireland would not necessarily need to be
a unitary state like the present Republic. Some of those
in favour of a united Ireland would accept a federal
system in which Northern Ireland Protestants might retain
a high degree of autonomy. There are several
possibilities in this respect. One would be a federal
system based on the four provinces in Ireland, leaving
Protestants with a small majority in Ulster. A second
possibility would be to have only two federal units
corresponding to the present Republic and Northern
Ireland. This would guarantee a substantial Protestant
majority in the northern unit. Although a federal system
would help overcome many of the objections of the Northern
Ireland majority to a united Ireland, and would presumably
be much more acceptable than a unitary state, the proposal
does not overcome the basic problem that Northern Ireland
Protestants do not see any positive advantage in
unification with the Republic. Federation might counter
the cultural and religious objections of Northern Ireland
Protestants to a united Ireland, but it would not placate

their economic objections. A united Ireland, whether federal or otherwise, currently holds little attraction for the Northern Ireland majority. A further disadvantage of the federal solution is that the major proponent of the idea until recently was Provisional Sinn Féin (i.e. the political wing of the IRA). This in itself would discourage Northern Ireland Protestants from actively considering the idea, due to an instinctive reaction against anything which is in any way associated with the IRA.

The alternative to a united Ireland by consent is to try to achieve it by military force. This is unlikely to be successful for two reasons. First, there does not appear to be sufficient commitment in the Republic of Ireland to the ideal of a united Ireland by force. On the contrary, the majority of opinion within the Republic would appear to be strongly opposed to the terrorist tactics of the IRA. The situation might be different in the event of a civil war in Northern Ireland: there are many, for example, who might be prepared to defend fellow Catholics in Northern Ireland if they were attacked by the Protestant majority. Nevertheless, the commitment required for a long and sustained offensive would appear to be lacking in the Republic. Second, even if the IRA or the Irish government could mobilise enough support to take the offensive, it is doubtful whether they could win a military victory given the numerical superiority of the Northern Ireland Protestants in east Ulster - the area of greatest population density. An Irish army would probably win control of much of the peripheral parts of Northern Ireland, but the Protestants would appear to be much too numerous, well armed and spatially concentrated in the greater Belfast region to be defeated. Further, even if a military victory was possible, it is extremely unlikely that the Irish army could control the area against a Protestant resistance movement given the problems which the much larger British army currently has in trying to control the area against the numerically much smaller

Irish nationalist paramilitaries.

A united Ireland, in short, does not appear to be a realistic short term possibility unless there is a massive and, at present, highly unlikely shift in the attitude of the Northern Ireland Protestants.

2) A United British Isles. Given the reluctance of the Northern Ireland majority to be separated from the rest of the United Kingdom, and given the desire of the majority in the Republic for a united Ireland, the formation of a new state comprised of the present United Kingdom plus the Republic of Ireland might appear to satisfy both sides. There would probably be little opposition to the idea from the Northern Ireland majority, but the proposal would presumably gain little support from the Republic because the new state would inevitably be seen as a de facto extension of the United Kingdom. It would therefore represent a return to the pre-1920 situation. It is extremely unlikely that people in the Republic would be prepared to surrender their independence, even in the interests of Irish unity. The idea of a united British Isles, even in the form of a federation, has never been seriously considered by either side, and is simply included here for the sake of completeness.

3) An Independent Ulster. Despite repeated assurances to the contrary, there are many who doubt whether the British government has a genuine commitment to defend the wishes of the Northern Ireland majority to remain within the United Kingdom. This has inevitably raised the question as to what would happen if the British government decided to withdraw. The IRA and various other groups in favour of a united Ireland are of the opinion that Northern Ireland Protestants, if faced with the prospect of being abandoned by Britain, would be forced to accept a united Ireland as the only viable alternative. Northern Ireland Protestants, however, would appear to be of a different mind and most would probably opt for an independent Ulster in the event of a British withdrawal

(i.e. a new independent state roughly corresponding to
what is now Northern Ireland). Most Northern Ireland
Protestants, it should be stressed, would only contemplate
an independent Ulster as a fallback solution in the event
of Northern Ireland being expelled from the United
Kingdom: they would much prefer a continuation of the
existing United Kingdom. Nevertheless, an independent
Ulster would be regarded as considerably more attractive
than a united Ireland.

An independent Ulster holds even less appeal for
Northern Ireland Catholics. Although some would favour an
independent Ulster because it might prove to be
economically non-viable, and therefore represent an
interim step in the eventual formation of a united
Ireland, most Catholics would be extremely apprehensive
about the formation of an independent Ulster. Such a
state would automatically have a significant Protestant
majority and a presumably irredentist Catholic minority,
therefore the fear would be that, free of all possible
interference from Britain, an independent Ulster would
become an even more repressive state than Northern Ireland
was at the height of Unionist power. Also, given the
possibility that an independent Ulster would suffer from
very severe economic problems, it is likely, given the
history of Northern Ireland, that the bulk of the
resultant hardship would be felt most in the Catholic
community.

It is unlikely that an independent Ulster could be
created peacefully. If the Northern Ireland Protestants
attempted to create an independent Ulster, it is probable
that they would have to face armed resistance from the
Northern Ireland minority (possibly supported by the
Republic of Ireland). In the event of a civil war, the
new state would probably be considerably reduced in
territorial extent, compared with Northern Ireland at
present, because of the numerical superiority of Catholics
in the more peripheral parts. Although the Protestants
would probably be able to maintain control of the heavily

populated core in the greater Belfast area, the loss of extensive rural areas might exacerbate the economic problems of the new state. An independent Ulster, irrespective of its impact upon the Catholic community, would therefore be economically disasterous for the Protestant majority. It would also be a political disaster for Irish nationalists: an independent Ulster, especially one which was formed during a civil war, would form a strongly entrenched barrier, even in a spatially restricted form, to an eventual united Ireland.

In short, despite its attraction as a fallback solution to the Protestant majority, an independent Ulster, although probably feasible, has little to recommend it as an alternative to the existing situation.

4) Retention of the Status Quo. This is the most likely scenario in the immediate future, given the lack of popular support within Northern Ireland for scenarios 2 or 3 and the hostility of the Northern Ireland majority towards scenario 1. However, although several alternatives are possible within this scenario (e.g. greater or lesser degrees of devolution of power from Westminster), the retention of the status quo does not by itself appear to provide any long-term solutions.

The Northern Ireland majority, as noted above, would regard this scenario as by far the most preferable, but the current crisis arises because it is unacceptable to both the Catholic minority within Northern Ireland and to nationalists in the Republic. Irish nationalists regard Northern Ireland as part of the national territory, therefore the only acceptable long-term solution for them is a united Ireland; so long as Ireland is partitioned there will always be dissatisfied Irish nationalists. The continuation of the status quo is also unacceptable to Northern Ireland Catholics for a second reason: Northern Ireland Catholics regard the Northern Ireland state as corrupt and beyond reform, therefore they believe that they will continue to be regarded as second class citizens as long as the Northern Ireland state continues to exist.

Most of the original demands of the Northern Ireland Civil
Rights Association in the late 1960s were conceded by the
early 1970s, but the legislative changes have failed to
make a major impression upon the relative deprivation of
Catholics. Catholics argue that Northern Ireland is a
Protestant state for Protestant people and that as long as
it continues as such, de facto if maybe not de jure,
it can never gain the allegiance, or even the acceptance,
of the Catholic population.

There is, of course, a possibility that the aspirations
of those in favour of a united Ireland might in time
change. There is, for example, a detectable body of
opinion within the Republic which, while not opposed to
the idea of a united Ireland, no longer regards
re-unification as a major political objective: social
reforms within the Republic are regarded as more
important. If this body of opinion were to gain further
support within the Republic, it would help remove the
external threat to the Northern Ireland majority and the
question of social justice within Northern Ireland could
be more readily disentangled from that of the national
question. Alternatively, if the Catholic minority within
Northern Ireland could be convinced that they are equal
citizens and that they would be economically better off
remaining within the United Kingdom, it is possible that
they might no longer aspire to a united Ireland. However,
both types of change, while not beyond the bounds of
feasibility, are unlikely to take place within the
immediate future given the continuation of the current
conflict. We therefore have a Catch-22 situation -
changing aspirations only become feasible as a solution to
the conflict if there is no conflict to begin with, yet
the continuation of the status quo will guarantee that
there will be a conflict so long as the Northern Ireland
question is interpreted within a nationalistic framework.
5) Repartition. This fifth scenario is not an
alternative to the other four, but rather could be
complementary to either scenario 3 or scenario 4. It

entails redrawing the boundary between Northern Ireland
and the Republic taking greater account of the local
inhabitants' national allegiances in order to ensure that
as many people as possible end up living on the 'correct'
side. Repartition, as mentioned above, would be almost
inevitable in the event of an attempt to create an
independent Ulster, but it could also arise through
negotiation between the two governments under a
continuation of the status quo. Either way, the net
result would probably be much the same and would entail a
net loss of territory to Northern Ireland.

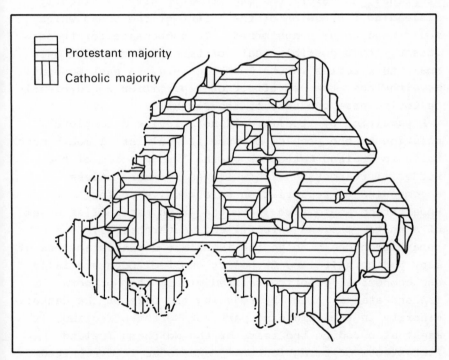

Protestant majority

Catholic majority

FIG. 3   Religious Affiliation In Northern Ireland.

The extent of the territorial loss can be gauged if one
assumes a high degree of correlation between national
identity and religious affiliation. Areas within Northern
Ireland with a Protestant or Catholic majority are shown

in Figure 3. If it is assumed that Catholics would opt to
join the Republic rather than remain in Northern Ireland,
Northern Ireland would clearly lose a considerable amount
of territory in regions close to the present border (e.g.
south Down, south Armagh, south Fermanagh and Derry's
Bogside). Northern Ireland would probably retain some
areas in Figure 3 with a Catholic majority to avoid the
creation of awkward enclaves within Northern Ireland (e.g.
in west Belfast and north Antrim). Also many of the areas
with a Catholic majority are mountainous areas of poor
land with a very low population density (e.g. the
Sperrins), therefore the map probably gives a slightly
misleading impression of the extent of the areas which
would need to be transferred. To compensate for these
losses, it is possible that Northern Ireland might gain
small territories in the Republic (e.g. in east Donegal).
Nevertheless, the net effect of repartition would clearly
be to increase the size of the Republic.

Repartition by itself would not provide a complete
solution to the problem because it would still leave most
Northern Ireland Catholics on the 'wrong' side of the
border, irrespective of how it was redrawn, unless
accompanied by repatriation on a massive scale.
Repartition would also leave the Irish nationalist dream
of a united Ireland unfulfilled. Nevertheless,
repartition could solve the immediate dissatisfactions of
many Northern Ireland Catholics who feel both spatially
and economically peripheralised within the Northern
Ireland state. Also, by reducing the size of the Catholic
minority in the remaining parts of Northern Ireland, it
might also reduce the fears of the Northern Ireland
Protestants of being 'outbred' and voted into a united
Ireland. This might then facilitate the development of
better relations between the two communities in Northern
Ireland, which in turn might result in a greater
acceptance of Northern Ireland by the Catholic minority.

TOWARDS AN ALTERNATIVE PERSPECTIVE

There would appear to be little possibility of a lasting solution to the conflict in Northern Ireland as long as both sides continue to see the problem in terms of nationalistic objectives. These nationalistic objectives are at present mutually incompatible, consequently there is very little scope for compromise. The objectives would also appear to be unattainable.

The ultimate goal of Irish nationalists is to achieve an independent united Ireland; any alternative outcome to the conflict would leave this goal unsatisfied and thereby create the conditions for further conflict. However, Irish nationalists do not have the military strength to capture and control the Protestant heartland in the greater Belfast area, even if the British government were to withdraw its troops from Northern Ireland. A united Ireland can therefore only be achieved with the consent of Northern Ireland Protestants, but this consent is unlikely to be forthcoming in the foreseeable future, partly because of the attempts of the IRA to achieve their objectives by force with what appears to Protestants to be the tacit support of the rest of the Irish nation.

Northern Ireland Protestants, on the other hand, do not have any unsatisfied nationalistic aspirations. However, although satisfied with the current political boundaries, their position is insecure and they are therefore under attack from the more militant sections of the Irish nation. Protestants do not have the military force to eliminate this threat to their security and economic well-being (without the loss of a substantial amount of territory in the event of a civil war), therefore their only alternative is to convince the Catholic minority in Northern Ireland that they have more to gain from supporting the continued existence of Northern Ireland than from campaigning for a united Ireland. This, however, is extremely unlikely under present conditions given a long record of second class citizenship for

Catholics within Northern Ireland since the creation of
the Northern Ireland state. Thus, in order to maintain
their independence from the Republic of Ireland, Northern
Ireland Protestants have to accept that the preservation
of partition must almost inevitably result in conflict
because the nationalist ambitions of the Irish nation are
left frustrated.

There is very little scope for compromise. Either
Northern Ireland is united with the present Republic of
Ireland or else it remains separate: there is no halfway
position which would be acceptable to both sides.
Consequently, given that neither side is capable of
defeating the other, the future for Northern Ireland would
appear to be one of continued unproductive violence and
counter-productive oppression for as long as the conflict
continues to be viewed from within a narrow nationalistic
framework. The only possibility of a solution would be
for both sides to approach the problem from a totally
different, non-nationalistic perspective. This book
represents an attempt to develop such a perspective.

This is not an easy task. There is a tendency,
especially strong in Ireland, to interpret the whole of
history from a nationalistic perspective because of the
dominance of nationalism as one of the most important, if
not the single most important, ideologies of the modern
era. However, nationalism is a relatively new ideology
which postdates many of the events which are frequently
interpreted from a nationalistic perspective;
consequently, the interpretation of these events from a
nationalistic perspective is often misleading, if not
actually meaningless. To understand the present conflict
in its entirety, it therefore becomes necessary to
interpret the events of the past within their proper
historical context.

The present 'troubles' are not only a conflict between
two groups of people: they are also a conflict between two
nationalistic ideologies. A complete understanding of the
conflict therefore requires one to understand how these

ideologies originated. This in turn requires one to
understand not only the reasons for the emergence of
nationalism in general, but to identify the reasons why
there should be two conflicting nationalistic ideologies
within Ireland. An understanding of the underlying root
causes of the present conlict in Ireland, from a
non-nationalistic perspective, will not by itself provide
a solution, but it is suggested that, unlike traditional
nationalistic interpretations, it does at least provide
the theoretical basis for an alternative initiative.

This book represents a preliminary attempt to trace the
origins and growth of two sets of national identity within
Ireland and the development of conflict between them from
a non-nationalistic perspective. The major theses of the
book may be summarised as follows:

1) There are two nations in Ireland, rather than one as
argued by Irish nationalists.

2) These nations cannot be traced back through history to
the beginning of time: they only came into existence
during the nineteenth century.

3) These two nations developed in Ireland in the
nineteenth century in response to struggles associated
with the growth and penetration of capitalism.

4) The major reason for the emergence of two nations in
Ireland is that northeast Ulster developed different
economic structures from the rest of Ireland during the
nineteenth century. The economic requirements in
northeast Ulster were consequently different from those in
the rest of Ireland. Different economic requirements gave
rise to different political requirements and ultimately a
different national identity.

5) There has been economic convergence between northeast
Ulster and the rest of Ireland during the present century.
The material basis for two different national identities
is therefore declining, but national identities have not
adjusted to reflect the changed circumstances because the
continuing conflict polarises people according to
'traditional' (i.e. nineteenth century) allegiances.

26

ORGANISATION OF THE BOOK

The remainder of this book is divided into eight
chapters. Concepts such as nation, state and nationalism
are reviewed in Chapter 2 to facilitate discussion of the
question of the number of nations in Ireland (i.e. thesis
1). Chapters 3 to 8 contain a historical review of the
political geography of Ireland since the early Christian
period. Chapter 3 looks at the period before the
establishment of effective English (later British) control
in Ireland by the Tudors and Stuarts. Chapter 4 then
discusses some of the implications of the establishment of
this control upon land-ownership and movements of
population into Ireland from Britain in the seventeenth
century. Chapter 5 examines the events in the eighteenth
century which culminated in the 1798 rebellion and the
union with Britain in 1801. These events provide an
important base-line because, it is argued, they clearly
demonstrate the then absence of either a single Irish
nation or of the present two nations (thesis 2), although
they were to prove instrumental in the later development
of national consciousness in Ireland. Irish nationalism
and Ulster unionism did not develop until the nineteenth
century. The growth of Irish nationalism is discussed in
Chapter 6 while the growth of Ulster unionism is discussed
in Chapter 7. It is argued that both developments reflect
a convergence of class interests within each area (thesis
3), but that these interests differed between north and
south because of a divergence in the nineteenth century
regional economies (thesis 4). The implications of the
conflict between the two nations in the present century,
as reflected by the creation of the Irish Republic and
Northern Ireland and the ways in which each has developed
politically and socially, is discussed in Chapter 8. It
is argued in the final chapter that changing conditions
have undermined the material basis of both Irish
nationalism and Ulster unionism, and that the continuing
conflict is therefore, in essence, historically irrelevant

(thesis 5). The book concludes with some speculations
about the implications of this analysis for the future.

CHAPTER 2
Nations, States and Nationalism

Irish nationalists often argue that almost everyone living in Ireland is a member of the Irish nation and that a minority of this nation (i.e. the unionists) do not have the right to opt out of the Irish nation state (i.e. the Republic of Ireland). Ulster unionists, on the other hand, usually argue that they are part of the British nation and that they consequently have a right to remain within the United Kingdom. The question as to whether there is one nation or two in Ireland therefore constitutes one of the most central areas of disagreement between Irish nationalists and Ulster unionists. This question is considered in the present chapter. The objective, however, is not to argue that one side is right and the other is wrong, but to lay the foundations for an analysis which can transcend both nationalistic (i.e. nationalist and unionist) interpretations.

Before discussing the question of the number of nations in Ireland, it is first necessary to consider what is meant by the term 'nation'. Irish nationalists and Ulster unionists are in general agreement about the major facts of the situation, but they disagree about how these facts should be interpreted. The debate as to the number of nations consequently arises because each side has a different concept of what constitutes a nation, although in each case the term 'nation' is rarely defined explicitly. An attempt is therefore made in the first section of this chapter to clarify what is meant by 'nation' and related concepts. The objective is not to define a 'nation' in such a way as to support the arguments of one side against the other, but to clarify the meaning of concepts, as used in this book, in order to avoid ambiguity. The question of the number of nations (as defined in section one (p.30)) in Ireland is then examined in the second section (p.39).

One reason why the debate as to the number of nations is so pertinent to the Irish national conflict is that both sides implicitly accept the principle of the right of nations to self-determination. The argument about the number of nations, therefore, is not purely academic: it is central to the attempts of both sides to legitimise their respective territorial claims by an appeal to a widely accepted democratic principle. However, this implicit acceptance of the right of nations to self-determination is also indicative of an unquestioning acceptance by both sides of a general nationalistic world outlook. A central theme of this book, in contrast, is that a full understanding of the Irish national question requires one to go beyond nationalistic interpretations. The third section in this chapter (p.49) therefore sets the scene for the remainder of the book by reviewing the growth of nationalism as a pervasive world ideology.

NATIONS AND STATES

The terms 'nation' and 'state' are frequently used in everyday conversation as if they were synonyms, but geographers and other social scientists normally acknowledge a fundamental distinction between the two concepts. A state loosely corresponds to what most people think of as a country, whereas a nation refers to a group of people who share certain characteristics (as discussed below). France, for example, is a state; whereas the French are a nation. The two terms, however, have become confused because nation-states (i.e. states largely

composed of a single nation) have become the predominant
state-form in recent times throughout the world. The term
'nation' is consequently used in many situations where the
term 'state' would be more accurate - the United Nations
Organisation, for example, should strictly speaking be
called the United States Organisation (although this would
obviously give rise to confusion of a different type!).
Both terms are now examined in more detail.

A state may be defined as an inhabited territory
effectively controlled by an indigenous sovereign
government. This definition contains several elements.
The first is territory - a state cannot exist without
territory. The boundaries between states may be subject
to dispute, but a state must have at least some territory
under its effective control otherwise it would cease to
have any existence. A second element is population - the
territory must be inhabited. A state cannot exist without
citizens. Thirdly, the territory must be effectively
controlled by an indigenous government (using the word in
its broadest sense to include the entire administrative
apparatus). It is incidental whether the government is
democratic or a dictatorship, but it must be indigenous -
i.e. it must originate from within the territory. The
major distinction between a colony and a state is that the
government of a colony is imposed from outside. Finally,
the government of a state should be sovereign. In other
words, the government of a state should be the supreme
authority beyond which there is no legal appeal.
Sovereignty is essentially a legalistic concept: in
practice the independence of a sovereign state may be
compromised by interference from other more powerful
states, or even partially surrendered in the course of
making international (i.e. inter-state) agreements.
Nevertheless, a territory does not constitute a state
unless its government is at least in theory the supreme
authority. This is the principal distinction between a
state and local government.

The term 'state' has increasingly been used in a second

sense in recent years. A state, as defined above, is an actual real-world political unit (i.e. a 'country'); the term 'the state' is frequently used in a more abstract generic manner to refer to the government (in its broadest sense) of states in general. The state can consequently be thought of as a collective name for the various structures and institutions required to govern a state. These include: the head of state; the executive; the legislature; the civil service; local government; the judiciary; the armed forces and police; and various other state and semi-state bodies and agencies. Recent research has tended to focus on the relationships between these various elements and also on the relationships between the state and society as a whole. The precise nature of the relationship between the state and the economy is still the subject of considerable debate, but it is clear that the state has increasingly intervened into almost every sphere of life in recent times and that control of the state is intimately related to social and economic power.

The word 'nation' has been used in various ways throughout history. It had a totally different meaning in the medieval period, for example, than it does at present. Also, historians sometimes use the word 'nation' loosely to refer to the inhabitants of a country in periods before these people fully acquired all of the characteristics of a modern nation. Historians, of course, are acutely conscious of the historical context of the period with which they are dealing and therefore implicitly recognise time-related variations in the meaning of words such as 'nation', but non-historians are often unaware of these shifts in meaning and may therefore erroneously assume a modern meaning which is inappropriate to the period under discussion. To avoid ambiguity, the word 'nation' will only be used in this book in its modern sense.

Although most social scientists make a clear distinction between a nation and a state, the term 'nation' has proved somewhat elusive to define. There is consequently no universally accepted definition of what a nation is,

although there is general agreement about some things
which it is not:
1) A race. Race is biologically determined by heredity
and is reflected by physical characteristics such as body
stature, facial features and skin colour; a nation, on the
other hand, is the product of social and political
processes. Common racial characteristics may act as a
stimulus to the development of a sense of national
identity, but they are by no means essential. Most
nations, in fact, are racially mixed.
2) A nation is not simply the name given to all the
inhabitants of a state. Despite the dominance of the
nation-state idea in the modern world, several states
remain multinational in composition (e.g. Yugoslavia).
Further, most nation-states contain minorities who would
not regard themselves as part of the dominant nation in
that state (e.g. the Magyars in Romania). Indeed, if a
nation was simply the name given to the inhabitants of a
state, the principle of the right of nations to
self-determination would be reduced to meaningless
tautology: the inhabitants of existing states would be the
only people with a recognised right to form a state and
this right would only continue so long as the state
continued to exist.
3) A nation is not simply the name given to the
inhabitants of a physical geographical region. The idea
of natural territorial frontiers is implicit in the
nationalist ideology of several nations (e.g. the French),
but all the people who live within these 'natural'
boundaries are not necessarily members of the same nation.
The existence of 'non-nationals' within the 'national'
territory, in fact, is a frequent source of conflict
between nations.
     Attempts to define a nation generally follow one of two
approaches. The first could be called the 'checklist'
approach. Checklist definitions define a nation as a
group of people who share a number of specified
attributes. The attributes vary from one definition to

another, but frequently used criteria include :
1) A common language;
2) A common culture (literature, folk traditions, etc.);
3) A common ideology (e.g. religion);
4) A common history, especially one in which the group was united against a common external threat;
5) An integrated economy; and
6) An identity with a common territory.

Stalin, for example, defined a nation as 'a historically evolved, stable community of language, territory, economic life and psychological make-up manifested in a community of culture' (Stalin, 1913). In other words, to be regarded as a nation under this definition, a group of people must satisfy a checklist of four 'objective' conditions (i.e. common language, territory, economy and culture).

The checklist approach reflects a positivist approach to science. The objective is to minimise subjectivity by defining a nation in such a way that the decision as to whether a group of people constitute a nation or not may be made by reference to a fixed set of objective criteria by someone external to the group. However, one of the major problems with checklist definitions is that they are inflexible and may therefore be misused for political objectives so as to argue that a particular group does not constitute a nation if they do not satisfy all of the criteria. The principal purpose of Stalin's definition, for example, was to argue that the Jewish Bund were not a nation because they did not have a territory, and that they therefore had no rights to self-determination. However, the same definition, and indeed any definition which makes a common language an essential condition, would deny that the Swiss are a nation due to the fact that the Swiss do not have a common first language - German, Italian, French and Romanche are spoken in different parts of Switzerland - yet the Swiss clearly regard themselves as a nation and are recognised as such by other nations. The major limitation of the checklist

approach is that it is impossible to identify a single set
of objective criteria to define a nation which would be
acceptable to everyone.

Checklist definitions are also deficient in other
respects. The fact that emphasis is placed upon objective
criteria often tends to detract from the importance of
subjective criteria - especially the belief within a group
that they are in fact a nation. Checklist definitions
consequently tend to define nations as if they were
natural and readily identifiable subdivisions of mankind,
irrespective of whether or not the people within each of
these subdivisions feel an affinity towards one another.
The quest for objectivity may therefore cause one of the
most pertinent features of a nation (i.e. a sense of
common identity) to be disregarded. Also, the fact that
checklist definitions tend to define nations as natural
subdivisions of mankind carries an implication that
nations, as we know them today, have always existed. Such
definitions are consequently inconsistent with a
perspective which accepts that nations have evolved into
their present form in the course of history.

The second approach is to let nations define themselves.
Following this approach, a group of people may be regarded
as a nation if they believe themselves to be a nation.
Seton-Watson, for example, argues that 'a nation exists
when a significant number of people in a community
consider themselves to form a nation, or behave as if they
formed one.' (Seton-Watson, 1977, p5). In other words, the
essential condition for a nation, under the
self-definition approach, is a sense of common identity.
A nation is therefore a type of community. However, it is
a special type of community: it is a community in which
the group cohesiveness is provided by a nationalist
ideology. The concept of a nation, following the
self-definition approach, cannot be fully understood
without examining what we mean by nationalism. Let us now
explore both concepts in more detail.

As in other types of community, the members of a nation

must feel an affinity towards other members of the group -
i.e. there must be a feeling of 'us'. This, however,
necessarily entails notions of exclusiveness: 'us' can
only be defined relative to 'them'. In other words, the
members of a nation must not only believe themselves to
have something in common with other members of the nation,
but they must also believe themselves to be different from
outsiders. These feelings of common identity and
distinctiveness may be strengthened by the existence of
some of the features listed in checklist definitions (i.e.
a common and distinctive language, culture, etc.), but
these features, with one exception, are not essential
prerequisites for the development of a nation.

The exception is territory: one of the major differences
between a nation and some other types of communities is
that nations are territorial communities. In other words,
the members of a nation not only identify with other
members of the group, but also with a particular territory
(the 'homeland'). This territory may be vaguely defined,
or it may even be contested with other nations, but a
territorial dimension is present in the identity of every
nation.

This gives rise to a second type of distinction between
nations and some other types of communities. The members
of a nation not only identify with a particular territory
- they also seek to maximise their political control over
it. Nations are therefore political communities. This
control might take the form of an independent nation-
state, but smaller nations may be prepared to accept a
more limited form of autonomy within a multinational
state.

A nation, however, is a particular type of
political-territorial community. Nations differ from
other types of political-territorial groups (e.g. tribes)
because their internal cohesiveness is provided by a
nationalist ideology, rather than by kinship or any other
cementing factor. Each nation has a unique nationalist
ideology which instils a common pride in the supposed

achievements and perceived positive qualities of that
particular nation, and which generates a desire to
maintain the group and to work together for the future.
National myths and legends often play an important role in
this respect: the story of William Tell, for example,
glorifies certain values perceived as important by the
Swiss nation. However, there are also a number of
implicit beliefs common to all nationalist ideologies.
These beliefs, which could be collectively termed the
'national ideal', include: a belief that legitimacy for
political power derives from the people (i.e. the nation);
a belief that nations are natural and unique subdivisions
of mankind; and a belief that each nation has a natural
right to self-determination. It is the acceptance of this
general nationalistic outlook (which is discussed in more
detail in the third section of this chapter) which
distinguishes a nation from other types of political and
territorial communities. Nations cannot exist without
nationalism. Given that nationalism is historically a
fairly recent phenomenon, it follows that nations as we
know them today are also relatively new.

Drawing these various points together, a nation could be
defined as 'a community of people, united by a nationalist
ideology, who identify with a territory and who seek to
maximise their political control over that territory'.
The essential feature is that the members of a nation
believe themselves to be a nation. The decision as to
whether a particular group of people constitute a nation
or not, following the self-definition approach, is made
internally by the group itself; whereas following the
checklist approach it is made externally by reference to
objective criteria.

An apparent limitation of the self-definition approach
is that it is incompatible with an unconditional
acceptance of the right of nations to self-determination.
If it is argued that each nation has a basic democratic
right to self-determination, and if one accepts (following
the self-definition approach) that any group of people

which thinks of itself as a nation is a nation, then one
might find oneself arguing that any group of people, no
matter how small, has an absolute right to self-
determination provided that they call themselves a
nation. The problem is unlikely to arise in practice
because a group of people are unlikely to regard
themselves as a nation unless they are likely to be
accepted as a nation by other nations, but a problem does
appear to exist - at least in theory.

This problem only arises if one accepts that all nations
have a natural right to self-determination. This,
however, is inconsistent with the philosophy underlying
the self-definition approach. The objective of the
exercise is not to define the features that a group of
people must have in order to qualify to have the right to
self-determination, but to indentify the salient features
of groups of people who in practice regard themselves as
nations. A nation is a real-world phenomenon which cannot
be defined out of existence; nor can a nation be said to
exist simply because certain objective criteria happen to
be present in a given instance. The purpose of a
definition is to descibe the principal features of these
real-world phenomena so as to clarify the conceptual
differences between nations and other types of groups,
rather than to set up a set of criteria which may be used
to decide if a particular group is or is not a nation.
The question as to whether one should support the demands
of a particular nation to self-determination is a
separate, and logically subsequent, issue. It would seem
to be more logical to evaluate the rights of each nation
to self-determination on its own merits, rather than to
assume that every nation has a natural right to
self-determination and then have to evaluate whether a
particular group which demands self-determination is or is
not a nation.

To summarise, although the checklist approach would at
first appear to be more objective, it is found to be
subject to a number of difficulties; the self-definition

approach, on the other hand, is more arbitrary, but it is
also more flexible and realistic. The self-definition
approach is therefore preferred here. Unless otherwise
stated, the term 'nation' is used in this book as defined
above following the self-definition approach.

Finally, some authorities make a distinction between a
'nation' and a 'nationality', where the term 'nation' is
reserved for groups who have achieved political
independence in the form of a nation-state, and the term
'nationality' is used to refer to groups who still aspire
to independence. However, this distinction does not
appear to be particularly useful: the principle of the
right of nations to self-determination, for example, would
be reduced to an empty tautology similar to that noted
earlier. The term 'nation' is therefore used in this book
to refer to both types of group, whereas the term
'nationality' is used simply to indicate membership of a
nation (e.g. a member of the French nation might be
referred to as having French nationality). Nationality,
as used here, should not be confused with the more
legalistic concept of 'citizenship' which refers to the
inhabitants of a state.

IRELAND: ONE NATION OR TWO?

Having considered what is meant by a nation, let us now
turn to the question of the number of nations in Ireland.
As noted above, there are basically two approaches to
defining a nation. Although the self-definition approach
is preferred, the question is considered here from both
perspectives so as to establish the number of nations in
Ireland as conclusively as possible in order to provide an
unambiguous starting point for the analysis in the
following chapters.

The definition of a nation, following the checklist
approach, obviously depends upon the set of objective
criteria which are used. This creates the possibility

that a checklist definition of a nation using one set of
criteria might lead one to conclude that there is only one
nation in Ireland, whereas another checklist definition
using a different set of criteria might lead one to
believe that there are two nations in Ireland. However,
advocates of the two-nation hypothesis argue that the
conclusion must always be the same - that there are two
nations in Ireland (or else only one in Britain and
Ireland together) - irrespective of whichever criteria are
chosen. Let us examine this argument relative to each of
the major criteria:

1) Ethnicity: Irish nationalist writers in the late
nineteenth century frequently referred to the 'Irish
race'. The idea of a pure Irish race is now recognised as
absurd, but the idea that the Irish are racially different
from the English probably has some validity. The Irish
population contains a mixture of racial types, reflecting
the assimilation by Gaelic and pre-Gaelic peoples of later
groups of colonists and invaders including Norse Vikings,
Anglo-Normans, Saxons, and other smaller groups (e.g.
Huguenots). The Gaelic and pre-Gaelic strains, however,
remain dominant. The English population is also racially
mixed, reflecting an integration of early Celtic peoples,
Angles, Saxons, Danes, Normans and more recent arrivals,
but the balance between these groups is different from
that in most of Ireland. Racial composition consequently
provides a possible criterion for making a distinction
between the Irish and the English. However, ethnicity
does not provide a very strong argument in support of the
one-nation hypothesis, due to the fact that most Northern
Ireland Protestants are ethnically different from the rest
of the people in Ireland. Most Northern Ireland
Protestants are the descendants of seventeenth century
English and Scottish settlers. Although highland Scots
have a strong Gaelic strain in their ethnic composition,
most of the Protestant Scots who migrated to Ulster were
from lowland Scotland (Galloway, Ayr, Renfrew, Lanark, the
Lothians, and the Borderlands). Apart from the Scots who

migrated from the western coastal areas in lowland
Scotland which had been previously colonised from highland
Scotland (e.g. Galloway), comparatively few of the Scots
who migrated to Ulster would have had a strong Gaelic
component in their ethnic composition. Northern Ireland
Protestants, like lowland Scots, consequently are
ethnically more similar to the English than they are to
people living in the rest of Ireland.

2) Language: Although everyone in Ireland can speak
English, Irish nationalists emphasize the fact that the
principal language of the Irish people until relatively
recent times was Irish Gaelic. Indeed, the Irish language
is regarded by most Irish nationalists as one of the most
important elements of the Irish national heritage and it
is consequently official policy (if maybe not practice) to
encourage the use of Irish. Selected areas known
collectively as the Gaeltacht, containing 2.2 per cent of
the population in the Republic, are designated for special
grants because a high percentage of their inhabitants
(about 82 per cent) claim to be native Irish speakers
(Coakley, 1980). The importance of the Irish language is
also recognised by the Irish Constitution. Article 8 of
the Constitution states: 'The Irish language as the
national language is the first official language'. About
75 per cent of people living in the Irish Republic claim
some ability to speak Irish (Irish Times, 27th. June,
1983).

The Irish language provides an important focus of
distinction between the Irish nation and the British, but
in so doing it contradicts the one-nation hypothesis due
to the fact that the Irish language is regarded as alien
by most Northern Ireland Protestants. The ancestors of
some Northern Ireland Protestants, especially those who
came from Galloway, may have been able to speak Scots
Gaelic (which is related to Irish Gaelic) when they first
came to Ulster in the early seventeenth century, but the
vast majority would have spoken either English (if they
were from England) or Lallans (a lowland Scots dialect

related to English). The ancestors of some of the first
Scots settlers may have spoken Gaelic in even earlier
centuries, but the historical link between Northern
Ireland Protestants and the Gaelic language is extremely
tenuous. Apart from a few Protestants who learned Gaelic
as a foreign language (and indeed who were prominent in
the Gaelic revival in the nineteenth century), Gaelic has
not been spoken by Protestants for at least three
centuries; nor is there any perception that it is a lost
part of their cultural heritage.

Thus, if an identification with the Irish language is
regarded as an important distinguishing characteristic of
the Irish nation, Northern Ireland Protestants cannot be
regarded as part of the Irish nation. On the other hand,
if the Irish language is not regarded as an essential
distinguishing characteristic of the Irish nation, then
there is no basis for making a linguistic distinction
between the Irish nation and the British nation.

3) Religion: Religion, as explained in later chapters,
played a very important role in the development of a
distinctive Irish identity. Although the Irish national
movement has always contained a substantial pluralist
element, particularly in its republican wing, many Irish
nationalists regard the Irish nation as a Catholic nation.
In the words of Éamon de Valera : 'Since the coming of St.
Patrick ... Ireland has been a Christian and a Catholic
nation ... She remains a Catholic nation ... ' (Irish
Independent, 18th. March, 1935). The contradiction
between this interpretation and the one-nation hypothesis
which claims that the Protestants in Northern Ireland are
part of the Irish nation is obvious. In order to include
Northern Ireland Protestants within the Irish nation, the
religious qualification would need to be broadened to
'Christian'; but this would also eliminate the possibility
of using the religious criterion as a means of
distinguishing the Irish from the British (unless, of
course, one was to argue that the Irish are more/less
Christian than the British).

4) <u>Culture</u>: The growth of Irish nationalism in the
late nineteenth century was parallelled by the development
of a distinctive Irish culture in which aspects of
traditional folk culture which were uniquely Irish were
consciously fostered: Gaelic games (e.g. Gaelic football,
hurling and camogie) were codified; traditional folk
music, folklore and mythology were recorded; and the Irish
language, which had previously been associated with a
backward peasantry, gained social acceptability (see
Chapter 6 for further details). These developments helped
to create the awareness of a distinctive Irish cultural
identity, but in so doing they also helped to create a
divide between the Irish nation and Northern Protestants
who, due to their different ethnic origins, could not
identify with the cultural values which were being
espoused. Northern Protestants, for example, feel no
affinity for traditional Irish games (such as hurling),
whereas they feel quite at ease with 'foreign' games such
as soccer, rugby and hockey.
5) <u>History</u>: The history of Ireland provides few, if
any, real examples of Protestants and Catholics uniting
together in the face of a common external threat. Irish
nationalists can rightfully point to a period at the end
of the eighteenth century when some Northern Protestants
sought common ground with Irish Catholics in a struggle
against British domination, but many Northern Protestants
also fought on the opposite side (see Chapter 5). More to
the point, most conflicts in Ireland since the Northern
Protestants first began to settle in Ulster have found
Protestants and Catholics on opposite sides (e.g. the 1641
rising, the Cromwellian wars, the Williamite wars, the
Repeal and Home Rule agitations, and the IRA campaigns in
the present century). The criterion of a common history
of struggle against some external enemy consequently
provides little support for the one-nation hypothesis.
Irish nationalist historiography emphasizes a prolonged
struggle against people regarded as foreign usurpers, but
Northern Protestants as a unified group have never played

an active role in this struggle. Indeed, it would
probably be more accurate to regard them as part of the
enemy against whom this struggle was waged. This would
certainly correspond more closely with the attitude of
Northern Catholics towards Northern Protestants, but it is
inconsistent with an advocacy of the one-nation
hypothesis.

6) Economy: The Irish economy provides little support
for the one-nation hypothesis. The economy of north-east
Ulster has been linked more closely to Britain than to the
rest of Ireland for at least two hundred years. This, in
fact, was probably the single most important factor
underlying the original growth of Ulster unionism in
opposition to Irish nationalism (see Chapter 7).

Considering the various criteria in conjunction, there
would appear to be little doubt that Northern Protestants
are different in many respects from the rest of the people
in Ireland, but it could be argued that these differences
are of minor importance: after all, there are regional
variations within every nation. However, the crucial
point is that Northern Protestants are not only different,
but that they are more similar to people living in Britain
than they are to people living in the rest of Ireland.
This is not to say that Northern Protestants are totally
different from Irish Catholics, but it is impossible to
define a nation following the checklist approach in such a
way as to include Northern Protestants and Irish Catholics
in the same nation while at the same time preserving a
distinction between this united Irish nation and the
British. The evidence, I would argue, forces one to
conclude that there are either two nations in Ireland or
else only one in Britain and Ireland as a whole.

Advocates of the two-nations hypothesis would not deny
the existence of a distinctive Irish nation; rather, they
argue that the very features which serve as a mark of
distinction between this Irish nation and the British also
serve as a mark of distinction between this Irish nation

and Northern Ireland Protestants. The only feature which
Northern Ireland Protestants and Irish Catholics have in
common which is not also shared by people living in
Britain is the fact that they live on the same island.
This provides an excellent reason for co-operation between
the two groups; it also provides a potential focus around
which a sense of common identity might conceivably develop
at some point in the future; but it does not by itself
provide sufficient justification to disregard the claims
of the smaller group to a separate existence.

   If one accepts that a nation can be adequately defined
following a checklist approach, the evidence would appear
to confirm the contention that there are two nations in
Ireland. However, it was argued in the previous section
that the self-definition approach is more appropriate.
Let us now examine the question of the number of nations
in Ireland following the self-definition approach.

   Viewing the question from the perspective of the two
groups themselves, we find that each group defines the
'we' group differently. Most Irish nationalists tend to
think of the Irish nation as comprised of almost everyone
living in Ireland (including Northern Protestants),
whereas politically Northern Ireland Protestants regard
themselves as British rather than Irish. In other words,
Irish nationalists generally think in terms of a single
(although politically divided) Irish nation, whereas
Northern Ireland Protestants think in terms of two
distinct nations.

   There is of course a certain degree of diversity within
both groups. A minority of people in the Republic of
Ireland would accept that Northern Ireland Protestants are
not a part of the Irish nation, although this minority is
divided as to the implications of this conclusion: some
would accept the right of Protestants in Northern Ireland
to remain outside the Irish state; but others argue that
the Protestant 'colons' should be 'repatriated' to Britain
in order to facilitate the reintegration of the Irish
national territory. However, the overwhelming majority of

people in the Republic would appear to regard the Northern Ireland Protestants as part of the Irish nation.

The overwhelming majority of Northern Ireland Protestants, as noted, regard themselves as British. However, the self-definition approach is complicated by doubts as to whether the self-definition of the British nation by people in England, Scotland and Wales would include the Northern Ireland Protestants: many mainland British would appear to regard the Northern Ireland Protestants as Irish, if for no other reason than the fact that they live in Ireland. There is consequently a degree of ambiguity about the nationality of Northern Ireland Protestants, depending upon the group which one selects for self-definition purposes: Northern Ireland Protestants see themselves as part of a larger group (i.e. the British nation); but other members of that group do not appear to unambiguously recognise Northern Ireland Protestants as fellow members.

This ambiguity, I would suggest, reflects a more widespread duality between the political and cultural dimensions within the British national identity. The political dimension of British nationality is represented by an allegiance to the state, whereas the cultural dimension is reflected by an allegiance to the 'we' group. The political dimension gives rise to a sense of common British identity based upon a shared allegiance to the British state (i.e. the United Kingdom), but the cultural dimension is reflected by the continuation of an identification with distinct smaller groups (i.e. the English, Scots and Welsh). British nationality can therefore be thought of as two tiered: there is a political tier reflecting an allegiance to the modern British state; and below that there is a cultural tier which reflects an allegiance to smaller groups in which the 'we' group is self-defined by cultural and historical criteria.

The political tier, by virtue of being based on a common allegiance to the state, does not necessitate the same degree of internal cohesiveness as the cultural tier: membership of the political nation is in a sense open to any group which gives allegiance to the state. The lower degree of internal cohesiveness reduces the perceived need to defend the unity of the political nation: part of the British state could in theory secede without an identification with the state being unduly upset for those who remain. However, a threat to the unity of the 'we' group at the cultural level could not be accommodated so easily: any change in the composition of the 'we' group would automatically change the object of group allegiance. There consequently tends to be a stronger group identification with the cultural nation than with the political nation. Although the sense of common identity with Northern Ireland Protestants is not particularly strong amongst the English, Scots or Welsh, it is probably not much weaker than the sense of common identity that they share with one another.

This two-tier sense of national identity is found within the Northern Ireland Protestants themselves. Political allegiance is given to the British nation and state, but the 'we' group in cultural terms is the smaller group. Northern Ireland Protestants realise that by themselves they are powerless to defend the territorial integrity of the British state, but they are determined to defend what they believe themselves capable of defending, namely the 'we' group and its territory, against the perceived threat of a larger external group (i.e. the Irish nation - defined by Northern Ireland Protestants to exclude themselves). This 'we' group, referred to up to now as 'Northern Ireland Protestants', can be regarded as comprising an Ulster nation which is directly analogous to the English, Scots and Welsh nations (i.e. at the cultural level). The within-group cohesiveness is provided by a unionist ideology. Although unionism is directly opposed to Irish nationalism, it is itself a type of nationalist ideology (as defined above). However, the Ulster nation, it must be stressed, does not aspire to political

independence (any more than do the majorities within the
English, Scots or Welsh nations): the political allegiance
of the Ulster nation is to the British state.

The term 'Ulster' introduces some terminological
difficulties. Although Northern Ireland Protestants often
refer to Northern Ireland as 'Ulster', Ulster is strictly
speaking the name historically given to the six counties
in Northern Ireland plus three counties in the Republic
(Cavan, Donegal and Monaghan). Also, as defined here to
refer primarily to Protestants, the Ulster nation is
comprised of only slightly more than half the people in
Ulster as a whole. Nevertheless, 'Ulster' is the term
most frequently used by Northern Ireland Protestants to
refer to themselves, as for example in the names given to
Protestant paramilitary organisations (e.g. Ulster
Volunteer Force, Ulster Defence Association) and in names
of official state bodies (e.g. Royal Ulster Constabulary,
Ulster Defence Regiment).

Irrespective of the terminological niceties, there is
one point which cannot be overstressed: Northern Ireland
Protestants do not regard themselves to be part of the
Irish nation, either politically or culturally. They do,
it is true, regard themselves as 'Irish' in some
non-political spheres of activity: the Irish rugby team,
for example, is organised on an all-Ireland basis and
receives the support of Northern Ireland Protestants.
This, however, does not imply an identification with the
Irish nation. Although 'Irish' in the politically trivial
sense that they happen to live on an island called
Ireland, Northern Ireland Protestants have never
identified with the goals and cultural values which Irish
nationalists used to define the Irish nation at the time
of its creation in the nineteenth century. In fact, the
perceived external threat posed by the Irish nation to the
culture and way of life of Northern Ireland Protestants is
possibly the single most important factor in maintaining
group cohesiveness within the Ulster nation. This
explains why Northern Ireland Protestants would probably

opt for an independent Ulster (despite the likely economic
consequences) in the event of a 'British withdrawal',
rather than consider the possibility of a united Ireland.
The perceived need to defend the group (i.e. the Ulster
nation) also explains why Northern Ireland Protestants
have even threatened to resort to force of arms against
the British Government (i.e. the government of the state
to which they give allegiance) on those occasions when
British government policies appeared to threaten the
preservation of the group.

To summarise, if we adopt a self-definitional approach
to the question of the number of nations in Ireland, we
end up with two possible answers. If we adopt the Irish
nationalist perspective, we would conclude that there is
only one nation; whereas, if we adopt the Ulster unionist
perspective, we would conclude that there are two nations.
However, the Irish nationalist perspective contradicts the
essential feature of the self-definitional approach,
namely that the members of a nation must believe
themselves to be a nation, due to the fact that the Ulster
unionists do not regard themselves as part of the Irish
nation. We must therefore conclude that there are two
nations in Ireland, irrespective of whether we adopt the
checklist or self-definitional approach.

NATIONALISM: THE HISTORICAL DIMENSION

The conclusion that there are two nations in Ireland
could be construed, subject to various assumptions
(especially that of the right of nations to
self-determination), as a vindication of the unionist
position. However, it was argued in the previous chapter
that the present conflict cannot be resolved within a
nationalistic framework. If we are to transcend existing
nationalistic interpretations of the conflict, including
that of the Ulster unionists, we must move move beyond a
simple acceptance that there are two nations in Ireland

towards an understanding of why there are two nations in
Ireland. Given that the group cohesiveness of a nation is
provided by a nationalist ideology, this requires us to
examine the reasons why there are two conflicting
nationalist ideologies in Ireland. The remainder of this
book consequently examines the historical evolution of
Irish nationalism and Ulster unionism. These
developments, however, must be viewed within the context
of broader historical changes, not only in Ireland but
also elsewhere. To help place these developments in
perspective, this section reviews the growth of
nationalism as a major world ideology.

People have organised themselves into groups
characterised by different languages, cultures and
political structures since the earliest times. However,
although these groups often commanded strong loyalties
from their members (i.e. there was a well developed sense
of 'us' and 'them'), they differed from modern nations in
a number of important respects. For example, many of
these groups (e.g. nomadic tribes) did not have a strong
identification with a particular territory; whereas others
identified with territories which were very localised
compared to the territories of modern nations and which
were often surrounded by uninhabited and unclaimed
frontier areas - land did not have the same use value
throughout most of history because population density was
much lower. Also, although some groups were characterised
by highly developed group ideologies which fostered a
desire to defend the group against external threats (e.g.
the Jews in the Old Testament), these ideologies differed
in many important respects from modern nationalism. The
Jews, for example, did not have any concept of the
nation-state as the ideal, natural or normal form of
political organisation (Kamenka, 1973). Likewise,
although there were some very sophisticated political
structures in the Ancient World (e.g. the Roman Empire),
people's loyalties to these structures were not the
product of a nationalist ideology. Nationalism, in the

context of world history, is a very recent innovation.

The evolution of modern nations in western Europe can be traced back to the medieval period. Feudal society was hierarchically organised into a number of distinct strata on the basis of landholding. Each stratum in society held land from higher strata in return for payments in kind or services, the nature of which varied depending upon the level in the hierarchy. The serfs, who comprised the bottom tier in the system, were tied to the land and were unable to move around freely. The top tier in the hierarchy was dominated by numerous kings, bishops, princes and other feudal nobility, with the result that political units tended to be both spatially small and highly fragmented.

People's identities operated at two spatial scales during this period. At an 'international' level most people gave universal allegiance to the Catholic Church: almost the whole of western Europe was united by a common religious belief and, in the case of the educated, by a common language (Latin). However, allegiances were also expressed at a more local level: given the lack of spatial mobility within the feudal system, most people's immediate loyalties were to their tribe, village, city or feudal lords and rulers. Identities and loyalties in the early medieval period consequently contained elements of both universalism and localism.

The growth of an identity with a group of intermediate scale (i.e. what we now recognise as a 'nation') required two conditions: a decline in universal allegiance to the Catholic Church; and a decline in the localised control of feudal lords and barons. Both conditions were fulfilled by the emergence of centralised states under the absolute control of powerful dynasties by the late medieval period.

This process of spatial consolidation, which took centuries to complete, was motivated by the ambitions of the more powerful kings, supported by the rising commercial classes, to extend their personal control by war, conquest, diplomacy, duplicity, marriage and

purchase, rather than by a desire by people with a common
culture to form a unified state. In fact, most of the
states which developed in the medieval period originally
contained diverse populations which only became culturally
homogeneous following the establishment of a centralised
authority (Shafer, 1972). As the political units grew
larger, there was an increased need for centralised
legislative, judicial and administrative systems. This
generated a need for improved means of physical and social
communication between the various parts of the state:
common vernacular languages, usually based upon the local
dialect of the core region of the expanding state,
consequently emerged to replace other regional dialects as
the language of the people and Latin as the language of
the ruling classes. This, in turn, facilitated the
gradual substitution of diverse regional cultures by a
more homogeneous 'national' culture.

The processes of spatial expansion and centralisation of
state authority invariably brought the king into conflict
with other elements of the feudal nobility whose power was
being usurped. However, as state power was consolidated,
the king increasingly gained a decided advantage through
his control over a large standing army funded out of
taxation. Strongly entrenched local loyalties were
gradually undermined by the gradual eclipse of the feudal
nobility and replaced by a closer identification with the
state following the growth of centralised authority. This
transfer of allegiance to the state was given a further
boost when later attempts at spatial expansion brought the
standing armies of different states into direct conflict:
the need to defend the state against foreign states helped
strengthen the identification of the people with king and
country, as for example in England at the time of the
Spanish Armada.

The emergence of strongly centralised states also
undermined the universal allegiance to the Catholic
Church. Under feudalism the Church had enjoyed
considerable social and political power; it therefore

resented the emergence of powerful dynasties which
threatened to upset the established order. The growth of
centralised state authority consequently often brought the
king into direct conflict with the Church. This was one
of the factors underlying the growth of Protestantism
following the Reformation, and in some instances it even
resulted in a distinctive national church. The Church of
England provides an obvious example, but religion was
sometimes 'nationalised' even in countries which nominally
remained Catholic. Although there was no formal break
between France and Rome, for example, the French monarchy
insisted upon exercising its jurisdiction over the
Catholic Church in France (e.g. in the appointment of
bishops). The emergence of centralised states thereby
fragmented the universal loyalty to the Catholic Church.
Later, religious differences acted as differentiae in
conflicts between states, and thereby helped strengthen
people's identification with the state.

By the end of the medieval period, most of western
Europe (excluding Germany and Italy) had been consolidated
into states with boundaries not too different from those
of today, but the populations of these states did not yet
constitute nations in the modern sense. Nevertheless, the
stability of these states in subsequent centuries helped
to facilitate the gradual evolution of a group identity
based upon a common allegiance to the state. However, the
growth of nations entailed more than an identity with the
state over a period of time: it also required the
development of a nationalist ideology. This, I would
argue, reflected fundamental societal changes and class
conflicts associated with the transition to capitalism.

As noted, the consolidation of the state in the medieval
period usually entailed a struggle between the
centralising monarchy and the feudal nobility. The
successful conduct of this struggle, from the king's point
of view, depended upon having sufficient finances to
support a standing army and a centralised bureaucracy.
This was often facilitated by the formation of an alliance

between the monarchy and an emerging class of wealthy
merchants, who as a class had a vested interest in the
overthrow of the remaining feudal restrictions on trade
and who as individuals were often prepared to advance
money for a military campaign in the expectation of a
healthy return on their investments. The interests of the
state therefore became increasingly identified with the
interests of the powerful merchants, culminating in the
seventeenth and eighteenth centuries in the doctrine of
mercantilism. Under mercantilism, the state became an
active agent for the development of trade: the army and
navy were used to acquire and defend overseas colonies
which became a source of cheap raw materials and a market
for manufactured goods, while legislation was passed to
protect home industries from outside competition
(including that of the colonies).

Once the challenge from the feudal nobility (now
fossilised as the landed aristocracy) had receded, the
kings' major challenge came from the rising commercial
classes (i.e. merchants, commercial farmers, small
commodity producers, etc.). This struggle, which took
many complex forms, was reflected in the seventeenth
century in England, for example, by the Civil War and the
Whig Revolution. These events can be viewed, in the
context of world history, as incidents in the transition
from feudalism to capitalism. This transition resulted in
the emergence of the industrial bourgeoisie as the
dominant class in western society by the late nineteenth
century, following the industrial revolution. The growth
of nationalism was in part a by-product of this struggle
for social and political power between the bourgeoisie and
the monarchy (which now sought an alliance with the landed
aristocracy).

The American War of Independence, triggered by the
resentment of the American colonists against the use of
mercantilist restrictions to levy taxes for military
purposes by the British, had a profound impact upon public
thinking in Europe because it demonstrated that political

control in an area could be seized by its inhabitants. A
few years later the French bourgeoisie and allied classes
deposed Louis XVI to seize power in the name of the French
people. This also had a profound impact upon the
development of nationalism because the French Revolution
formalised the proposition that political power did not
rest with the king by divine right but was held in the
interests of the people (i.e. the 'nation'). The state,
in other words, became an instrument of the people (or, to
be more precise, those who owned property), rather than of
the monarchy. Previously the inhabitants of states had
been subjects; now they became elevated to the status of
citizens. State power, according to the French, could
only be legitimised by the nation.

The French Revolution clearly threatened the stability
of the old regime in other countries, especially as the
French openly advocated that other nations should free
themselves following their revolutionary example. The
French consequently soon found themselves almost
continuously at war with the other major European powers
in the following two and a half decades. These wars
resulted in a marked increase in national consciousness
throughout Europe, although not always in the way that the
French had hoped. Rather than being regarded as
progressive liberators, the French armies were more often
regarded simply as foreign invaders, causing those whom
they had hoped to liberate to rally to the defence of
their respective kings and 'nations'.

The French revolutionaries regarded the nation as little
more than the collective name for the inhabitants of a
state: the French concept of a nation did not carry any
connotations of common ethnicity or culture. These
attributes were added in the late eighteenth and early
nineteenth centuries by German nationalist philosophers
such as Fichte and Herder. Germany and Italy at this time
each remained politically fragmented into a number of
states; consequently the German philosophers developed a
new concept of the nation which reflected their own

particular situation by placing the emphasis upon common culture rather than upon common citizenship. It was the German philosophers who first propounded the idea that the whole of humanity is naturally divided into a number of nations, each of which can be recognised by its unique cultural attributes and each of which has a special contribution to make to the development of mankind. Under the German conceptualisation, each nation is more than the sum of its component parts: it is an organic unity with a divine destiny to fulfil. This destiny can only be achieved through national self-realisation in the form of an independent nation-state. Personal self-fulfilment is conditional upon the freedom of the nation; consequently the will of the individual must be subjugated to the political struggle for the creation of an independent nation-state. Nationalism was viewed as the awakening of national self-consciousness.

The German version was adopted by others groups desiring an independent state throughout Europe (especially Italy and eastern Europe) and later the rest of the world. The Young Germany, Young Italy and Young Poland movements in the 1830s were particularly influential in this respect. Although the German version lost some of its mystical qualities when it was modified to suit local conditions elsewhere, many of its features have been preserved to form what we identified earlier as the national ideal: the idea that nations are natural subdivisions of humanity; that they have existed throughout history (albeit in latent form); that each is primarily identifiable in terms of its cultural traits; that nations are the legitimate units for state organization; that each nation has a natural right to self-determination; and that loyalty to the nation should override all other loyalties. In short, it would not be untrue to say that nationalism, as we now know it, was largely invented by the Germans in the early nineteenth century.

Nationalists, following the German philosophers, regard nations as eternal subdivisions of mankind, and

nationalism as the conscious recognition of their
existence. This, as pointed out by Gellner, is to invert
historical reality: 'nationalism is not the awakening of
nations to self-consciousness: it invents nations where
they do not exist.' (Gellner, 1964, p168). In the
nineteenth century, nationalism was instrumental in the
creation of new nations which began to demand
independence, resulting in the course of time in the
creation of a large number of new states. However, the
fact that these nations usually claimed a much longer
history should not blind us to the fact that the nation,
as we now know it, only came into existence in the
nineteenth century. This is true even of states, such as
France, with a long history. Following the consolidation
of France by the Capetian, Valois, and Bourbon dynasties
in the medieval period, the French 'nation' in the
sixteenth and seventeenth centuries meant simply the
subjects of the king of France; by the late eighteenth
century it would have entailed a conscious group identity
within the propertied classes; but it was not until the
nineteenth century that the nation became an object of
common identity for the whole population.

The reasons why nationalism became such a pervasive
ideology at this particular point in history are complex
(e.g. see Smith (1971) for a useful review of the more
important theories), but it is necessary to outline at
least some of the major features for present purposes.
The growth of nationalism, I would suggest, may be viewed
as an ideological manifestation of underlying material
conditions associated with the transition to industrial
capitalism. However, these material conditions varied
from region to region, depending upon specific local
conditions, with the result that the growth of nationalism
took different forms in different areas.

In the case of Germany, political fragmentation into a
number of small petty states interfered with the growth of
industrial capitalism. Trade, for example, was hampered
by imposition of customs duties between these petty

states. The creation of a large (i.e. 'national') home
market was an essential precondition for the growth of
German capitalism if it was to be competitive with that in
the advanced European countries. The political system
also had to be restructured if the bourgeoisie were to
eliminate the remaining feudal restrictions on capitalist
expansion. The German bourgeoisie, in short, had a strong
vested interest in the creation of a larger political unit
- one which corresponded in spatial extent with the German
cultural group rather than with the existing German
states. This consequently created a predisposition for
the Germans to think of a nation in terms of common
culture rather than as the inhabitants of a state. German
nationalism reflected these materialist needs of the
bourgeoisie in a mystified form, and thereby facilitated
the mobilisation of support from other sections of society
for German unity. Seventeen German states formed a
customs union (Zollverein) in 1833 to create a larger home
market; this formed the basis for the creation of a united
German state in 1871.

The growth of nationalism followed a different course
elsewhere. In eastern Europe, for example, nationalism
preceded the final victory of capitalism; and instead of
creating larger market areas it had the opposite effect of
fragmenting pre-existing Empires into much smaller
nation-states. The German model of the growth of
nationalism is clearly inappropriate in this context.
However, the general contention that the growth of
nationalism was an ideological reflection of material
needs arising out of the transition to capitalism is still
valid. Capitalism did not evolve independently in
different regions by a process of replication; rather, it
evolved in parts of western Europe and penetrated outwards
into other regions which were transformed under conditions
dictated by the more developed areas. Eastern Europe
consequently began to feel the effects of the penetration
of capitalism long before it became identifiably
capitalist.

The penetration of capitalism was reflected in numerous ways which are sometimes collectively referred to as 'modernisation'. The penetration of commodity relations, which preceded the advent of industrial capitalism in most parts of eastern Europe, had a major disruptive effect on traditional peasant society. Structural changes associated with the commercialisation of agriculture, for example, often resulted in the displacement of population, whilst the intimate inter-personal relations of traditional society were replaced by the functional relations of the market. 'Gemeinschaft' society, in short, was transformed into a 'gesellschaft' society. This was particularly the case where the penetration of capitalism took the form of industrial urbanisation. These disruptions to traditional society created a psychological vacuum: people have an instinctive desire to belong, but traditional local identities were being broken down by modernisation. Meanwhile, the introduction of improved means of mass communications helped to broaden peoples' horizons with the result that they now had a greater awareness of, and identity with, regions which extended beyond their local area. The conditions were thereby being created within which nationalism could develop.

However, the growth of nationalism was not simply a product of the social upheaval associated with the penetration of capitalism: it was a function of its uneven development. Capitalist development resulted in an improvement in living conditions for some sections of society, but it also had the opposite effect upon many other sections of society. More importantly, in the present context, it often created expectations which were not fulfilled even when living conditions did rise. Many sections of society consequently either felt threatened by the changes taking place or else felt that they should have been doing better than they were. Given the uneven spatial development of capitalism, this disillusionment was usually more acute in peripheral regions.

Disillusionment created a predisposition towards increased local political autonomy, which in turn became reflected by a growth in nationalism.

Nationalism, however, was not reinvented in each of these peripheral regions. Rather, the basic nationalist ideology which had developed in Germany (i.e. the 'national ideal') was adopted and modified to local conditions. The spread of nationalism can therefore be regarded as a diffusion process. This diffusion, however, did not take the form of regular concentric waves radiating out of Germany, but rather tended to be spatially uneven reflecting the penetration of capitalism. Nationalism only took root where the local material conditions created a favourable receptive environment. To explain the growth of nationalism in any particular region it is necessary to identify the material reasons why people in that region should have been predisposed to the general nationalist ideology.

However, it is important not to overstate the degree of consciousness involved in the diffusion of nationalism. People did not rationally weigh up the material advantages and disadvantages of increased local autonomy before consciously deciding to become nationalists; rather, their material conditions created a predisposition towards the acceptability of certain ideas. People who felt that they were being bypassed by the benefits of development, or who felt their position was being eroded, would have found much to identify with in an ideology which glorified 'traditional' values (i.e. culture) while simultaneously advocating the restructuring of the political system in the interests of future progress. Nationalism was not consciously adopted as a disguise for more basic objectives; rather, it was adopted because it had a strong emotive appeal given the nature of local material conditions. This appeal was particularly strong in peripheral areas which were ethnically or historically different from the more developed core areas. If these differences did not exist they were sometimes invented -

most national separatist movements were preceded by
cultural and linguistic revival movements, associated with
a nationalist reinterpretation of history.

The diffusion process also had an important 'vertical'
dimension. Nationalism in most instances was initially a
middle class phenomenon, which later diffused 'downwards'
to the other classes. This did not indicate that the
middle classes had more grievances (either real or
perceived) than other sections of society; rather, it
reflected the fact that the middle classes, especially
those sections which comprised the intelligentsia, had a
greater awareness of the growth of nationalism in other
countries and also of the history of their own region.
They were consequently better equipped to adopt the
general nationalist ideology to their own particular
circumstances. However, a nationalist struggle can only
be successful if it has popular support: it therefore
became necessary to mobilise the 'masses'. To do this,
the middle classes had to persuade the other classes, who
had grievances of their own, that they had something to
gain from national liberation. Material grievances were
therefore blamed upon foreign overlords and national
liberation became implicitly linked with promises of
social reform.

The growth of nationalism sometimes appears to have
reflected a convergence of different class interests
within a region, but closer analysis often reveals that
the national struggle was often manipulated by various
groups for their own ends. Nationalism, in fact, is often
a very powerful tool in the hands of the dominant classes,
even after national independence has been achieved,
because it tends to emphasise conflicts between societies
(i.e. nations) and thereby distracts attention from the
conflicts within societies - especially those arising out
of class exploitation.

SUMMARY

Two approaches to defining a nation were identified in the first section: the checklist approach and the self-definition approach. Although the self-definition approach is preferable, the question of the number of nations in Ireland was considered using both types of definition in the second section. It was argued that, no matter how one defines a nation, one is forced to conclude that there are either two nations in Ireland or else only one in Britain and Ireland as a whole. However, to understand fully the present conflict between these two nations, it is necessary to understand why there are two nations to begin with. This requires us to examine the reasons why there are two conflicting nationalist ideologies within Ireland. The historical evolution of Irish nationalism and Ulster unionism is therefore traced in the following chapters, utilising the framework outlined in the final section.

CHAPTER 3

The Conquest and Unification of Ireland

Irish nationalist historiography, in its crudest form, often depicts Ireland in the first millennium A.D., prior to its conquest by foreign invaders, as culturally homogeneous and politically united under the leadership of a centralised monarch referred to as the high king. The period is also regarded as the golden age of Irish civilisation: at a time when the rest of western Europe was being overrun by heathen tribes of barbarians, Ireland survived as an outpost of civilisation and, acting as a centre of Christianity and learning, it played a major role in the recovery of Europe in the early middle ages. However, following its conquest by the Anglo-Normans in the twelth century, Ireland was relegated to a position of subservience to England and prevented from achieving its full potential social and economic development. Irish greatness, it is implied, can only be recovered once Ireland is reunited as an independent nation as before.

The Irish nationalist interpretation (presented here in a grossly oversimplified form) contains a certain amount of truth: Ireland, especially in the second half of the first millennium, did exhibit a very high degree of cultural homogeneity; also, development undoubtedly has been hindered by a long history of external domination. However, it is debatable whether the island has ever been both politically united (in any meaningful sense) and independent at any one time in its entire history. In fact, it would probably be more accurate to say that

Ireland has only ever been politically united under
British rule and that the present disunity (in the form of
partition) is a direct, if undesired, consequence of Irish
nationalist aspirations for independence.

The present chapter reviews the political history of
Ireland up to the beginning of the early modern period.
The principal objective is to trace the process of
political unification in Ireland so as to provide a
background to the events discussed in later chapters.
However, as a secondary objective, this chapter also
examines the extent to which the people living in Ireland
during this period could be regarded as comprising a
nation. Most of the discussion deals with Ireland as a
whole and is at a fairly high level of generalisation, but
Ulster is discussed in slightly more detail due to the
emphasis later placed upon its regional distinctiveness
and close connections with Scotland by Ulster unionists.

The chapter is divided into five sections organised by
historical sequence, followed by a brief summary.

EARLY CHRISTIAN IRELAND

Little is known about Gaelic Ireland before the fifth
century; indeed, even the information available for the
period before the seventh and eighth centuries is somewhat
hazy. However, it is clear that Ireland was not
politically united in the early historical period, but
rather was divided into about 150 petty kingdoms known as
tuatha. The term 'tuath' means 'a people', but the
members of a tuath were not necessarily of common descent
(Mac Niocaill, 1972). Rather, they were a group which saw
themselves as sufficiently large and distinct from other
groups to form their own political structures. Each tuath
was located in a fixed locality (i.e. they were not
migratory tribes), but the territorial boundaries appear
to have been poorly defined and subject to change. This
would suggest that population pressure was not sufficient

to make land a highly valued resource. Each tuath was
ruled by a king (rí) who was elected by the freemen in
the tuath from the derbfine (i.e all the male descendants
down to the fourth generation) of a previous king. Gaelic
society therefore contained limited democratic structures,
but it was essentially a very stratified society in which
there was a complex hierarchy of social strata ranging
from nobility, through freemen, to serfs and slaves (Mac
Niocaill, 1972).

The political organisation was also hierarchical. The
kings of the tuatha usually gave allegiance to more
powerful overkings (ruiri). The relationships between
kings and overkings varied, but they generally entailed
payment of tribute in return for protection. The
overkings in turn gave allegiance to even more powerful
provincial kings (rí ruirech - king of overkings) and,
towards the end of the first millennium, some of the more
powerful provincial kings claimed the title 'high king'
(ard rí) - i.e. king of the whole island. This, however,
was a claim rather than a de facto or de jure
position.

Sovereignty, in so far as the concept is applicable to
Gaelic Ireland, rested with the kings of the tuatha. The
loyalty of individuals was a personal loyalty to their own
tuath, and hence to their own rí, rather than to the more
powerful overkings. In the words of Mac Niocaill (1972),
'anything they found themselves obliged to do as a result
of their king's submission was done by virtue of their
subordination to their own king'.

Although Ireland was politically fragmented, there was a
very high degree of cultural homogeneity. This, however,
should not be interpreted as indicating that the Gaels
were the original, or indeed the only, inhabitants of
Ireland. On the contrary, archaeological evidence
suggests that Ireland has been settled by successive waves
of people since the first Mesolithic peoples arrived about
6,000 B.C. Each wave either assimilated, or was
assimilated by, the pre-existing groups. This

archaeological evidence is echoed by legends in Irish
mythology which tell of heroic deeds and struggles between
various early peoples referred to as Partholonians,
Nemedians, Fomorians, Fir Bolg, Tuatha Dé Danann and
Milesians.

The most recent of the pre-historic waves of invaders,
corresponding to the Milesians in mythology, were
Celtic-speaking groups which arrived in the late Bronze
Age and early Iron Age. The Celts migrated from their
original core area, somewhere near Bohemia or Bavaria, to
places as far apart as Galatia in Asia Minor and Iberia.
The first Celts probably began to arrive in Ireland as
early as the sixth century B.C. (Byrne, 1967), but later
waves included the Gaels who established themselves by 150
B.C. (Mitchell, 1967). Different groups of Celts spoke
different dialects. Britain, for example, was settled by
Celtic groups, referred to as the Ancient Britons, who
spoke a dialect known as P-Celtic; whereas the Gaels who
settled in Ireland spoke a dialect known as Q-Celtic. The
Britons were subsequently displaced to peninsular parts of
Britain and France (where P-Celtic survives today as
Welsh, Cornish and Breton) by later invaders (e.g. Jutes,
Angles and Saxons), whereas Q-Celtic survives today as
Irish and, due to later colonisation from Ireland, as Manx
and Scots Gaelic. Many pre-Celtic peoples (known as
Pritani to P-Celts and as Cruithin to Q-Celts) survived
the Celtic invasions, including the Picts who remained a
major political force in Scotland until quite late into
historical times.

In Ireland many of these pre-Celtic peoples survived as
tuatha (typically with names having the prefix Dál or
Corco or the suffix -raige or -ne) which gave submission
to Gaelic overkings, but by the early historical period
they had been completely Gaelicised. Ireland was
consequently characterised by a high degree of cultural
uniformity which included a common language and a highly
developed and complex legal system known as brehon law.
It has been suggested that brehon law may have been worked

out to formalise the relations between the Gaels and their
subject peoples and that, by defending the rights of the
latter, may actually have hindered the later development
of Ireland into a unitary Gaelic state (Mac Niocaill,
1972). Brehon law, for example, recognised the positions
of rí, ruiri and rí ruirech, but it did not recognise
the legality of ard rí (Ó Corráin, 1972).

Cultural uniformity also included a common religion.
Christianity was introduced into Ireland in the fifth
century, supposedly by St. Patrick who established an
episcopal system. However, by the sixth century the Irish
Christian Church had adapted to the fragmented political
system by adopting monasticism as its principal form.
Monasteries were founded in the territories of the more
powerful kings, and strong political connections were
forged between kings and abbots. Indeed, by the eighth
century the abbots of most monasteries were members of the
local dynastic families, and their appointment was often
the source of political conflict.

The Gaelic political system was never very static.
Kingships were violently contested by rival branches of
the derbfine, and overkingships were frequently contested
by rival kings. Few kings consequently enjoyed a lengthy
reign. However, the dynamism of the system extended
beyond a fluctuating state of dynamic equilibrium: long
term trends towards centralisation were also apparent.
Major dynasties (e.g. the Eóganacht, Connachta and Uí
Néill) began to emerge as early as the fifth century A.D.
and by the eighth century many of the weaker tuatha would
appear to have lost their legal independent status. The
kings of these tuatha were often referred to by the
inferior title 'dux' (Ó Corráin, 1972). Power was
consolidated in the higher tiers of the political
hierarchy and from the ninth century onwards the more
powerful provincial kings increasingly tried to enforce
their claim to the title of high king.

The early history of Ulster is fairly typical of Ireland
as a whole. Most of the northern half of Ireland was

ruled in the first four centuries A.D. by the Ulaid (from whom the name Ulster is derived). The Ulaid, who had their capital at Emain Macha, near Armagh, may originally have been P-Celts who entered Ireland via Scotland. Their subject peoples included groups of Cruithin, the largest of which was probably the Dál nAraide (Heslinga, 1962).

In the fifth century, however, the Ulaid were displaced by the emergence of the Uí Néill dynasty, and were subsequently confined to east Ulster (i.e. to an area roughly corresponding to modern counties Down and Antrim). The Uí Néill were Q-Celts and, although little is known about their origins, it is believed that they may have been an offshoot of the Connachta dynasty. Different branches of the Uí Néill established themselves as the provincial kings of Ailech (the northern Uí Néill) and of Meath (the southern Uí Néill). The overkingship of the Ulaid was usually contested by the kings of the Dál Fiatach and the Dál nAraide, but the Ulaid generally remained subservient to branches of the Uí Néill. Former subject peoples of the Ulaid formed a crescent-shaped belt of tuatha, known as the Airgialla, between the Ulaid and the northern and southern Uí Néill (Figure 4).

One of the Ulaid peoples, the Dál Riata, began to colonise Argyll in Scotland in the late fifth century, possibly due to population pressure arising from the emergence of the Uí Néill. The Dál Riata kingdom straddled the North Channel for three centuries before being severed in the ninth century by the emergence of a Viking kingdom in the Western Isles of Scotland. Although the Dál Riata never played a major role in Irish politics, they played a significant role in Scotland (where they were known as the Scotti). Apart from giving Scotland its modern name, the Dál Riata were responsible for introducing the Q-Celtic dialect which later developed into Scots Gaelic and they played a major role in the re-introduction of Christianity into Scotland through the missionary work of St. Columba (an exiled Uí Néill) from

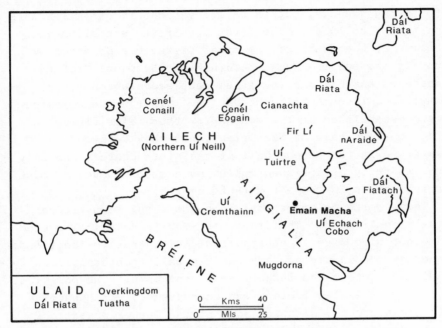

FIG. 4   Political Units In Gaelic Ulster.

563 onwards. The kingship of the Scotti eventually
evolved into the kingship of Scotland after Kenneth
McAlpin, the king of the Scotti, through marriage also
became king of the Picts, the dominant military force in
highland Scotland, in 843. The P-Celtic Britons in
Stathclyde and the Germanic Angles in the Lothians were
later integrated into the Scottish kingdom (Mackie, 1964).

THE VIKING INVASIONS

Ireland was unaffected by the Germanic tribes which
began to arrive in Britain from the fifth century onwards,
but at the end of the eighth century the first overseas
invaders in historic times - Norse Vikings - began to
arrive. The first raiding parties, probably seeking ships
provisions, raided monasteries off the Irish coast in 795.

These were followed by other raiding parties in the
following decades, but in 841 they began to establish more
permanent colonies. The first attempt to establish a
colony at the mouth of the river Liffey was defeated by
the Irish, but the Norse returned in 853 under Olaf the
White to establish a fortified settlement which later
developed into the city of Dublin. Other Norse colonies
were established at the mouths of other major rivers in
the southern half of the island, but they suffered
reverses in the second half of the ninth century and only
became fully established following a second wave of Norse
colonisation in the early tenth century.

These Norse colonies contained the first towns to be
built in Ireland. The fragmented Gaelic political system
did not give rise to centralised administrative functions;
whereas the Gaelic economy was basically pastoral, locally
self-sufficient and largely self-contained. The political
economy of Gaelic Ireland was consequently not conducive
to urban growth, although some of the larger monastic
settlements may have had populations of over a thousand
and therefore presumably acquired some urban functions.
The Norse, on the other hand, maintained close contacts
with Norse colonies elsewhere, giving rise to long
distance trade. Their fortified settlements consequently
developed into important trading towns. Given their
locations at the mouths of major rivers which provide
access to rich agricultural lands in the interior, it is
hardly surprising that many of these foundations have
persisted as some of the largest towns in modern Ireland
(viz. Dublin, Cork, Limerick, Waterford and Wexford - see
Figure 5).

The Vikings, differing in appearance and in language
from the Gaelic Irish, would clearly have been regarded as
foreigners, but resistance to the Norse was local or
provincial rather than national. The fact that the Norse
made very little impact upon the northern half of the
island, except possibly in the coastal parts of east
Ulster where their presence is reflected by a few

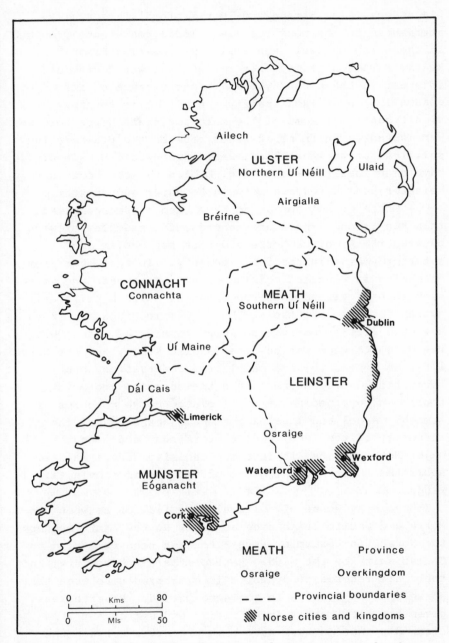

FIG. 5   The Principal Viking Settlements In Ireland.

placenames (e.g. Strangford, Carlingford), is usually
attributed to the more resilient local resistence provided
in the north by Mael Sechnaill, the powerful king of
Meath, although it may also reflect a lower degree of
interest in the north by the Vikings because of its
generally poorer land quality. Also, it is perhaps
significant that some of the more important Norse colonies
were situated in frontier zones between the pre-existing
political units where local resistance would presumably
have been less resilient (e.g. Dublin between Meath and
Leinster; and Waterford between Leinster and Munster).

The Norse do not appear to have been any more united
than the Irish. There are records, for example, of wars
between the Limerick Norse and both the Dublin and
Waterford Norse in the tenth century. In fact, far from
appearing as a united foreign army of conquest, the Norse
seem to have fitted into the fragmented Irish political
system fairly comfortably. Local Gaelic kings appear to
have had little reservation about forming alliances with
the Norse to wage war on other Gaelic kings, and the Norse
likewise appear to have had little reservation about
recruiting Gaelic support when the occasion arose for
their own internecine wars. Isolated Norse colonies at
Armagh, Cashel and Thurles must have acknowledged the
authority of the local Gaelic overkings, and even the
major Norse cities, following a decisive defeat in 941,
submitted to the overkingship of the Gaelic provincial
kings.

There is evidence of cultural assimilation between the
Norse and Gaelic Irish even as early as the ninth century:
the Norse, for example, appear to have been converted to
Christianity by the middle part of the ninth century, and
there are records of dynastic intermarriages between the
Norse and the Osraige in the same period. Nevertheless,
given the differences in ethnicity and settlement types, a
clear distinction must have been preserved between the
Gaels and Norse for centuries. However, these cultural
differences do not appear to have affected political

identities: people's political affiliations were still to
the smaller political units rather than to their cultural
or ethnic group. The poet-historians (filí) employed by
the more powerful provincial kings appear to have used the
penetration of outsiders in an attempt to create a sense
of common Irish identity (i.e. a feeling of 'us' in
contrast to 'them') to help legitimise the aspirations of
their masters to the high kingship in the eleventh and
twelfth centuries (O Corráin, 1977), but there is little
evidence to suggest that the Irish sense of nationality
included any real notion of political solidarity or a
perceived need to defend the 'nation' against foreign
invaders. This is clear if we briefly consider the events
leading to the battle of Clontarf (1014).

The battle of Clontarf is usually depicted in
nationalistic school history books as a heroic struggle in
which the Irish, led by their high king Brian Boru,
successfully defended Ireland against an invasion of
'Danes'. Apart from the fact that the Vikings at Clontarf
were Norse rather than Danes, the situation was in fact
much more complex than these history books suggest. The
battle of Clontarf was not a struggle between the Irish
and an army of foreign invaders (who at that stage had
been living in Dublin for almost two centuries), but
between Brian Boru, the king of Munster, and Mael Mordha,
the Gaelic king of Leinster. Brian Boru was probably the
first king who could claim the title of high king with any
degree of realism. In the previous decade he had waged
wars against all the other provincial kings, forcing each
to submit to him in turn. The last, the king of Cenél
Conaill in Ulster, submitted to him in 1011. However, in
1013 he was faced with rebellion in Leinster where Mael
Mordha enlisted the support of Sitric, the Norse king of
Dublin, who was one of his underkings. Sitric in turn
enlisted support from Norse kingdoms in the Isle of Man
and the Orkneys. Brian Boru's army, on the other hand,
far from being a united Irish army as depicted in some
history books, was drawn almost entirely from Munster.

Mael Sechnaill, the king of the southern Uí Néill and a
previous claimant of the high kingship, had promised his
support to Brian but withdrew it before the battle
following a quarrel, while most of Connaught and Ulster
did not become involved at all. Indeed, in Ulster the
king of Cenél Eógain was at that time trying to
establish his authority over both the Ulaid and Cenél
Conaill as the first step in his own aspirations to the
high kingship. Brian did however receive the support of
two Viking kings, Wolf the Quarrelsome and Ospak, who
fought on the side of the 'Irish' at the battle of
Clontarf.

Brian's army won the battle of Clontarf, just outside
Dublin, fairly decisively. Brian, however, was killed and
his successor did not have sufficient military power to
retain the high kingship for Munster. Any semblance of
national unity which had existed quickly collapsed. In
fact, far from being welcomed as national heroes, Brian's
victorious army was attacked by the Osraige on the
Leinster-Munster frontier on their march back to Munster.

THE ANGLO-NORMANS

Irish national disunity was again evident in the
following century and was instrumental in an invasion
which changed the course of Irish history - the invasion
of the Anglo-Normans in 1169. Between 1156 and 1166
political supremacy in Ireland was contested between Rory
O'Connor, the king of Connaught, and Murtough
MacLochlainn, the king of Ailech. Tiernán O'Rourke , the
king of Bréifne, gave allegiance to O'Connor; whereas
Dermot MacMurrough, the king of Leinster, was allied with
MacLochlainn. O'Rourke, however, had a long standing
grudge against MacMurrough, and when Rory O'Connor
eventually established himself as the most powerful king
in Ireland following MacLochlainn's death, O'Rourke took
the opportunity to attack MacMurrough and force him into

exile in 1166. While in exile, MacMurrough went to France to seek the support of Henry II, who was then the King of England, Duke of Normandy, and Lord of Anjou, Maine, Poitou and Aquitaine, with sovereign claims over Toulouse, Wales and Scotland (Martin, 1967). Henry gave MacMurrough permission to recruit any of Henry's subjects who would be willing to help him and MacMurrough subsequently managed to gain the support of powerful Anglo-Norman families in south Wales.

MacMurrough returned to Ireland with a small army in 1167, but was again defeated by O'Connor and O'Rourke. However, his Norman allies brought over a second army comprised of Norman, Welsh, French and Flemish mercenaries in 1169. This landed in south-east Ireland and quickly took the Norse cities of Wexford and Waterford before proceeding north to take Dublin in 1170. Following his death in 1171, Dermot MacMurrough was succeeded as the king of Leinster by the Norman leader Strongbow (Richard Fitzgilbert de Clare, the Earl of Pemboke) in accordance with an agreement they had made. This resulted in renewed conflict: Strongbow's succession was contested by Dermot's nephew Murtough MacMurrough, supported by O'Connor, O'Rourke, O'Carroll from Ulster and the Norse from Man and the Hebrides; but the Anglo-Normans emerged victorious following an unsuccessful attempt by the 'Irish' to besiege Dublin.

Meanwhile, Henry II feared that Strongbow and the other Anglo-Norman barons might establish a kingdom in Ireland which was not only outside his control but which might even pose a threat to his kingdom in England, so he came to Ireland in late 1171 with an army, supposedly of 10,000 men, to establish his authority. Henry waged a very successful campaign and secured not only the submission of the Norman barons, but also that of the Norse and Gaelic kings. Henry decided to retain the strategic and commercially important cities of Dublin, Wexford and Waterford under direct control, but Strongbow was permitted to retain most of Leinster as a vassal to the

king. Meath, however, was granted to Henry's loyal
subject Hugh de Lacy to serve as a precautionary
counterbalance to Strongbow to the south and as a curb on
O'Connor to the west. Rory O'Connor acknowledged Henry as
his overlord and it was agreed that he should remain as
high king in the then unconquered areas. However, Henry
was unable to curb the expansionist tendencies of the
Norman barons, and within a few years they began to expand
into other parts of Ireland. Disregarding his earlier
agreements, Henry postjustified the aggression of his
supposed subjects by granting them title to further Gaelic
lands, whilst retaining the cities of Cork and Limerick
for himself.

The Norman conquest of Ireland, in contrast to that of
England in the previous century, was haphazard,
unco-ordinated and mainly conducted by land-hungry
adventurers, acting on their own account over a period of
decades, rather than under the centralised authority of
the king. The number of Norman invaders was relatively
small, but they were militarily superior to the native
Irish whose resistance was considerably weakened by
internal divisions. Indeed, the conquest was facilitated
by the willingness of the local Gaelic leaders to form an
alliance with the Normans in order to settle old scores
against their Gaelic rivals, thereby illustrating the
absence of a perceived need to defend the Gaelic Irish
'nation' against foreign incursions. The Normans
consolidated their supremacy in the areas which they
overran by building fortresses, initially of wood on
earthen mounds (mottes) but increasingly taking the form
of stone castles after about 1200. Conquest, in most
areas, entailed the superimposition of Norman authority
upon the existing political units rather than wholesale
displacements of large populations. Many of the Gaelic
territorial units were preserved as territorial divisions
within the Norman administrative system (e.g. many tuatha
became baronies), but the political and economic
structures introduced by the Normans were quite different

from those of Gaelic Ireland.

The Normans were largely responsible for the introduction of feudalism into Ireland, although there are indications that feudalism might have developed without the assistance of the Normans. Ireland had been considerably influenced by the political and economic changes taking place in western Europe as a whole in the half century prior to the arrival of the Normans. The Catholic Church, having consolidated its authority in the spiritual sphere, was then pursuing a policy aimed at increased political control in the temporal sphere to be effected through a few powerful monarchs acting as feudal vassals to the Pope. In Ireland, the decentralised Gaelic monastic system, which had evolved in association with the tuatha, had been largely replaced by a system of episcopal sees following the synods of Rath Bresail (1111) and Kells (1152). Many of these sees corresponded with the territories of Gaelic overkingdoms (e.g. Ossory corresponded with the kingdom of the Osraige, Kilmore with Bréifne), reflecting the trend towards a smaller number of larger political units. The Irish Church also become more closely linked with Rome, as reflected by the introduction of continental monastic orders such as the Benedictines in 1127 and Cistercians in 1142. Rome, however, seems to have been anxious to speed up the reforms in Gaelic Ireland and Henry II was authorised by the Pope in the papal bull Laudabiliter (1155) to conquer Ireland in order to 'enlarge the boundaries of the Church, to proclaim the truths of the Christian religion to a rude and ignorant people, and to root out the growths of vice from the field of the Lord' (Curtis and McDowell, 1943, p17). As a result, Henry's claim to the lordship of Ireland was unanimously accepted by the Irish bishops at the synod of Cashel in 1172 and, far from being regarded as a foreign invader, Henry seems to have been welcomed as the mechanism for inevitable feudal reforms, not only in the Church but in society as a whole.

Areas of effective Norman control, which were mostly in

the areas of better land quality, were converted into feudal manors, and English (i.e. Norman) concepts of common law, feudal obligation and political structures were introduced. Norman settlement, in contrast to the dispersed settlement of the Irish, was nucleated: manorial villages were established in agricultural areas; and fortified towns were built in areas of strategic or economic importance to supplement the towns already established by the Vikings. New ports, for example, were established at Dundalk, Drogheda, New Ross, Dungarvan, Kinsale, Dingle, Tralee, Galway and Sligo (Orme, 1970). The towns were granted charters (Dublin being the first to receive a charter as early as 1172) and were inhabited by freemen who generally tended to owe allegiance to the king of England rather than to local feudal barons. Norman agriculture, in contrast to the subsistence pastoralism of the Gaelic Irish, placed much more emphasis upon mixed farming: fruit and vegetables became much more important, and a three field system of crop rotation was introduced which placed emphasis upon cereal production for export. Many of the towns consequently developed into important trading centres, and thereby attracted further colonisation from England.

Although few in numbers, the Anglo-Normans dominated about three-quarters of Ireland by the mid-thirteenth century, although central and west Ulster remained one of the most Gaelic parts of Ireland throughout the entire medieval period (Figure 6). The history of east Ulster, however, was quite different and illustrates in microcosm many of the features of the Norman invasion as a whole, although it was also complicated by the close links between eastern Ulster and Scotland. Let us now consider the events in east Ulster in more detail.

Soon after the Normans had established themselves in the southern and eastern parts of Ireland, John de Courcy, acting on his own account, moved north from Dublin with a small army and established an Anglo-Norman colony in east Ulster after defeating the Ulaid in 1177. This colony was

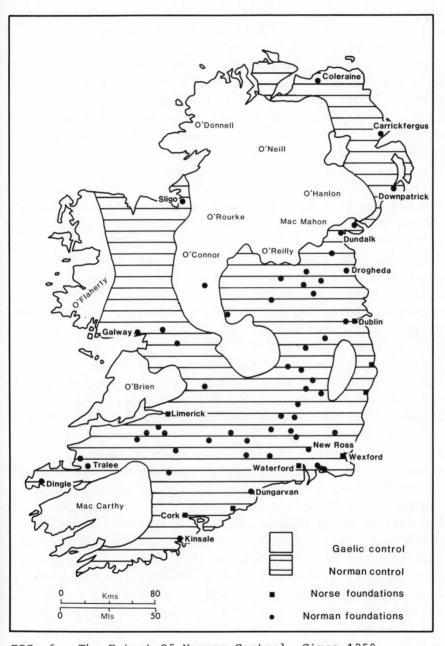

Coleraine
O'Donnell
Carrickfergus
O'Neill
O'Hanlon
Downpatrick
Sligo
O'Rourke
Mac Mahon
O'Connor
O'Reilly
Dundalk
Drogheda
O'Flaherty
Dublin
Galway
O'Brien
Limerick
New Ross
Tralee
Wexford
Dingle
Waterford
Mac Carthy
Dungarvan
Cork
Kinsale

	Gaelic control
	Norman control
■	Norse foundations
●	Norman foundations

0 Kms 80
0 Mls 50

FIG. 6   The Extent Of Norman Control, Circa 1250.

mainly confined to the coastal region and was defended by
a series of castles which could be provisioned from the
sea. The core area of the colony was Lecale, near
Downpatrick, but boroughs were established as far north as
Coleraine. Central and western Ulster, on the other hand,
remained under Gaelic control, but the major clans in the
late medieval period, the O'Neills of Tyrone and the
O'Donnells of Tyrconnell (both descended from the northern
Uí Néill), were divided by a bitter rivalry for the
provincial hegemony of Ulster.

De Courcy was dispossessed in 1205 by King John of
England and his lands were granted to Hugh de Lacy who
became the first Earl of Ulster. De Lacy introduced a
number of Scottish Normans to help defend the colony,
including Walter Bisset, a Scottish Norman noble and
ancestor of the present Earl of Antrim. De Lacy, however,
fell into disfavour and he was defeated in 1210 by King
John with the aid of Scottish Norman barons, including the
Earl of Atholl and the Earl of Carrick, who were rewarded
with estates in Antrim.

Political and military alliances in the early thirteenth
century, as elsewhere in Ireland, were generally complex
and tended to cut across what we would regard today as
national divisions. For example, seeing that the O'Neills
of Tyrone were hard pressed on their eastern side by the
Anglo-Norman colony in east Ulster, the O'Donnells
attacked them from the west with the support from the east
of the Scottish Norman Earl of Atholl and the MacDonnells
(known as the McDonalds in Scotland) who were the lords of
the Western Isles of Scotland, and were ethnically of
mixed Scots Gaelic and Norse Viking descent. The O'Neills
suffered some setbacks, but were strong enough to resist
this 'Scottish' invasion (with the aid of the Norman de
Lacy family). Nevertheless, the MacDonnells, and other
Scots Norse clans (e.g. the MacSweeneys), continued to
play a significant role in Irish politics as they were
frequently employed as mercenaries (known as
'gallowglass') by the major Gaelic clans, throughout the

late thirteenth and fourteenth centuries, because of their military prowess.

Walter de Burgo, of Connaught, became Earl of Ulster in 1264 and both he and his son Richard, the 'Red Earl', extended the authority of the Normans in Ulster. The colony was extended across the north coast of Ulster to the Inishowen peninsula, thereby driving a wedge between the O'Neills and O'Donnells. The de Burgos became the effective overlords of most of Connaught and Ulster, and many of the Gaelic leaders in Ulster were forced to pay the Earl maintenance for a fixed number of troops, including the O'Neills who were obliged to support 80 men (Dolley, 1972). The de Burgos were even able to interfere in the succession of some of the O'Neill kings. They also cultivated powerful connections in Scotland: Richard's daughter, for example, married Robert the Bruce, who as the Earl of Carrick held land in Ulster, but who is better remembered as the king of Scotland who defeated Edward II, the king of England, at the battle of Bannockburn in 1314.

Robert's brother, Edward the Bruce, landed near Larne with an army in 1315 to continue the battle against the supporters of Edward II in Ireland. This was to signal the major turning point in the fortunes of the de Burgos in Ulster. Bruce received the support of many of the more important Gaelic leaders, including Donal O'Neill of Tyrone, and he inflicted a defeat upon the Earl of Ulster at Connor in 1315. This encouraged many of the Earl's Gaelic underkings, especially the O'Connors in Connaught, to rebel. Although Edward the Bruce was defeated and killed soon after in 1318, his early success was instrumental in further encouraging a Gaelic resurgence.

THE GAELIC RESURGENCE

Anglo-Norman power in Ireland began to wane in the late thirteenth century and by 1400 the area of Norman control had shrunk to about one third of the island, mainly in the south and east. The Black Death, which decimated the population in 1348-9, may have been an important precipitating factor in their decline. If, as seems reasonable, we believe contemporary accounts of a much higher death rate in areas of nucleated settlement, the Normans must have been much more adversely affected than the largely pastoral Gaelic Irish. Given that the colonists introduced by the Normans had not been too numerous to begin with, their higher mortality from the Black Death may have been sufficient to swing the balance of power in many of the more marginal areas.

By the mid-fifteenth century English crown control had contracted yet further and was mainly confined to the Pale - an area which extended inland by about 30 miles from the ports of Dublin and Drogheda. The area outside the Pale was politically fragmented and generally either under the control of the local Gaelic clans or the descendants of Norman barons whose loyalty to the king of England could no longer be guaranteed. However, many of the towns outside the Pale held out against the Gaelic resurgence as isolated islands which remained loyal to the king.

A strong sense of nationality appears to have existed in the late fourteenth and fifteenth centuries (Cosgrove, 1981). The descendents of the Norman colonists, for example, maintained a group identity which rigorously excluded the Gaelic Irish. The colonists also made a distinction between the 'English by blood' (i.e. themselves) and the 'English by birth' (i.e. those living in England). The English, in turn, made a distinction between the 'wild Irish' (i.e. the Gaelic Irish) and the 'Anglo-Irish' (i.e. the colonists in Ireland); whereas the Gaelic Irish made a distinction between 'Gaedhil' (natives), 'Gaill' (foreigners, i.e. Anglo-Normans) and 'Saxain' (English).

However, although historians may legitimately speak of two nations in medieval Ireland, it is important to qualify the meaning of the term 'nation': medieval nationality was quite different from that of today.

Nationality in medieval Ireland was more a reflection of
social position than of cultural attributes or political
affiliation. Feudalism was a very conservative social
system which placed an emphasis upon social stability and
order: social status was determined by birth and jealously
guarded. The colonists were consequently anxious to
maintain a distinction between themselves and the Gaelic
Irish in order to preserve their privileged position by
excluding the Gaelic Irish from the benefits of English
law (except in a few special cases where the Irish were
granted special charters from the king). The Irish were
prohibited, for example, from becoming members of trade
guilds, and thereby prevented from participating in urban
life. The Gaelic nobility, for their part, appealed to
brehon law to justify their claims to land, and therefore
found it equally convenient to make a distinction between
themselves and the 'gaill'.

Despite the distinctions made between the two nations by
both sides, it would be wrong to assume that either side
was politically united in opposition to the other. The
Gaelic resurgence in the fourteenth and fifteenth
centuries resulted in a transfer of power in many areas
from the Normans to the Gaelic Irish, but the Gaelic Irish
nation was by no means united in its struggle against the
'foreigners'. Rather, the resurgence was as piecemeal as
the original conquest had been and entailed autonomous
attempts by the Gaelic leaders in each local area to
re-establish their former authority. Indeed, alliances
were frequently forged between Anglo-Norman and Gaelic
leaders as each fought to defend their own interests,
often in opposition against other leaders from their own
'nation'.

Also, despite the emphasis placed upon nationality by
both the Anglo-Norman and the Gaelic Irish, they were not
always ethnically or culturally easy to distinguish.
There was a considerable degree of intermarriage, usually
to forge political alliances, between the Anglo-Norman and
Gaelic nobility. In such cases, unless a special charter

was received from the king, the children of the union inherited the nationality of their father. Also, many of the Anglo-Normans were culturally assimilated by the Gaelic Irish and became 'more Irish than the Irish themselves', especially in the west where Norman colonisation was particularly sparse. The de Burgos, for example, who were the Norman lords of Connaught, adopted Irish dress and customs, spoke Gaelic and generally became indistinguishable from their Gaelic Irish vassals; branches of the Burkes (as they became known) subsequently managed to survive the resurgence to retain control over large parts of Connaught.

The acculturation process, it should be noted, was by no means one-way. By the fifteenth century, the Gaelic political system was in a state of decline and was becoming increasingly feudalised. Inheritance by primogeniture became accepted in practice, if not by brehon law, in many Gaelic areas, and the Gaelic nobility increasingly adopted the dress and manners of the Anglo-Norman nobility in the late medieval period.

In Ulster, the Gaelic resurgence was reflected by the emergence in the mid-fourteenth century of the O'Neills of Clandeboye as the dominant force in south Antrim and north Down. The origins of the O'Neills of Clandeboye are obscure, but it would appear that they broke away from the O'Neills of Tyrone following a dynastic struggle. The O'Neills of Clandeboye subsequently remained bitter rivals of the O'Neills of Tyrone and they generally formed a natural alliance with the O'Donnells of Tyrconnell. Following the emergence of Clandeboye, with the aid of gallowglasses, the Anglo-Norman colony in east Ulster was forced back and virtually eclipsed, although it survived in residual form in east Down until the early sixteenth century (Nicholls, 1972).

Meanwhile, in north Antrim, the Anglo-Norman estates of the Bissets passed by marriage to the MacDonnells in 1399. The MacDonnells were the Lords of the Isles in Scotland and they subsequently established a semi-autonomous kingdom which straddled both sides of the North Channel until the early sixteenth century, when the Scottish end of their domain was crushed by the emergence of the strong centralising monarchy of the Stuarts (especially James IV) in Scotland. The MacDonnells, however, remained a major political force in Ulster throughout the sixteenth century.

THE TUDOR CONQUEST

By the early sixteenth century political power in Ireland was very fragmented (Figure 7). The direct authority of the king was mainly confined to the Pale and to the larger towns. Outside the Pale, political control rested with the local lords, both Gaelic and Anglo-Norman, who gave different degrees of allegiance to the king. Most of Ulster was under the control of the O'Neills and O'Donnells, whereas most of Connaught and the Midlands was either under the control of other Gaelic clans (e.g. the O'Connors) or Gaelicised Normans (e.g. the Burkes). Anglo-Norman control was mainly confined to east Leinster and east Munster, but by the sixteenth century the major Anglo-Norman families had become partly Gaelicised and increasingly autonomous. As royal authority in Ireland collapsed in the fifteenth century, the influence of the Pale diminished and the king was forced to depend upon the Anglo-Norman families outside the Pale to assert his authority. The major Anglo-Norman families therefore tended to act as political intermediaries between the king and Gaelic Ireland.

The major Anglo-Norman families in the first half of the fifteenth century had been the Fitzgeralds of Desmond and the Butlers of Ormond (between whom a bitter rivalry developed), but in the late fifteenth and early sixteenth centuries the Fitzgeralds of Kildare became the most powerful family. Three generations of Kildares (Thomas, Garret Mór and Garret Óg) served as the king's lord

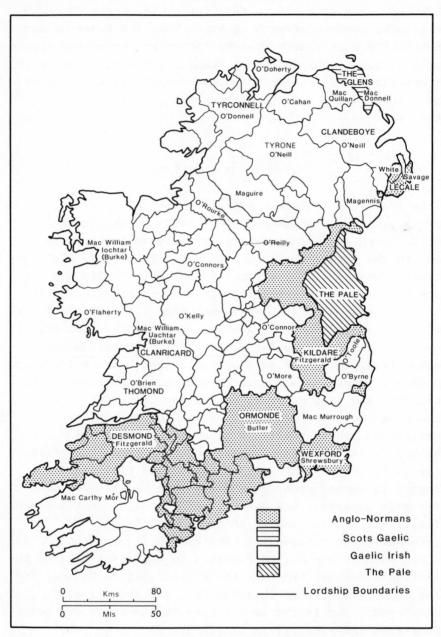

FIG. 7   The Lordships Of Ireland In 1532 (After
          Nicholls, 1976).

deputy and used the position and strategic marriages with some of the more powerful Gaelic leaders (including the O'Neills) to establish themselves as the effective rulers of Ireland from 1468 to 1533. Indeed, even though they had supported the house of York in the War of the Roses, such was their power that Henry VII, a Lancastrian, felt that it would be more prudent to retain them in the office of lord deputy than to attempt to displace them.

By the early sixteenth century England had been consolidated into an increasingly centralised state by the Tudor kings Henry VII (1485-1509) and Henry VIII (1509-1547). Scotland, meanwhile, had been largely consolidated around the same time by the Stuarts. Centralised states were likewise being established in other west European countries. In many instances the king was able to assert his authority over the feudal nobility with the support of the burghers whose wealth, accumulated in long distance trade (which was expanding rapidly due to new overseas discoveries), could be used to support standing armies and a centralised bureaucracy. However, in Ireland the self-sufficient nature of the Gaelic economy, coupled with the anarchical political situation in the late medieval period, had limited the scope for urban growth and long distance trade. The absence of a strong merchant class which could give financial support to the most powerful political leader consequently reduced the potential for an indigenous centralised Irish state.

Henry VII did not show much inclination to extend his domain to Ireland, but by the time of Henry VIII wars between absolute states highlighted the fact that Ireland provided a potentially useful base for the Tudors' continental enemies (especially France and Spain) to launch attacks on England. Henry VIII realised that it was strategically essential to re-establish royal authority over Ireland. Garret Óg Fitzgerald, the lord deputy, was summoned to London where he was dismissed from office and imprisoned. His son, Silken Thomas, consequently rebelled, but the rebellion was successfully

put down by an army sent over by Henry in 1535. Thomas
and five other leading members of the Kildare family (some
of whom were innocent) were executed for treason in 1537.

Having crushed the Kildares, Henry had himself declared
king of Ireland in 1541. The Gaelic and Anglo-Norman
leaders were asked to surrender to his authority on the
understanding that they would receive new title to the
lands which they controlled from the king. The more
powerful leaders also received English titles of nobility.
There was relatively little opposition from the Irish
leaders to Henry's policy of 'surrender and regrant',
especially given that Henry was often able to grant more
land than was being surrendered because of the
confiscations arising out of the dissolution of Irish
monasteries. Even Conn Bacach O'Neill, the powerful
leader of the O'Neills, surrendered and was created the
first Earl of Tyrone in 1542.

Difficulties arose, however, because lands and titles
were to be automatically inherited by the eldest son under
English law, whereas clan leadership under brehon law was
open (at least in theory) to all members of the derbfine.
As a result, the new earls frequently met with opposition
from other branches of their own families who were now
excluded from the succession, and who also contested the
right of the clan leaders to receive as personal property
lands which they had previously held on behalf of the
clan. For example, under English law Conn Bacach O'Neill
should have been succeeded by his eldest son Matthew, but
most of the O'Neills (including Conn himself) supported
his younger son Shane. Matthew was killed in the
resulting turmoil in 1558, but when Conn Bacach died in
1559 the English supported the claims of Matthew's eldest
son Brian. This initiated a long series of wars between
the O'Neills and the English, with the latter forming an
alliance with many of the O'Neills' traditional enemies,
including the O'Donnells. Elizabeth I ordered that Shane,
who had been inaugurated as the clan leader, should be
suppressed, but when Brian was killed in 1562 she allowed

Shane to take the unofficial title of Lord of Tyrone.
Shane, however, had higher ambitions and he proceeded to
try to enforce his claim to the provincial kingship of
Ulster. He initially inflicted heavy defeats upon both
the O'Donnells of Tyrconnell and the MacDonnells of Antrim
in 1565, but in 1567 he was defeated by the O'Donnells and
then murdered by the MacDonnells. His severed head was
placed on display in Dublin castle for four years to serve
as a warning to other rebels.

English authority, directed from Dublin, frequently met
with local opposition and rebellion. Many of the local
leaders, both Gaelic and Anglo-Norman, resented the
Tudors' centralisation of power and they therefore looked
to continental Europe for support. Henry VIII had broken
from the Church of Rome in 1534, and England became
increasingly influenced by the Protestant Reformation
under Edward VI and Elizabeth I. Doctrinal differences
did not generate the same degree of friction in sixteenth
century Ireland as they did elsewhere, but given the close
association which developed between the Protestant Church
and Tudor State in England, those opposing centralisation
in Ireland frequently appealed to the Counter-Reformation
for external support. Religion therefore became an
important rallying call and Catholicism later intensified
the degree of common ground between the Gaelic Irish and
Anglo-Normans, few of whom had been influenced by the
Reformation.

The English increasingly adopted a policy of introducing
loyal English settlers in areas where rebellions had been
suppressed. The first such plantation was in Laois and
Offaly, where the confiscated lands of the O'Connors and
the O'Mores were granted to English adventurers in 1556
(Figure 8). The major objective, in this instance, was
to provide a buffer zone between Gaelic Ireland and
the Pale. However, the English settlers were too few
in number and, apart from the survival of a few garrison
towns (Maryborough and Phillipstown, now Portlaoise
and Daingean), the plantation had little lasting effect.

90

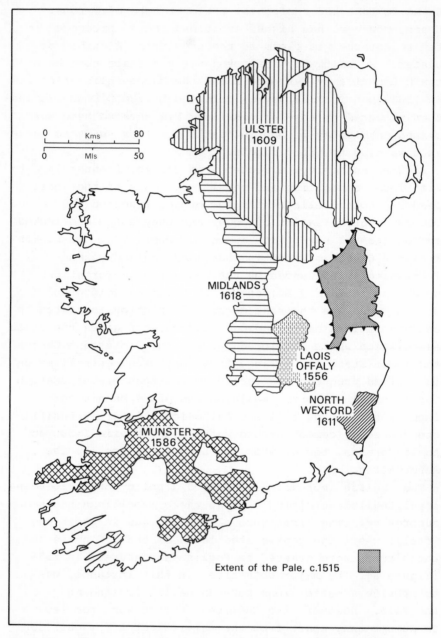

FIG. 8   The Principal Tudor And Stuart Plantations.

An attempt to plant parts of counties Monaghan, Armagh,
Down and Antrim in the 1570s (known as the Enterprise of
Ulster) was a total failure due to the military resistance
provided by the O'Neills of Tyrone, O'Neills of Clandeboye
and the MacDonnells of Antrim.

A lengthy rebellion by the Anglo-Norman Fitzgeralds of
Desmond, which was eventually suppressed in 1585, provided
an opportunity to plant large parts of Munster. 400,000
acres of confiscated land were divided into seigniories of
4,000 to 12,000 acres and granted to English adventurers
who undertook to introduce English settlers. However, the
plantation was again too thinly colonised to succeed. By
1592 only 13 out of the 58 English undertakers were
actually resident in Munster and only 245 families of
colonists had been introduced. Its fortunes were revived
slightly when Richard Boyle, later the Earl of Cork,
bought the estates of Sir Walter Raleigh (who had 42,000
acres) in 1602. Boyle established a number of industries
and fortified towns (e.g. Bandon).

Although these plantations were not very successful, the
English gained a lot of experience. This was used to
their advantage when an opportunity arose later in Ulster,
following the nine year war between the English and the
Gaelic clans who were united under the leadership of Hugh
O'Neill. Hugh O'Neill, who was the son of Matthew and
therefore the Earl of Tyrone under English law, had been
brought up in the English court and had fought for the
English against the Fitzgeralds of Desmond in Munster.
However, he had hopes of reviving the traditional claims
of the O'Neills to the kingship of Ulster. After he was
accepted as the leader of the O'Neills, who recognised his
outstanding military and leadership qualities, Hugh formed
an alliance with the other major Ulster clans, including
the O'Donnells of Tyrconnell, and waged war against the
English from 1595 to 1603. Hugh established himself as
the effective leader of Gaelic Ulster, but he realised
that outside support was required if he was to maintain
his position against the English and so he appealed to the

Pope and the king of Spain for assistance. Troops were eventually sent by the king of Spain, but the combined Spanish and Gaelic army was defeated by the English at the battle of Kinsale (1601). This marked the turning point of the war, eventually leading to the surrender of the Gaelic leaders in 1603.

The battle of Kinsale is often treated in school history books as a battle between the Irish and English nations. There were indeed strong nationalistic overtones. Hugh, for example, in furthering his own personal ambitions, appealed for solidarity between the Gaels, whose traditional way of life was being threatened by the consolidation of Tudor power and the imposition of English law. He also appealed for solidarity between Catholics against the Protestant English. However, although Hugh received widespread support from the Gaelic Irish in Ulster, he did not receive the total support or sympathy of either the Gaelic Irish or Anglo-Normans in the rest of Ireland. One of the 'English' generals at Kinsale, for example, was the Earl of Thomond - a member of the Gaelic O'Brien family. Also, one of the deciding factors in the battle was the fact that Kinsale, whilst easier for the Spanish to make a landing, was at the opposite end of Ireland from Hugh's power base in Ulster. Lacking significant support outside Ulster, Hugh therefore had to march his armies the length of Ireland through hostile territory. Even in Ulster, Red Hugh O'Donnell, who supported Hugh O'Neill, was challenged in Tyrconnell by his cousin Neill Garbh O'Donnell who supported the English. Red Hugh was therefore placed in a dilemma as to whether he should support the 'national' cause by marching his army south to Kinsale or whether he should try to retake Donegal castle which had been captured by Neill Garbh. Hugh O'Neill was by no means the leader of a united Irish nation.

The defeat of Hugh O'Neill can be regarded as a major turning point in Irish history for three reasons. First, it represented the decisive defeat of the Gaelic clan

system. Although the Gaelic way of life was by no means
totally destroyed by the defeat of Hugh O'Neill at
Kinsale, the Gaelic Irish never re-established themselves
as a major political force. Second, it left Ireland
effectively controlled by a central, albeit external,
authority for the first time in its history. Third, it
indirectly facilitated fundamental population changes in
Ulster. Ulster, as we shall see in Chapter 4, was
transformed in the seventeenth century from the most
Gaelic and rebellious part of Ireland into the area later
to become the most receptive to British influence.

SUMMARY

The Irish nationalist assumption that Ireland, as a
relatively small island, is a natural political unit is
not supported by historical experience. Ireland has never
at any point in its history formed an independent and
politically united state. Since the time of the
Anglo-Norman invasion, Ireland has either been totally or
partly ruled from England; whereas before the Anglo-Norman
invasion, and indeed throughout the medieval period,
Ireland was politically fragmented into a number of
autonomous units. Effective political unity in Ireland
has only ever existed under British rule, following the
consolidation of centralised political control by the
Tudors.

Further, even when it was independent (but disunited),
Ireland was not politically self-contained: there is a
very long history of political links between Ireland and
Britain, especially between Ulster and Scotland. This
could be construed by Ulster unionists as a historical
precedent for the present link between Northern Ireland
and Britain, but only to the extent that it illustrates
that there is nothing natural about Ireland being a
self-contained political unit. Many of these links, it
must be remembered, were between the Gaels in Ireland and

94

the Gaels in Scotland. The historical record would
therefore provide a stronger argument for including parts
of Scotland within an Irish state, than for including
parts of Ireland (i.e. Northern Ireland) within the
British state. Such an argument, however, merely serves
to illustrate the futility of trying to justify
nationalistic claims by historical precedents.

Although there was never an independent united Irish
state, we must also consider whether there was an Irish
nation in the period discussed above. The second of the
five theses identifed at the end of Chapter 1, it will be
remembered, is that the two nations in Ireland (as
identified in Chapter 2) did not come into existence until
the nineteenth century. Given that the ancestors of the
Ulster nation did not begin to settle in Ireland until the
seventeenth century, we need only concern ourselves here
with the ancestors of the Irish nation.

The Gaelic Irish exhibited a very high degree of
cultural homogeneity, extending even to the acceptance of
a common legal system. There must therefore have been a
strong group identity which would have enabled them to
make an easy distinction, in terms of cultural attributes,
between themselves and 'foreigners' such as the Norse and
Anglo-Normans. However, they were not welded into a
nation (in the modern sense). Cultural attributes were
not regarded as an important basis for political
affiliations throughout the medieval period, with the
result that there was no perceived need to defend the
culture group against foreigners. Indeed, Gellner's
contention that throughout history it was 'generally far
more acceptable to have an outsider at the top, than to
submit to the rival party (clan, baron, or whatnot)'
(Gellner, 1964, p152) is clearly supported by the history
of the Anglo-Norman invasion and the subsequent submission
of the Gaelic chiefs to Henry II. Hugh O'Neill, it is
true, attempted to rally support in his struggle against
the Tudor state by an appeal to common culture (i.e. the
Catholic religion and the Gaelic way of life); but this

appeal, given his earlier career in Munster, would appear
to have been governed more by pragmatic considerations
than by ideological idealism. Apart from the fact that it
failed to overcome totally the deep-rooted divisions
within Gaelic society, the appeal differed from modern
nationalism by being addressed to an élite rather than to
the Gaelic people as a whole. This was inevitable given
the hierarchical nature of Gaelic society: political power
was controlled by a small (but internally divided) élite
who followed their own interests rather than acting at the
behest of the people - the people were subjects rather
than citizens, consequently the preconditions were absent
for the creation of a political community with which
people could fully identify. The various other aspects of
the general nationalist ideology (such as the belief that
nations are the normal and natural units for political
organisation) which only emerged in the late eighteenth
and early nineteenth centuries (see Chapter 2), were also
obviously absent in medieval and early modern Ireland.

CHAPTER 4
The New English and the Ulster Scots

The defeat of Hugh O'Neill left Ireland politically united under the effective control of the British crown at the beginning of the seventeenth century. This by itself had relatively little direct impact upon the later course of Irish history, but it facilitated other changes throughout the seventeenth century which are important to an understanding of later events.

One of the most important changes was in the ownership of land. Irish landowners suspected of treason, or who for one reason or another failed to support the winning side in the Cromwellian or Williamite wars (generated by political and economic struggles in England), usually forfeited their estates and were replaced by new English landowners. This resulted in the creation of a new, non-Irish, landowning élite. A second major change, arising out of changes in landownership, was the introduction of a substantial number of settlers from Britain. Most of these settlers came from areas which had been influenced by the Reformation in the sixteenth century and were consequently Protestants, whereas most of the native Irish remained Catholic.

The resentment felt against the new landlords and settlers, who were never fully assimilated by the existing population due to religious and social differences, later had a major influence upon the development of Irish nationalism. Irish nationalism, when it developed in the middle and late nineteenth century, was characterised by a strong Catholic ethos, fired by feelings of dispossession. Protestants, popularly identified by Catholics as usurpers, consequently felt alienated from the Catholic Irish nation created by Irish nationalism. This alienation was particularly strong in Ulster, where Protestants lived in much larger numbers than in other parts of Ireland because of extensive colonisation associated with the Ulster plantation in the early seventeenth century.

The present chapter, divided into three sections arranged by historical sequence followed by a brief summary, describes these changes in the seventeenth century in more detail. The first section looks at the Ulster plantation, the second examines the impact of the Cromwellian wars in the middle part of the century, and the third discusses the Williamite wars towards the end of the century.

THE ULSTER PLANTATION

When Hugh O'Neill surrendered in 1603, he thought he was surrendering to Elizabeth I. However, Elizabeth had died six days previously and James VI, the Stuart king of Scotland, had succeeded her as James I of England. The unification of the crowns of England and Scotland had a major influence upon government policy in Ireland. Previously the English had tried to keep the Scots, especially the MacDonnells, out of Ulster because they feared a growth of French influence in Ireland as a result of the close links between Scotland and France (Collins, 1980), but after 1603 Scots settlers were allowed to move into Ulster without English opposition. These new Scots, however, differed from those who had settled in earlier centuries. The earlier Scots were mostly pre-Reformation Catholics from highland Scotland, where the Gaelic clan system still dominated; whereas the new Scots were Protestants from lowland Scotland, where more advanced forms of commercial agriculture were practised.

There were two types of Scottish colonisation in Ulster in the seventeenth century. One was an official government-planned plantation in central and west Ulster; the other was an unofficial, unplanned, 'spontaneous' colonisation in east Ulster. Both, however, were a direct consequence of the defeat of Hugh O'Neill.

These colonisations had a major impact upon later political developments, culminating in the creation of Northern Ireland, but it is important not to oversimplify the relationship between the Ulster plantation (see Figure 9) and what was later to become Northern Ireland. Only four of the six planted counties are located in present day Northern Ireland (viz. Armagh, Fermanagh, Londonderry and Tyrone): the other two (Cavan and Donegal) are in the Republic. Monaghan, also in the Republic, was not included in the plantation because the local Gaelic leaders, the MacMahons, had shown loyalty to the crown since their surrender and regrant in 1591. The two counties which now comprise the core area of Northern Ireland (i.e. Antrim and Down) were also excluded from the plantation, but they were the major reception area for the unplanned Scottish settlement.

The unofficial Scottish colonisation of east Ulster began when two Scottish lairds, James Hamilton and Hugh Montgomery, secured lands in north Down from the O'Neills of Clandeboye, partly in return for using their influence with the king to arrange the release of their leader, Conn O'Neill, from Carrickfergus jail and to secure him a pardon. Tenants from Ayrshire were introduced onto these estates from 1606 onwards. Meanwhile, Randal MacDonnell (now the Earl of Antrim) also brought over large numbers of lowland Scots to tenant his estates in north Antrim. The area in between (i.e. the Lagan valley and the north shore of Belfast Lough) was granted to the lord deputy, Sir Arthur Chichester, and to other English gentlemen who introduced English settlers.

Scottish settlers were attracted to Ulster by the opportunities offered to commercially-orientated tenant

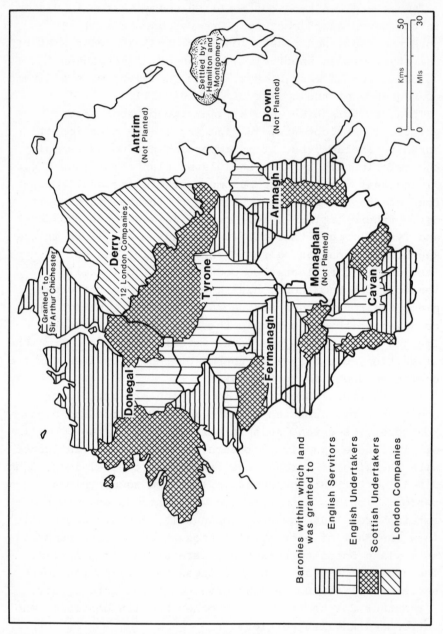

FIG. 9   Land Allocations In The Ulster Plantation (After
         Robinson, 1982).

farmers. Scotland suffered problems of overpopulation in
the early seventeenth century; consequently, when the
threat of attack by the Gaelic clans in central and west
Ulster receded, many Scots were enticed to settle in what
appeared to them as under-utilised land in east Ulster.
Conditions for agriculture were initially harsh, but the
colonists were able to clear forests and convert rough
pasture into arable land. Grain grown in Ulster found a
ready market in Scotland, where news of the opportunities
available in Ulster filtered back and gradually attracted
further tenants. Migration from Scotland to Ulster,
however, only built up slowly and probably did not reach
its peak until the second half of the seventeenth century.

The unofficial settlement of Antrim and Down acted as a
bridgehead colony from where many settlers were later
enticed to move further west into the area of the official
plantation. The official plantation did not begin until
1609. Although defeated in 1603, the leaders of the
Gaelic clans in central and west Ulster were initially
treated favourably by the new king. They were allowed,
for example, to retain their English titles and their
desmesne lands as freehold estates, and to receive a fixed
rent from their sub-chiefs (Robinson, 1982). This,
however, was a source of disappointment to the king's
servitors (i.e. civil servants and military personnel) in
Ireland who had hoped that the lands in central and west
Ulster would have been confiscated and divided between
them in the same way as the lands of the Desmond
Fitzgeralds had been at the time of the Munster
plantation. The Gaelic aristocracy in Ulster were
consequently harassed by the Dublin administration and,
believing that the English officials were conspiring to
eliminate them, they decided to flee to Spain en bloc
in 1607 rather than risk going to London to answer charges
made against them that they were planning another
rebellion. The 'Flight of the Earls' was regarded by the
authorities as evidence of treason, and the lands of the
Gaelic leaders were confiscated. A plan devised in 1608

102

to plant the confiscated lands in six Ulster counties
(viz. Armagh, Cavan, Coleraine (later renamed
Londonderry), Donegal, Fermanagh and Tyrone) was put into
effect in the following year.

The Ulster plantation was more successful than earlier
plantations. This was partly due to better planning.
Having learned from the mistakes made in Laois-Offaly and
Munster, land in Ulster was granted in much smaller
parcels in an attempt to maximise the number of settlers.
The largest grants were for 3,000 acres, but most grants
were for units of 1,000 to 2,000 acres. Those receiving
grants were divided into four categories: servitors
(mostly English); undertakers from England; undertakers
from Scotland; and Irish natives. The servitors received
their grants within the same baronies as the native
grantees, so that they could oversee the Irish, and were
not required to plant their estates with tenants from
Britain (Robinson, 1982). The undertakers, on the other
hand, were not allowed to take Irish tenants and were
required to plant at least 24 men, from at least 10
families of English or lowland Scots, on every 1,000
acres. Scottish and English undertakers were allocated
land in different baronies (see Figure 9). In all areas
grantees were required to build towns or villages, and
stone or brick houses with fortified enclosures known as
bawns. The plantation was organised slightly differently
in county Coleraine. Here most of the confiscated land
was allocated to twelve London companies, who received it
under the same conditions as the undertakers (although the
estates were generally larger - about 3,000 acres). A
substantial amount of land was also allocated to the
Church of Ireland bishops and to Dublin University.
Robinson (1982) estimates the division of land between the
various categories (excluding county Coleraine/
Londonderry) as follows: Church 24%; English undertakers
22%; Scottish undertakers 21%; Irish natives 15%;
English servitors 13%; Dublin University 3%; corporate
towns etc. 2%.

Many of the grantees, unlike those in the earlier plantations, had relatively small holdings in Britain and therefore proved more willing to actually settle in Ulster. However, the major reason for the success of the Ulster plantation, compared to earlier plantations, was the fact that there was a more abundant supply of tenants from Britain because of the close proximity of Ulster to Scotland. Nevertheless, tenants sometimes proved difficult to attract to central and western Ulster, and many undertakers were forced to break the conditions of their grants by taking native Irish tenants. Although landownership was dominated by English grantees, it is estimated that Scots tenants outnumbered English tenants by a ratio of about 5 to 1, with the result that the overall settlement patterns showed little resemblance to the distribution of landownership between English and Scots.

These settlements made a lasting impact upon the economy and environment. Large areas of forest were cleared and converted to agricultural use, and the mainly pastoral economy of the Gaelic Irish was replaced by a more mixed and market-orientated agricultural economy. This in turn facilitated the gradual economic development of towns and other market centres, including a number of fortified corporate towns which were built as part of the plantation scheme (e.g. Armagh, Ballyshannon, Cavan, Derry, Donegal, Dungannon, Dungiven, Killybegs, Lifford, Limavady and Omagh). Ulster was consequently transformed from being the least to being the most urbanised part of Ireland by the end of the eighteenth century.

These seventeenth century migrations also left a lasting impression upon the religious map of Ireland. Most of the new settlers, whether English or Scots, had been influenced by the Reformation and had been converted to Protestantism, whereas most of the native Irish had not been influenced by the Reformation and therefore remained Catholic. Present day religious and national affiliations consequently reflect, to a large extent, movements of population in the seventeenth century, although there are a few exceptions on both sides: some of the colonists were Scottish or English Catholics and are today Irish nationalists, whereas some of the native Irish were later converted to Protestantism and are today Ulster unionists (Stewart, 1977). The different origins of the settlers themselves is also reflected to some extent by religious differences: most of the lowland Scots tenants had been converted to Calvinism by John Knox, whereas the English settlers were mainly Episcopalian. Presbyterians still tend to be more dominant in areas of former Scots settlement (e.g. Antrim, north Down and parts of Derry), whereas Episcopalians (i.e. Church of Ireland, the Irish equivalent of the Church of England) are more numerous in a belt of former English settlement stretching from the Lagan valley west through north Armagh into Fermanagh.

The different natures of the two types of settlement in Ulster had several important long-term implications. The official plantation had a much lower density of settlers than the unplanned colony in east Ulster: Protestants were consequently much more numerous, both proportionately and in absolute numbers, in east Ulster than in central and west Ulster. Also, given that the lands in the planted counties had been confiscated, and given that the previous inhabitants had been displaced (although not to the extent that is sometimes depicted), the grievances of the native Irish were much greater in central and west Ulster. East Ulster consequently became, in effect, an extension of lowland Scotland and thereby the core area of British settlement in Ireland, whereas central and west Ulster always remained more a frontier zone due to the relatively even numbers of Protestants and Catholics, coupled with a higher degree of sectarian animosity based upon grievances and insecurity. In fact, the plantation was almost wiped out by a rebellion of the Gaelic Irish in 1641, and many of the colonists in central and west Ulster had to flee back to east Ulster where they received the protection of an army sent over by the Scottish parliament in 1642.

THE CROMWELLIAN CONFISCATIONS

The Gaelic uprising in Ulster in 1641 was part of a more complex and widespread chain of events. Charles I's attempt to rule in England as an absolute monarch had disintegrated into an open conflict between the king and the English parliament. When parliament had attempted to limit the power of the king by restricting his financial resources, Charles had retaliated by governing without parliament for eleven years. However, he was forced to seek alternative sources of finance. Sir Thomas Wentworth, Charles's lord deputy in Ireland, attempted to raise money by confiscating the estates of, or imposing large fines upon, those who could not prove full legal title to their lands. The Irish landowning nobility, both Catholic and Protestant, consequently developed a considerable antipathy towards Wentworth.

The situation was further complicated by religious considerations. Although a Protestant, Charles I adopted a tolerant attitude towards Irish Catholics (in return for their financial support); but he adopted a much tougher line against the nonconformist Presbyterians in Scotland. The fact that the Scots Presbyterians would not conform with the Church of England, of which Charles was the head, was regarded by Charles as a challenge to his claim to rule by divine right. Charles's attempt to coerce the Scots met with disastrous defeats in the two Bishops' Wars (1639 and 1640). The terms of the second defeat forced Charles to convene the English parliament in the hope that it might support him against the Scots; but parliament took advantage of the king's weak position to press its own demands. Relations between the king and the English parliament deteriorated, culminating in the English civil war (1642-1646).

Meanwhile, the Gaelic Irish, led by Rory O'More in Leinster and Sir Phelim O'Neill in Ulster, also took advantage of the confused situation in England to stage a rebellion in 1641 in an attempt to recover their former

lands. The uprising in Leinster failed, but central and
west Ulster was quickly captured by the Gaelic Irish,
resulting in the massacre of thousands of English and
Scots settlers. The Irish initially attacked only English
settlers, but the rebellion degenerated into a sectarian
attack on all Protestants. Although the territory was
regained by the settlers within a few years, accounts of
the massacre occupied a prominent position in the folk
memory of Ulster Protestants in subsequent centuries and
were instrumental in the creation of a 'siege mentality'
amongst Protestants in the planted counties: the 1641
rebellion was pointed to in later years as an example of
the supposedly untrustworthy, violent and destructive
nature of Irish Catholics, in contrast to self-perceived
Protestant virtues of hard-work, thrift and dependability.
This crude stereotype is in some ways reinforced at the
present by IRA bomb attacks on small Protestant
businesses.

The Old English (i.e. the descendants of the
Anglo-Normans, most of whom remained Catholic) proclaimed
their loyalty to the king and their willingness to defend
the Pale, but the English administration in Dublin was
suspicious of all Catholics. The Old English consequently
allied with the Gaelic Irish, to form what is usually
referred to as the Catholic Confederation or Confederation
of Kilkenny (1642), but they maintained that their
rebellion was not against the king (who, they recognised,
was much more tolerant of Catholicism than the Puritan-
dominated English parliament). Owen Roe O'Neill,
a nephew of Hugh O'Neill, returned from Spain to lead the
Gaelic forces in Ulster and Colonel Thomas Preston, an
experienced soldier of Old English stock, was brought in
to lead the Old English in Leinster. However, the
Catholic Confederation never really operated in a cohesive
manner.

The Protestant opposition to the Confederation was even
more fragmented. The Earl of Ormond acted as the king's
representative throughout and managed to control Dublin

and the Pale for most of the war. However, when
eventually faced with defeat, he surrendered Dublin to the
parliamentarians (also Protestant) rather than let it be
taken by the Catholic Confederation. Large parts of
Munster were controlled by Lord Inchiquin, a Protestant
member of the Gaelic O'Brien family. Inchiquin began the
war supporting the king, defected to the parliamentarians,
and then switched back to the royalists (although many of
his supporters remained on the side of the
parliamentarians). In Ulster, the Scots settlers,
reinforced in 1642 by a Scottish army under General Munro,
followed the Scottish parliament by supporting the English
parliamentarians in the first part of the war, but then
later opposing the imposition of the republic by
Cromwell's English parliament in the later stages.

The war in Ireland generally took the form of a struggle
between Protestants and Catholics (although a lengthy
truce was established between Ormond and the Old English
on the basis of common loyalty to the king); but in the
late 1640s the Gaelic Irish and Old English were joined by
Ormond and Inchiquin in opposition against Cromwell, who
was supported by the administration in Dublin. Following
the defeat and eventual execution of the king, Cromwell
came to Ireland in 1649. During a short campaign he
captured the royalist towns of Drogheda and Wexford. The
massacre of their garrisons (about 2,000 in each case) and
many of the inhabitants (especially in Drogheda),
frightened most of the other royalist towns into easy
surrender before he returned to England in 1650. The
Cromwellians, under the leadership of Cromwell's
son-in-law, Ireton, completed the subjugation of Ireland
by 1652.

Cromwell, having waged a long war against royalists,
Scots and others, in both Britain and Ireland, was faced
with heavy debts. He therefore confiscated the lands of
those who had not supported him in Ireland in order to pay
his soldiers and to repay the loans of the adventurers who
had financed his campaigns (Figure 10). Those who had

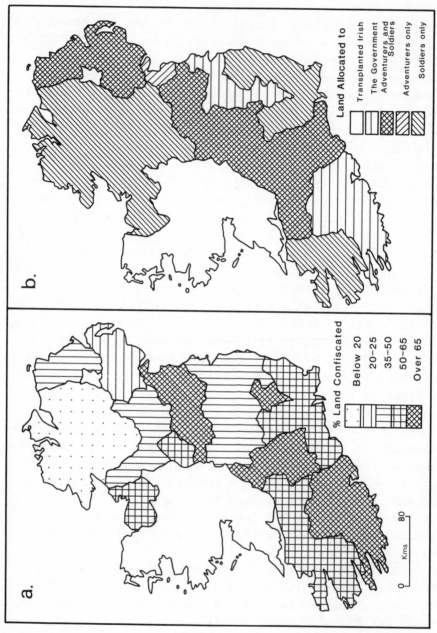

FIG. 10   (a) Land Confiscated And (b) Land Allocated By
          Cromwell.

fought against him had all of their lands confiscated, and those who could not prove that they had actively supported him had a portion of their lands confiscated and were later obliged to move to estates of a similar size (but of much poorer land quality) in Connaught. The confiscations only applied to large landholders: those with holdings valued at less than £10 per annum were exempted. Nevertheless, the confiscations resulted in a massive transfer of land ownership from Gaelic Irish and Old English to a new group of English landlords, sometimes called the New English. (The New English are generally referred to in later centuries as the Anglo-Irish. The term 'Anglo-Irish' is sometimes applied to the Anglo-Normans in the late medieval period, but the term is used here to refer only to post-Reformation New English in the eighteenth and nineteenth centuries to avoid confusion). A total of 11 million acres (out of a total area of slightly more than 20 million acres) changed hands, compared with only half a million acres in the Ulster plantation. Given that both the Gaelic Irish and Old English were Catholic and the New English were mainly Protestant, the confiscations resulted in a dramatic shift in religious composition of the dominant class in Irish society.

Unlike the Ulster plantation, the Cromwellian confiscations did not entail a very large influx of new tenants: they merely entailed a change in landownership. The existing tenants, generally speaking, were not displaced, although some chose to follow their previous landlords to Connaught. Many of the former landowners whose lands had been confiscated remained as tenants to the new landlords. Given that little attempt was made to convert the tenants to Protestantism, the confiscations resulted in the introduction of religious divide between a numerically small but powerful landlord class and a large and increasingly impoverished tenantry. This divide became a significant factor shaping the nature of Irish nationalism in the nineteenth century.

110

THE WILLIAMITE WARS

England was effectively ruled by Cromwell until he died
in 1658, but a after his death the English parliament
invited Charles II to return as king in 1660. The
restoration of the monarchy did not affect the situation
in Ireland significantly: a few dispossessed royalist
landlords had their former estates partly restored, but
Charles was forced to accept the Cromwellian settlers as
one of the conditions for the restoration.

Charles II was an astute king who recognised the
vulnerability of his position, but he was succeeded by his
brother James II who had aspirations of restoring the full
authority of the monarchy. James soon generated
opposition from the English parliament, which he adjourned
in 1685. James, a Catholic, also alienated the
conservative Protestant nobility by attempting to
introduce Catholics into key civil and military positions.
It was therefore decided to invite William of Orange, who
was married to James's Protestant daughter Mary, to come
to England with an army to preserve England's
'constitutional rights and the Protestant religion'.
James retreated to France and William, whose main concern
was to get the support of England in his struggle with
France, arranged for the election of a new parliament.
The new parliament invited William and Mary to occupy the
throne jointly as constitutional monarchs on terms drawn
up by parliament in the Declaration of Right (1689).
Under these terms the king was obliged to hold frequent
parliaments, was not allowed to raise taxes without
parliament's consent, and was not allowed to suspend laws
on his own authority. The struggle between James and
William in England was not simply one between rival kings
with different religious affiliations: it was a
revolutionary struggle between the forces of absolutism
(the Jacobites) and limited democracy (the Whigs).

Most of the more important battles between James and
William were fought in Ireland, where allegiances tended

to divide along religious lines. The Catholic nobility supported James because they were hopeful that their former property and social power might be restored under a Catholic king. Indeed, James's lord deputy, the Earl of Tyrconnell, set up a Catholic-dominated Irish parliament (the 'Patriot Parliament') which in 1689 passed legislation to confiscate the property of 2,400 Protestants (Beckett, 1966). The Episcopalian landowners consequently looked to William to protect them. The Presbyterians in Ulster also supported William because he offered them a greater degree of religious freedom than James.

James landed in Ireland in 1689, but his hopes for a rapid victory were frustrated by the stuborn resistance of the Protestants in Enniskillen and Derry. Derry withstood a siege lasting 105 days before supplies could be brought in to relieve a population reduced to eating rats, and the Williamites of Enniskillen intercepted and defeated a Jacobite army at Newtownbutler which was on its way to Derry from Dublin. James's failure to control the north enabled Williamite armies of Dutch, German, Danish and Huguenot soldiers to land in Ulster before proceeding south to defeat James at the battle of the Boyne in 1690. James fled to France, but Irish Catholics continued to fight and were not defeated until after the battle of Aughrim and the surrender of Limerick in 1691.

The Treaty of Limerick, which signified the end of the war, provided the defeated Catholics with favourable terms of surrender. Soldiers in the defeated army were offered the choice of returning home or leaving the country: 11,000 left for France to serve Louis XIV, 2,000 remained at home, and 1,000 chose to serve William. The treaty also guaranteed that Catholics would have the same degree of religious toleration that they had enjoyed under Charles II, and that their estates would be protected against confiscation. However, the terms of the treaty had to be ratified by the Irish parliament which, following William's victory, was now solidly Protestant.

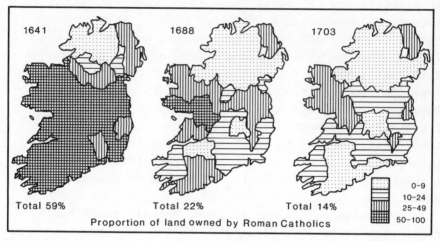

FIG. 11   Changes In The Religious Affiliations Of
Landowners In The Seventeenth Century (After
Simms, 1958).

Parliament refused to honour the treaty; in fact, in the
following years it passed legislation (the Penal Laws)
which discriminated very strongly against Catholics (see
Chapter 5). About one million acres of land were
confiscated from those who had supported James, with the
result that by the early eighteenth century Catholics
owned less than one sixth of the land in Ireland (Figure
11)

SUMMARY

Many of the seeds for later national conflict were sown
in the seventeenth century. The defeat of Hugh O'Neill,
followed by the flight of the Gaelic aristocracy,
facilitated the planned and unplanned colonisations of
Ulster by Scottish and (to a lesser extent) English
settlers. Most of these settlers had been converted to
Protestantism before they came to Ireland. Given that
relatively little effort was made to convert Catholics to

Protestantism, distinctions between the existing
inhabitants and the new settlers - which were not as great
as are sometimes depicted (see Buchanan, 1982) - were
subsequently preserved by differences in religious
affiliation.

Religious differences were also an important
contributory factor in the changes which took place in
other parts of Ireland. The struggle between emerging
capitalism and the remnants of feudalism throughout
western Europe often took the form of a religious war
between Protestants and Catholics: it was therefore only
natural that the Catholic Gaelic Irish and Old English
landowners should appeal for external Catholic support in
their struggle to maintain their position against the
centralising influences of the Protestant English state.
The defeat of the Catholic Irish landowners by Cromwell
and William of Orange resulted in a massive transfer of
landownership to new groups of Protestant and English
landowners who, although small in numbers, were to
dominate social and political power in Ireland throughout
the eighteenth century.

The movement of population into Ulster and the changes
in landownership were both important factors in the later
growth of Irish nationalism and Ulster unionism. However,
although each entailed the introduction of new Protestants
into Ireland, it is important to make a clear distinction
between their different regional effects. The
colonisations in Ulster resulted in a substantial
Protestant majority in many areas (especially in east
Ulster), whereas the confiscations associated with the
Cromwellian and Williamite wars simply entailed a transfer
of landownership from a Catholic élite to a new Protestant
élite: there was relatively little change in the overall
religious composition outside Ulster (except Dublin where
there was a large Protestant population associated with
the centre of political power). Second, the Protestants
who moved into Ulster were drawn from all sections of
society: the overwhelming majority were originally tenant

farmers rather than landowners. The Protestants who moved into the rest of Ireland, on the other hand, were mainly drawn from the higher levels in the social pyramid: a very high percentage were either landowners or their agents. Finally, a high percentage of the Protestants in Ulster were nonconformists, reflecting the Scottish origins of most; whereas most of the Protestants outside Ulster were Episcopalians, reflecting not only the fact that most of them were from England but also that conformity in religion was usually a condition for receiving land. These differences between northern and southern Protestants were to become important in the eighteenth century, as we shall see in the following chapter.

CHAPTER 5
The Protestant Nation and Irish Republicanism

In contrast to the wars, land confiscations, large scale population movements and general turmoil of the seventeenth century, Ireland enjoyed a long period of apparent stability in the first three-quarters of the eighteenth century. Even the Jacobite risings in 1715 and 1745 caused little incident in Ireland. However, this apparent stability disguised a number of deep-rooted tensions which eventually gave rise to widespread rebellion towards the end of the century. These events are important because they indicate to what extent nationalism and national identities had evolved by the late eighteenth century.

To understand these events, it is necessary to consider the tensions which induced a spirit of rebellion. There were two major types of tension. First, there was resentment towards England arising out of Ireland's inferior and exploited position as a British colony. Second, there was considerable inter-class friction arising from political inequalities and restrictions within Ireland. A violent solution to both types of tension was encouraged by major events elsewhere. The American War of Independence encouraged and provided the opportunity for the Irish colony to demand greater autonomy within the British colonial system. These demands were made in the late 1770s and early 1780s by a body known as the Irish Volunteers. The French Revolution, in turn, inspired demands for social reforms

within Ireland in the 1790s. These were made by the
United Irishmen and culminated in the 1798 rebellion.
This chapter is divided into five sections. The first
two sections consider the two types of tension mentioned
above in more detail: section one discusses social
injustice within Ireland; whilst section two deals with
the grievances arising out of Ireland's colonial status.
The next two sections deal with the major upheavals in the
last three decades of the eighteenth century: section
three discusses the events associated with the Irish
Volunteers; and section four considers the rebellion of
the United Irishmen. The final section discusses some of
the implications of these events, especially with respect
to the light that they cast upon the growth of nationalism
and national identities.

THE PROTESTANT ASCENDANCY

The Treaty of Limerick, agreed between the Williamite
and Jacobite generals in 1691, provided for religious
toleration of Catholics and gave a guarantee that those
who agreed to acknowledge William as king would not
forfeit their estates. However, the Treaty had to be
ratified by the Irish parliament. William probably
intended to honour the agreement of his general, but the
king could not afford to ignore the feelings of parliament
and neither the English nor the Irish parliament looked
upon Catholics very favourably. The English parliament
associated Catholics with the counter-revolutionary
Jacobites and it therefore passed legislation in 1691
which prohibited Catholics from sitting in either the
English or Irish parliament. The Irish parliament which
was convened in 1692 was consequently exclusively
Protestant. Having recently survived the attempt of the
Patriot parliament to confiscate the estates of
Protestants, the new Irish parliament was not favourably
disposed towards ratifying the Treaty of Limerick.

Instead, it passed a series of discrimatory Acts between
1695 and 1727 which became collectively known as the Penal
laws.

The Penal laws banished the Catholic bishops to the
continent, and permitted only one Catholic priest to
remain to serve each parish. This in theory should have
eventually resulted in the total demise of the Catholic
Church in Ireland because new priests could not be
ordained without bishops, but in practice these laws were
not rigidly enforced. Catholics were also prohibited from
voting in elections and from holding public positions.
They were not allowed to teach or open schools, carry arms
or own a horse worth more than £5. However, the most
important and rigidly enforced laws related to
landholding. Catholics were prevented from buying land,
and if they owned an estate it had to be divided between
all the heirs on the death of its owner - unless one of
the heirs became a Protestant, in which case he could
claim the whole estate. Catholics were also prohibited
from leasing land for more than 33 years.

Penal laws were then common in many European countries
(both Catholic and Protestant), but Ireland was
exceptional in two respects. First, the Irish penal laws
discriminated against the majority rather than a minority.
Second, the Irish penal laws were not designed to
eliminate a religious practice. Life was certainly made
more difficult for the Catholic Church as an institution,
but no Catholics were ever executed under the Penal laws
because of their religious beliefs, nor was any serious
attempt ever made to convert large numbers of Catholics to
Protestantism. The major purpose of the Penal laws was to
exclude Catholics from political and economic power in
order to protect the privileged position of the Protestant
ascendancy (i.e. the Episcopalian landlord class). Their
net effect was a further reduction in the amount of land
owned by Catholics to less than 5 per cent as many of the
Catholic landowners became Protestants to avoid the Penal
restrictions. 'Converts' included the Earl of

Clanrickarde (descended from the Gaelicised Anglo-Norman Burke family) and the Earl of Antrim (of the MacDonnells).

The privileged position of the Episcopalian landlord class was maintained by their almost total control of the Irish parliament. Each county and each borough returned two members of parliament, but many of the boroughs were either 'rotten' (i.e. had no inhabitants) or were 'pocket' (i.e. effectively controlled by the local landlord). It is estimated, for example, that only seventy-two of the three hundred members of the Irish House of Commons in 1783 were freely elected (albeit by a very restricted franchise). Most of the others were selected by the local landlord. Ninety-one M.P.s were selected by fifty-two commoners and one hundred and twenty were chosen by fifty-three lords: Lord Shannon, for example, returned sixteen M.P.s; Lord Hillsborough nine; and the Duke of Leinster seven.

Given the powerful position of the landlords, the relationship between the landlords and their Catholic tenants often became extremely exploitive. Irish tenants, unlike their English counterparts, did not have the protection of long standing feudal traditions governing landlord-tenant relations because most Irish landlords had held their estates since only the seventeenth century. Many landlords looked upon their estates as a source of income and had little regard for the welfare of their tenants, although some, it must be said, adopted an extremely caring and paternalistic approach. Given that many of the landlords also held estates in England, there was a high degree of absenteeism. Estates in such instances were either managed by agents or leased to middlemen who sub-leased farms to tenants. The middlemen, many of whom were Catholics, were often guilty of rackrenting (i.e. maximising their profits by ruthlessly increasing the rents of the tenants). Most tenants, particularly the small holders, held land on very short leases (frequently one year) and when the lease expired they were obliged to pay whatever rent increases were demanded or else face eviction. Those who were evicted lost without compensation any improvements which they had made to the property. The system was obviously not conducive to the development of good farm management by small holders.

Although the Penal laws ensured a Protestant domination of land ownership and social power, a minority of Catholics were able to maintain a considerable degree of affluence: apart from the Catholic middlemen, there were substantial numbers of Catholic merchants and large commercial tenant farmers holding farms of 100 acres or more, especially in areas of good land in the south and east. However, most Catholics lived in increasingly destitute conditions. The large farm areas in the south and east were characterised by large numbers of landless labourers, whereas other areas, especially in the west, were characterised by large numbers of cottiers trying to scrape a subsistence existence from a few acres of poor quality land. The number of cottiers and landless labourers increased throughout the eighteenth century in tandem with net increases in population (from about 2.5 million in 1700 to about 5 million by 1800). This resulted in the further subdivision of small farms and intensified the gap between rich and poor.

The gap between rich and poor was also widened by the commercialisation of agriculture, reflecting the growth of commodity production associated with the transition to capitalism. This resulted in enclosures of common land and wholesale evictions of tenants by 'improving' landlords who adopted the latest scientific methods for maximising output. As in England, Ireland became a country of 'thin men and fat beasts' in the eighteenth century. The poor lived a marginal existence, and thousands died of starvation in years of bad harvests (e.g. 1728-9, 1740-1). The landlords, on the other hand, accumulated large amounts of capital which were expended on conspicuous consumption. Large mansions surrounded by attractive landscaped demesnes in rural areas and town

houses built in Dublin to the highest architectural
standards survive today as monuments to the super-
exploitation of the Irish tenantry in the eighteenth
century.

The tenants did not always accept their position
peacefully. Throughout the eighteenth and nineteenth
centuries the tenants frequently banded together in
retaliatory secret societies, especially in the rich
commercial farming areas in the south and east.
Collectively known as 'whiteboys', because of their
practice of wearing white shirts over their clothing at
night, these societies opposed evictions by intimidating
new tenants and fought against enclosure and commercial
cattle ranching by destroying fences and maiming cattle.
However, these societies operated at a localised level and
never developed into a cohesive national movement with a
concerted plan of action. They were therefore easily
suppressed by the authorities.

Landlord-tenant relations were somewhat different in
Ulster. Although most of the landlords were
Episcopalians, the tenants (both Catholic and Protestant)
were protected from the landlords by a custom known as
Ulster tenant right (or Ulster custom). This had no
standing in law, but a practice had evolved whereby
tenants were protected against eviction if they paid their
rents, were given longer leases (and therefore protected
against rack renting) and had the right to sell any
improvements which they made on their farms if they moved.
It is not too clear when this custom developed, but it was
probably during the seventeeth century when the landowners
in central and west Ulster had to offer terms which would
attract Protestant tenants from east Ulster in sufficient
numbers to protect their estates from the Gaelic Irish.
The Ulster custom was mutually beneficial to landlord and
tenant alike: due to their greater security the tenants
were able to improve their holdings and thereby increase
their output; this in turn increased their ability to pay
rent.

Although tenants in Ulster generally enjoyed a higher standard of living than most of their southern counterparts, Ulster Presbyterians felt considerable resentment towards the landlord Protestant (i.e. Episcopalian) ascendancy and the Dublin parliament. Presbyterians (and other Nonconformists) suffered a similar, although milder, form of disrimination to Catholics, under the Test Act passed by the Irish parliament in 1704. Although Presbyterians were legally entitled to own land, carry arms and vote, they were not allowed to hold state offices, become officers in the army or to sit in parliament or other elected bodies. Marriages conducted by Presbyterian ministers were not recognised in law, with the result that the inheritance of the children was sometimes jeopardised because legally they were illegitimate. Discrimination against Presbyterians was relaxed after 1719, but the legislation remained on the statute books until 1780. However, the thing which irritated Presbyterians most was the fact that they were forced to pay various taxes which helped maintain the ascendancy. These included a county cess (administered by the major landlords for the upkeep of roads, etc.) and a tithe to the Established (i.e. Episcopalian) Church of Ireland. The grievances of the Prebyterian and other Protestant tenants on occasions erupted in violence. The enforced payment of tithes, cess and other taxes, for example, resulted in an outbreak of whiteboy activity by Protestant tenants known as Oakboys in Armagh and Tyrone in the 1760s. Evictions and the introduction of cattle ranching on the Donegall estates in 1769 gave rise to similar activities by some of the Presbyterian tenants in Antrim and Down calling themselves the Hearts of Steel.

Following a series of large rent increases, Presbyterians began to emigrate to the American colonies in large numbers from 1717 onwards. Catholics, because of their more destitute condition, did not generally have sufficient resources to emigrate and large scale Catholic emigration did not begin until the mid-nineteenth century. The proportion of Presbyterians in Ulster consequently declined, and some areas which formerly had Presbyterian majorities were 'recolonised' by Catholics. It is estimated that up to a half a million Presbyterians emigrated to the American colonies - where they became known as Ulster-Scots or Scotch-Irish - by the beginning of the outbreak of the American War of Independence. There, because of the strong dislike that they had developed of the British colonial authorities in Ireland, many Ulster-Scots played a prominent role on the side of the Americans in the War of Independence. Five of the signatories, for example, on the Declaration of Independence (which was printed by an emigrant from Strabane) were Ulster-Scots. American settlers from Scotland, in contrast, tended to side with the British government.

COLONIAL IRELAND UNDER MERCANTILISM

Ireland, as we saw in the previous chapter, was completely subjugated by England by the mid-seventeenth century. From then, until the beginning of the nineteenth century, Ireland became a fully dependent colony of England governed by a small executive headed by the lord lieutenant, who represented the king, and a chief secretary, who reported to the English (after 1707, British) cabinet. Both were appointed by Westminster and were normally English.

The Irish parliament, like that in England, had two houses. The House of Lords comprised Irish peers and Church of Ireland bishops. However, many of the peers were absentee and therefore the bishops often formed a majority. The appointment of bishops was consequently dictated by political considerations - most were English and were selected because they could be trusted to follow the instructions of the lord lieutenant. The House of

Commons could also be manipulated by the administration. As noted above, the Commons was controlled by a small number of landlords who were in a position to nominate a substantial number of the M.P.s. The administration could therefore secure a majority, when required, by offering titles and other inducements to the landlord oligarchy.

The executive did not often need to manipulate the Irish parliament. Under a law passed in 1494, known as Poynings Law, the Irish parliament could only meet when authorised by the king and could only pass legislation which had first been approved by Westminster. Also, under the Declaratory Act of 1719 (sometimes known as the 'Sixth of George I'), the British parliament claimed the authority to make laws for Ireland. In addition to being undemocratic and corrupt, the Irish parliament was therefore essentially powerless.

The English parliament, in contrast, was becoming increasingly powerful. At the beginning of the seventeenth century England had been an absolute monarchy under Elizabeth I, but by the end of the century political concessions had been forced upon the king by parliament following the Whig revolution. This growth in parliamentary power was only part of a wide-ranging series of changes associated with the growth of merchant influence, during which the state was gradually transformed from serving the interests of the king to serving the interests of the powerful merchant classes. These changes were reflected by the emergence of mercantilism as the dominant political economic doctrine.

Mercantilism merged the interests of the merchant classes with those of the state by emphasising the importance of a healthy trade balance to the economic growth of the state. It also emphasised the need for state intervention to achieve this objective. Legislation was passed to protect English industries from overseas competition by imposing high import duties and other restrictions on manufactured goods which competed with English goods. Cheap imports of food and raw materials

essential to English industry were facilitated by the
payment of government subsidies. The state apparatus was
also used to acquire colonies through military conquest in
order to provide cheap food and raw materials and to act
as a market for English exports. The dependency of the
colonies upon England was enforced by a series of
Navigation Acts (e.g. 1651, 1663, 1670). These required
trade with other colonies or foreign countries to be
conducted via England, where the goods were subject to
both import and export taxes. State taxes were used to
support a standing army and navy which could be be used to
defend the colonies against the predatory interventions of
the other colonial powers.

Ireland, as an English colony, suffered as a result of
English mercantilist legislation, and many of Ireland's
later economic woes can be traced to the systematic
destruction of some of her more important industries in
the second half of the seventeenth century and the first
half of the eighteenth century because they competed too
strongly with those in England. For example, Ireland had
developed a profitable export trade in fat cattle to
England by the mid-seventeenth century, but this was
prohibited by the Cattle Acts of 1663 and 1666 following
protests by graziers in the west of England. These
remained in force until 1759. (Their repeal,
incidentally, encouraged cattle ranching and enclosure in
the 1760s and resulted in a rapid growth of whiteboy
activities). Manufacturing industries were also adversely
affected. The Irish woollen industry, although still
small, began to challenge the sale of English woollens on
the continent in the 1690s. An Act was therefore passed
in 1699 to prohibit the export of Irish woollen goods to
any country other than England. This effectively killed
the industry because Irish woollens were not competitive
in England due to high import duties. Similar protective
legislation was passed to the detriment of other Irish
industries (e.g. brewing, glass making and sugar
refining).

Although the Irish economy was seriously weakened by English mercantilism, it must be stressed that Ireland was not singled out for special discriminatory treatment. The English legislation was designed to enhance the English economy, not to destroy that of the colonies, and to that extent all colonies suffered equally. Indeed, it was this type of treatment of the American colonies which generated the American War of Independence.

Colonial industries were only discriminated against when they came into competition with those of England. Economic activities which did not compete with English industries were allowed to develop unhindered. In the case of Ireland the two major survivors were the provisions trade and the linen industry. The provisions trade, which was beneficial to the expanding British navy, encouraged the growth of ports with rich agricultural hinterlands, mainly in the south and east of the country (e.g. Dublin, Waterford and Cork). This facilitated the growth of a relatively prosperous class of merchants, many of whom were Catholics. The linen industry, which was at this stage still cottage based, thrived mainly in Ulster (centred on north Armagh). Exports in the first half of the eighteenth century were mostly through Dublin, due to the availablity of banking facilities, but in the second half of the century Newry and later Belfast began to develop as the major ports for the industry. This again facilitated the development of a strong educated middle class.

With the exception of the linen industry, mercantilist legislation generally reduced Ireland to a supplier of unprocessed raw materials and food: Irish manufacturing industries were usually uncompetitive because of prohibitions and high tariffs, with the result that there was little point in reinvesting capital accumulated in Ireland in Irish industries. Capital accumulated by the landlords, middlemen and merchants consequently tended to be invested either in land and property or in English industries and government stocks. This is one of the reasons why Ireland (with the exception of east Ulster) was bypassed by the industrial revolution which totally transformed England in the late eighteenth and nineteenth centuries. Nevertheless, the second half of the eighteenth century was generally a period of increasing prosperity for commercial agriculture, due to increasing demand for grain and other agricultural products in the growing industrial urban areas in England. This was reflected by a massive improvement in communications between the major ports and their hinterlands through the construction of turnpike roads and canals.

THE IRISH VOLUNTEERS

A form of colonial 'nationalism' developed amongst the Protestants in Ireland against this background of colonial domination by Britain in the eighteenth century. The Protestant ascendancy had always had an ambivalent attitude towards Britain: it realised that British support was required to maintain its dominance over the large Catholic majority; but it also resented the fact that Ireland was politically and economically dominated by Britain. Colonial resentment had therefore existed amongst the ascendancy for some time, as indicated by the writings of William Molyneaux and Johnathan Swift in the early decades of the eighteenth century, but it developed into a mass movement in the 1770s following the mobilisation of the Protestant middle classes, to form what is sometimes referred to as the 'Protestant nation'.

The triggering event was the American War of Independence. Angered by the restrictions and taxes imposed upon their colonies by the British authorities, the Americans rebelled in 1775 and issued the Declaration of Independence in 1776. The American cause attracted a considerable degree of sympathy in Ireland because the Irish colony was hampered by very similar restrictions. Also, many Ulster families had relatives fighting for the

Americans against the British. This sympathy, however,
was not reflected by the majority in the manipulated Irish
parliament: on the outbreak of war, parliament declared
its support for the British and agreed to the withdrawal
of 4,000 troops from Ireland to fight in America. This
left Ireland virtually undefended and open to attack by
France, Spain and the Netherlands who, taking advantage of
Britain's weak position, entered the war on the side of
the Americans.

   Ireland's vulnerable defences were highlighted in 1778
when an American pirate, Paul Jones, sailed into Belfast
Lough and captured a British naval sloop. The merchants
of Belfast appealed to the government for protection, but
were informed that sufficient troops were not available.
Fearing an invasion by the French, they therefore
established a volunteer force initially comprised of three
companies. Volunteer companies were quickly formed in
other parts of Ireland, and within a year about 40,000 men
had joined the Volunteers in order to defend the colony
against Britain's European enemies. Most of the
Volunteers were Protestants because Catholics were still
prohibited from carrying arms by the Penal laws.
Companies were provided with colourful uniforms financed
by their local landlords or by public subscriptions from
civic minded citizens (including some prosperous Catholic
merchants) and they were normally officered by Protestant
clergymen and merchants in the towns and by the local
gentry in rural areas.

   Volunteer companies paraded in 1778 to celebrate the
battle of the Boyne and the birth of William of Orange,
but the motivations for these celebrations contained an
ambiguity which was later to split the Volunteer movement
into two factions. The battle of the Boyne was celebrated
because it represented the overthrow of Catholic
absolutism by Protestant-dominated parliamentary
democracy: it therefore symbolised not only the victory of
the Protestant ascendancy within Ireland, but also the
growth of parliamentary power within England. A

contradiction consequently emerged between those who
sought the retention, or even an expansion, of the power
of the Protestant landlord ascendancy, and those who
sought further democratic representation for the emerging
middle classes within the Irish parliament.

The conservative and reformist factions were both
represented within the Irish parliament. The majority
supported retention of the ascendancy, but a minority
opposition known as the 'Patriot' party, under the
leadership of Henry Flood, demanded greater autonomy for
the Irish parliament and a reduction in the restrictions
imposed by England upon Irish trade. Both demands were
kept in check by the manipulation of parliament by the
government (i.e. the executive). When Flood resigned to
take up a position in the government in 1775, he was
replaced as the leader of the Patriot party by Henry
Grattan who extended the demands to include parliamentary
reform and Catholic emancipation (i.e. repeal of the penal
laws), both of which recognised the need to extend the
ruling class to include the emerging middle classes of all
religions.

The government was not particularly happy about the
rapid growth of the Volunteers, especially given that many
of the leaders of the Volunteers were members of the
Patriot party. Their fears proved to be well founded. In
1779, following riots by hungry mobs in southern towns
where there was a food shortage because government
contractors were buying up supplies of beef, pork, butter
and flour to supply the British army, the Irish parliament
adopted a resolution in favour of free trade. When the
government refused to act on this resolution, Volunteer
companies paraded in Dublin with two cannon carrying
placards saying 'Free Trade - or this' (McDowell, 1967).
Given that the army was still engaged in fighting the
Americans, the government realised that they were in no
position to argue and free trade was consequently conceded
by Westminster in 1780. Ireland was now free to export
woollens and other previously proscribed commodities, and

to trade directly with foreign countries.

Having achieved the first of their objectives, the Patriot party and Volunteers turned their attention to the demand for legislative independence. Grattan moved a motion before the Irish parliament in 1780 that only the king and the Irish parliament had the right to make laws for Ireland, but the government manipulated a majority against him and the motion was defeated. Two years later, a convention of Volunteers in Ulster held in Dungannon passed a number of resolutions, including one which stated that 'a claim of any body of men, other than the King, Lords and Commons of Ireland, to make laws to bind this kingdom is unconstitutional, illegal and a grievance.' The Dungannon resolutions were quickly adopted by meetings of Volunteers, who now numbered about 80,000, in other parts of the country. When Grattan moved a motion in support of the Dungannon resolutions in the Irish parliament, he received no opposition whatsoever and the government, again faced with the threat of military force, was obliged to back down. The Irish parliament consequently repealed Poynings law and the British parliament repealed the Sixth of George I in 1782.

Ireland now became, at least in theory, more independent. However, it was still a monarchy. The king of England was still the king of Ireland, and he was still represented by a lord lieutenant who was appointed by the British parliament. Further, the government of Ireland (i.e. the executive) was not subject to Irish parliamentary control. If the government was defeated in a crucial vote, it was not obliged to resign. Rather, all it had to do was to win over further support and then introduce the bill again. This was facilitated by the fact that the Irish parliament was still under the control of a small number of powerful landlords and the Episcopalian hierarchy, many of whom were English and continued to owe their primary allegiance to Britain. Also, the government was usually able to acquire the required support by bribery, given that it controlled the appointment of state officials, nominated peerages and allocated pensions. Corruption was rife, and Irish independence, in the absence of a democratic reform of parliament, therefore tended to be notional, rather than real.

Having achieved legislative independence, the Irish Volunteers therefore began to demand a reform of the Irish parliament. The Irish parliament, not surprisingly, did not wish to be reformed and it rejected the Volunteers' demands. This created a major dilemma for the Volunteers. Until this point they had achieved their objectives simply by threat of armed force, and had been successful because the British army was engaged in fighting the Americans. The situation was now quite different: the government position in Ireland was strengthened by the end of the war in America, with the result that reforms could now only be gained by physical force. Also, instead of the government, the Volunteers now found themselves threatening their own parliament, for which they had only recently gained legislative independence. The Volunteers lacked the commitment required for an armed rebellion and therefore backed down. They subsequently declined as a force of any significance, although they remained in existence for a further ten years.

THE UNITED IRISHMEN

The eclipse of the Volunteer movement in 1783 left a number of demands unsatisfied. The major ones were for Catholic emancipation and for a reform of the Irish parliament. Many of the Penal laws, including those restricting religious practice and landholding by Catholics, were repealed in 1778, but Catholics were still excluded from sharing in political power. Likewise, the Protestant middle classes, although not legally prevented from sharing in state power, were de facto excluded by the undemocratic way in which the Irish parliament was

selected. This in turn meant that the Irish parliament
could be easily manipulated by the government in the
political and economic interests of Britain. Catholic
emancipation and reform of the Irish parliament therefore
remained as major sources of discontent throughout the
1780s, although widespread popular agitation for reform
did not emerge again until the 1790s.

As in the 1770s, the demands for reform within Ireland
were strongly influenced by events elsewhere. In this
case the triggering event was the French revolution. The
overthrow of Louis XVI and the seizure of state power by
the bourgeoisie on behalf of the 'nation' (i.e. the people
of France) in 1789 fostered a growth of revolutionary zeal
in Ireland.

Belfast and the adjoining counties of Antrim and Down
quickly emerged as the major centre of radical ideas in
Ireland. This area enjoyed a certain degree of
prosperity, relative to the rest of Ireland. Belfast was
then beginning to grow rapidly as the major port for the
linen industry and also as the centre of a factory-based
cotton industry. However, the emerging Belfast
bourgeoisie developed a strong antipathy towards the
Dublin-based parliament and administration.

This antipathy contained religious, class and regional
components. East Ulster was the heartland of
Presbyterianism in Ireland, and there was consequently a
strong resentment against what was regarded as the unjust
enforcement of tithes to the Established Church. Class
grievances arose from the fact that the Irish parliament
was controlled by a landed aristocracy which refused to
agree to reforms which would enable representation for the
bourgeoisie. This, in turn, was aggravated by the fact
that the Irish parliament met in Dublin and showed little
appreciation for the needs of developing capitalism in
east Ulster. Many of the radicals were consequently
either Belfast businessmen,dissatisfied at the incentives
provided for manufacturing and trade in the provinces by
the landlord-dominated Dublin parliament, or medium-sized

tenant farmers in Antrim and Down. Most of the latter farmed about 20 to 50 acres on leases of about 30 years and, compared with the bulk of the population in Ireland, they enjoyed a fair degree of financial security, but they strongly resented the imposition of tithes and the county cess. This resentment was directed towards the Episcopalian landlords and the state apparatus which supported them.

Radical ideas also gained some support from merchants and the professional classes in the other major cities, especially Dublin, due to their exclusion from political power. Many of these were Episcopalians, including Theobald Wolfe Tone, a Dublin barrister who published a number of leaflets arguing for a reform of the Irish parliament and equality for Catholics. These attracted the attention of the Belfast radicals who invited him to Belfast in 1791. The Society of United Irishmen was formed during his visit to lobby for a democratic reform of the Irish parliament and an extension of full citizenship to Catholics. Branches of the United Irishmen were soon established in Dublin and other centres.

The original intention of the United Irishmen was to secure liberal democratic reforms by peaceful means, but it soon became clear that reforms would not be conceded by the Irish parliament without a struggle. It was also recognised that reforms could not be implemented as long as the Irish parliament and government were controlled from England. Democratic reforms therefore became contingent upon political separation from England, which in effect meant deposing George III as the king of Ireland. Inspired by the Revolution in France, the United Irishmen consequently became increasingly republican and revolutionary in orientation.

The government feared that the Irish Volunteers, who were still strong in Ulster, might be used against them by the radicals, so they disbanded the Volunteers in 1793 and replaced them by a Militia under government control. The officers in the Militia were Protestant, but the vast bulk

of the rank and file were forcibly conscripted from the
Catholic peasantry. This conscription proved to be very
unpopular, and resulted in widespread disorder due to
peasant resistance.

The United Irishmen made approaches to France for
support. The French government sent William Jackson as an
emissary in 1794, but he was arrested whilst carrying a
memorandum from Wolfe Tone outlining the prospects for a
French landing. The government allowed Tone to go into
voluntary exile, due to a lack of suffient evidence
against him, but the United Irishmen were declared an
illegal organisation. However, they were reconstituted in
Belfast as a secret revolutionary body.

The United Irishmen hoped to secure the support of the
Catholic middle classes for democratic reforms. However,
the Catholic middle classes, having only recently gained a
repeal of most of the Irish penal restrictions, were
anxious not to provide any excuse for the Irish parliament
to reintroduce penal legislation. Also, many of the
educated Catholic middle classes, especially the clergy,
were very wary of republicanism following the persecution
of the Catholic Church by the French revolutionaries, and
were therefore predisposed against radical reforms.
Indeed, the lack of Catholic sympathy for republicanism
and the French revolutionaries (with whom Britain was at
war) encouraged the government to make further concessions
towards Catholics in 1793 in an attempt to defuse
potential support for the radical demands of the United
Irishmen. Catholics consequently received the same voting
rights as Protestants, and therefore the only thing which
continued to be denied them was the right to sit in
parliament and to hold the top positions within the state
apparatus (i.e. in the civil service, armed forces and
legal professions).

The United Irishmen also attempted to mobilise support
from the vast potential army of Catholic cottiers and
landless labourers, but most were too preoccupied with
simply trying to survive to identify with the liberal

bourgeois democratic demands of the United Irishmen.
However, both the United Irishmen and the government were
able to take advantage of sectarian conflict between
Catholic and Protestant (mainly Episcopalian) tenants to
rally support for their respective causes. This conflict
had originated in Armagh and adjoining counties in central
Ulster where Catholic tenants had moved in to take up
farms previously occupied by Protestants. The Protestant
tenants were upset because they were engaged in a struggle
against their landlords to hold down rents, whereas the
Catholics (who were more desperate) were prepared to pay
higher rents in order to get land. The Protestant tenants
therefore attempted to defend their interests by forming
whiteboy groups known as Peep o'Day Boys to drive out the
new Catholic tenants. The Catholics, in turn, organised
themselves into secret defence organisations called
Defenders. Violence escalated in the mid-1790s and,
following a battle in 1795 which left 25 Defenders dead,
the Peep o'Day Boys formed the Orange Society, named after
William of Orange, to defend their position against what
they regarded as Catholic encroachment.

The government recognised that the Orangemen could be
utilised to defend the ascendancy as a whole, and large
numbers of Orangemen were consequently enlisted in a new
military force known as the Yeomanry under landlord
control. Meanwhile, Defenderism rapidly spread throughout
the Catholic peasantry, partly inspired by news of social
revolution in France, but mainly because of fears of
attack by the ascendancy-supported Orangemen. However,
given the absence of middle-class Catholic support or
leadership, the Defenders tended to react incohesively
against local grievances rather than follow any concerted
plan of national action. The United Irishmen therefore
attempted to mobilise the Defenders under their leadership
with promises of an improvement of peasant conditions
following a radical reform of the Irish parliament.

Tone spent some time in the United States before going
to France in 1796 to request armed support. The French

eventually agreed to send an army of 14,000 men under General Hoche in December of the same year. However, Hoche became separated from the main force in a thick fog and when the rest of the force arrived in Bantry Bay they were unable to land because of rough seas. After waiting four days they reluctantly returned to France.

Although the French expedition failed, the government was seriously alarmed and a state of emergency was declared. The Habeas Corpus Act was suspended, and people other than peace officers or soldiers were ordered to surrender their arms. The tendering of secret oaths was made a capital offence and the army, comprised of Militia and Yeomanry as well as regular soldiers, began a campaign of terror under General Lake to disarm Ulster. This continued throughout most of 1797. Houses were arbitrarily searched for weapons and many who were even vaguely suspected of United Irish activities were brutally flogged or tortured to secure information. Given that little attempt was made to distinguish between the innocent and guilty, some government supporters were worried that Lake's methods might provoke a rebellion rather than prevent it, but in the event his methods proved highly effective. When the rebellion finally did take place in 1798, the United Irishmen in Ulster had already been broken and were easily defeated by the government forces.

A second attempt to land a French army was frustrated when the Dutch fleet which was to carry them was defeated by the British at Camperdown in 1797. The French promised that they would make a further attempt in the following year and the United Irishmen made preparations for a spring rebellion. However, the French army was required by Napoleon to fight a campaign in Egypt, and the United Irishmen therefore had to make preparations to rebel without foreign assistance. The government by then had infiltrated the organisation of the United Irishmen in Leinster, and were able to arrest most of the leaders in March, 1798. Lord Edward Fitzgerald, a brother of the

Duke of Leinster and commander-in-chief of the United
Irishmen, managed to evade capture for a few weeks but was
eventually caught in Dublin and mortally wounded whilst
resisting arrest. Meanwhile, the government forces
conducted a campaign of terror in Leinster and Munster
which was even more brutal than that conducted in Ulster
in the previous year.

The imprisonment of the leadership of the United
Irishmen seriously impaired the effectiveness of the
rebellion which eventually broke out in central Leinster
(i.e. counties Carlow, Kildare, and Wicklow - Figure 12)
in late May. This took the form of a series of small
local uprisings which were easily suppressed by the
authorities. However, a more serious uprising took place
a few days later centred in Wexford. This caught the
authorities by surprise because they had only learned of
the existence of a United Irish organisation in Wexford at
the last minute. The North Cork Militia had been ordered
to search for arms, and the subsequent rebellion appears
to have been more a defensive reaction by the local
peasantry against the excesses of the Militia than a
planned uprising. Frightened peasants persuaded local
priests, including Father John Murphy who less than two
months previously organised a petition declaring loyalty
to the government amongst his parishoners, to lead a
counter-attack. A vast peasant army, numbering at least
30,000 men, gathered over the next few weeks and captured
the towns of Enniscorthy and Wexford before being
scattered after a brave but futile attempt to take New
Ross.

The Wexford rebellion owed little to the idealism of the
United Irishmen: rather, it was the gut reaction of a
down-trodden peasantry who took the opportunity to avenge
past transgressions. However, given the religious
differences between landlord and tenant, it tended to
degenerate into a sectarian massacre of Protestants (with
the exception of Quakers whose charity in the past was
respected). These sectarian attacks revived memories of

137

FIG. 12   Places Associated With The 1798 Rebellion.

the 1641 massacre in Ulster and many of the Protestant
United Irishmen began to have second thoughts about the
viability of a secular Irish republic. However, despite
this, and the effects of General Lake's campaign,
rebellions were staged in Antrim and Down in early June.
An attack on the garrison in Antrim town by 3,000 men led
by Henry Joy McCracken, a Belfast cotton manufacturer, was
repulsed with the loss of 200 lives. Ballymena and
Randalstown were occupied by the United Irishmen, but were
easily recaptured by the government forces. Two days
later 7,000 United Irishmen attacked the garrison at
Ballynahinch in county Down, but they were defeated with
the loss of about 500 men. Henry Joy McCracken and the
leader of the Down rebellion, Henry Munro, a Lisburn linen
draper, were executed, but most of the rebels were allowed
to return home once they surrendered their arms.

The rebellion was effectively defeated once the
government secured control of Ulster and Leinster, but the
French landed a small force under General Humbert at
Killala (Co. Mayo) in the late summer. This proceeded to
capture Castlebar and then marched towards Dublin, but
Humbert was content to surrender at Ballinamuck (Co.
Longford), after Irish support had failed to rally in
sufficient numbers, upon condition that his army would be
repatriated to France. A few days later another small
force landed at Rutland Island in Donegal, but they sailed
off when they failed to gain any local support; and a few
weeks later a third French expedition was intercepted by
the British navy, resulting in the capture of Wolfe Tone
who was on the flagship. Tone later died in prison after
allegedly committing suicide to avoid being hanged by the
government.

The United Irishmen had by this time been
comprehensively defeated, although Robert Emmet, the
younger brother of one of the United Irish leaders,
organised a final small and totally unsuccessful rebellion
in Dublin in 1803. The British government, however, was
concerned at the state of affairs in Ireland and it

therefore decided that the only solution was to bring
Ireland under direct control. It therefore proposed a
legislative union between Ireland and Britain: Ireland
would cease to be a colony and to have its own parliament,
but would instead become an integral part of the United
Kingdom with the right to elect 100 M.P.s to Westminster.
The idea met with some resistence from the Protestant
ascendancy who realised that their position would be
considerably weakened, but the government was able to
induce a sufficient number of members of the Irish
parliament to vote for the Union. Ireland consequently
became part of the United Kingdom on 1st. January, 1801.

DISCUSSION

Irish nationalists and Ulster unionists often tend to
assume that their respective nations have a long ancestry
which can be traced back at least as far as Brian Boru, in
the case of the Irish nation, or to the Ulster plantation,
in the case of the Ulster nation. It is argued here,
however, that neither the Irish nation nor the Ulster
nation exhibited a strongly defined group identity before
the advent of Irish nationalism and Ulster unionism in the
nineteenth century. This, it should be remembered, is the
second of the five hypotheses outlined at the end of
Chapter 1. The events of the late eighteenth century are
therefore important because of the light which they shed
upon this contention.

The 1798 rebellion tends to be glossed over by
propagandist historians on both sides, but it is a more
obvious embarrassment to the unionists because it
illustrates that a strong feeling of group solidarity did
not exist between Ulster protestants in the 1790s. The
colonial 'nationalism' of the Irish Volunteers, it is
true, had created a Protestant 'nation' in the previous
decade, not only in Ulster but in Ireland as a whole. The
Protestant nation exhibited many of the features of a

modern nation: a group identity which cut across class
divisions; an identification with a territory (Ireland)
which extended beyond the local level, reflecting
improvements in communications; and a desire to maximise
the group's political control over that territory. This
desire, however, revealed a contradiction due to the fact
that the Protestant nation differed from a modern nation
by explicitly excluding the majority of the people living
in the territory from the group: further control over the
territory could only be achieved if this majority was
included within the nation on equal terms, but this would
have threatened the stability of the ascendancy. The
Protestant nation therefore became divided between those
who were prepared to forego further self-government in
order to maintain the status quo, and those who wanted
further independence precisely because of the effects
which it would have on the existing social order.

By the 1790s, the present Ulster nation was divided into
two mutually antagonistic factions: the Episcopalian
landlords and tenantry generally supported the government;
whereas the merchants and tenant farmers in Presbyterian
east Ulster were generally opposed to the government.
Unionist embarrassment is further compounded by the fact
that the Presbyterians were not only on the 'wrong' side
in 1798, but were actually the originators of Irish
republicanism. The Presbyterians in eighteenth-century
east Ulster can therefore be regarded as the fathers of a
tradition which is represented today (albeit in a modified
form) by the IRA.

The anti-British republicanism of the Presbyterian
United Irishmen clearly contradicts the belief that Ulster
unionism has a long pedigree. However, unionists cannot
even claim a long unionist or pro-British pedigree for the
pro-government Episcopalians: the Episcopalians fought in
defence of the Protestant ascendancy and the Episcopalian
-dominated Irish parliament in 1798, rather
than for Britain; and two years later the Act of Union was
opposed by many Episcopalians, including the Orange Order,

because they feared that it would threaten the Protestant
ascendancy in Ireland. The ancestors of the present
Ulster nation, in short, exhibited neither a group
solidarity nor a desire to be united with Britain in the
1790s.

The 1798 rebellion is also embarrassing to Irish
nationalist propagandists. Many Irish nationalist
historians like to emphasise the role of the Ulster
Presbyterians because they argue that it indicates the
existence of a single Irish nation, united in opposition
against the British in the 1790s, which has subsequently
been artificially divided by partition. This argument,
however, is not substantiated by the facts. The vast
majority of those who fought against the United Irishmen
were Irish themselves: of the 76,791 men available to the
government in December 1797, only 11,193 were English or
Scots - the remainder were Irish. Episcopalians, as
already noted, were generally opposed to the United
Irishmen, but it would not even be correct to assume unity
between non-Episcopalians: most of the Catholic middle
classes and clergy supported the government; whilst
Catholic peasants formed the majority of those who fought
for the government in the Militia. Many of these had
originally been conscripted against their will, but very
few defected to the United Irishmen, as hoped by Wolfe
Tone, when the opportunity actually arose. Indeed, some
of the worst atrocities against the Catholic peasantry
were committed by Catholic peasants serving in the
Militia, including those in the North Cork Militia whose
excesses sparked the rebellion in Wexford. The mainly
Catholic (and Gaelic-speaking) Monaghan Militia were
likewise prominent in the pogroms against the United
Irishmen in Ulster (Kee, 1972). The 1798 rebellion
therefore provides little evidence to support the notion
of an Irish nation united in the struggle for national
independence in the late eighteenth century.

It is also incorrect to regard the rebellion of the
United Irishmen as a struggle by nationalists. The fact

that republicanism has subsequently been absorbed as an
integral component of Irish nationalism - to the extent
that the two are now regarded by many as almost synonymous
- has resulted in the 1798 uprising being misrepresented
by Irish nationalists as primarily an attempt to gain
national independence. This, however, obscures the true
motivations. The 1798 rebellion was primarily a rebellion
against the Dublin government, rather than against
Britain, and it was motivated by the material grievances
of the emerging bourgeoisie against the landlord
oligarchy, rather than by a romantic desire for national
independence. The United Irishmen only turned to
separatism as a means of attaining their principal
objective - namely, to gain political power for the
bourgeoisie through a reform of the Irish parliament.
Although the United Irishmen frequently referred to the
Irish nation, they followed the French revolutionaries in
using the term 'nation' to refer simply to the subjects of
a kingdom (in this case the kingdom of Ireland) for whom
they sought liberal reforms; the term did not yet imply
any notion of the Irish as a distinctive people with a
natural right to self-government.

If the United Irishmen had been nationalists, one would
expect them to have been upset by the prospect of Ireland
being further integrated into Britain by the Act of Union.
This was not the case. Samuel Nielson, for example, while
in prison for United Irish activities, wrote in 1799:

'I see a union is determined on between Great
Britain and Ireland. I am glad of it. In a
commercial point of view it cannot be injurious;
and I can see no injury the country will sustain
from it politically.' (Quoted in BICO, 1975, p18).

Likewise, Hamilton Rowan, another United Irish leader,
wrote in the same year:

'In that measure (the Union) I see the downfall
of one of the most corrupt assemblies I believe
ever existed (i.e. the Irish parliament), and
instead of an empty title, a source of

industrious enterprise for the people.'
(Ibid., p18)
Irish independence was simply a means to an end, not an
end in itself; when this means was blocked, and an
alternative presented, the 'nationalist' goal of
independence was quickly abandoned.

The events of the late eighteenth century cannot be
meaningfully interpreted from a nationalistic perspective
because the conflict was not between pre-existing nations,
but between various groups of people following their own
perceived material interests. Given that the landlord
oligarchy was supported by the British government, the
struggle against the ascendancy took on an appearance of
being anti-British; but it was not a nationalist struggle
in the sense that the rebels were simply united by a
strong desire to be ruled by fellow Irishmen.
Nationalism, as explained in the following chapters, did
not emerge until the nineteenth century.

CHAPTER 6
The Growth of
Irish Nationalism

It was argued in the previous chapter that the rebellion
of the United Irishmen in 1798 was not a nationalist
rebellion and that the Irish nation (as we now know it)
had not yet come into existence by the late eighteenth
century. This chapter considers the growth of Irish
nationalism, and consequently the emergence of the Irish
nation, in the nineteenth and early twentieth centuries.

It is suggested that the growth of Irish nationalism
must be examined within the context of changing economic
conditions in Ireland arising from the growth of
industrial capitalism in Britain, and that the analysis
must take account of the various implications which these
changes had for different classes in different parts of
Ireland.

The chapter is divided into eight sections, followed by
a short summary. With the exception of the first section,
which outlines the economic background in the first half
of the nineteenth century, these are organised by
historical sequence.

THE PRE-FAMINE ECONOMY

Ireland enjoyed an economic boom in the last two decades
of the eighteenth century: Irish industries revived to
some extent under protective legislation passed by the
Irish parliament, whereas agricultural exports increased

145

dramatically in response to the increased demand generated by rapid industrial urbanisation in England.

This prosperity continued into the second decade of the nineteenth century. Agricultural exports to Britain before 1815 were boosted by the Napoleonic wars which cut off the supply of food from Europe. Given that it was already a net importer of food, Britain was prepared to pay high prices for Irish grain to feed its inceasingly urban population. The acreage in Ireland under tillage consequently continued to expand in response to the artificially high demand. High prices were also paid for Irish pigs and pigmeat, and after 1800 high prices also encouraged increased output of sheep and dairy produce (Ó Tuathaigh, 1972).

This apparent boom, however, disguised important regional and class disparities. The main beneficiaries were the landlords who creamed off most of the increased income through rent increases: in some areas the rents quadrupled between 1760 and 1815 in response to rising prices. The larger tenant farmers also managed to share in the rising prosperity. The situation was different, however, for the poorer rural classes. Although the growth in tillage created a demand for farm labour, this was counterbalanced by a very rapid increase in the population (probably initiated by the changes in the economy): the population increased from about 5 million in 1800, to 6.8 million by 1820, to over 8.1 million in 1840. This increase was greatest in the labouring classes, with the result that increased competition forced labourers to work without wages in return for small plots of land which would enable them to grow enough potatoes to provide subsistence for their families. Further population increases were accommodated by a subdivision of the land into smaller and smaller plots, with the result that more and more labourers lived an increasingly marginal existence. With the exception of Ulster, where cottage-based textiles supported a large rural population, rural population densities generally increased, and living

conditions generally deteriorated as one moved from east
to west (Figure 13).

The situation changed for the worse after 1815. Prices
for Irish agricultural goods declined rapidly following
the restoration of peace in Europe. The price of grain,
for example, declined by one third between 1815 and 1821:
Irish grain farmers consequently received a much lower
income, even though the output of grain continued to rise
until the 1840s. This had widespread repercussions
because declining incomes were not generally matched by a
proportionate decline in rents. The larger farmers were
forced to take a more ruthless attitude towards their
subtenants, whilst many of the smaller farmers were forced
into the ranks of the landless labourers and cottiers.
Higher prices for cattle encouraged farmers who had
sufficient capital to switch from tillage to livestock.
This was reflected by a fourfold increase in the number of
live cattle exported between 1820 and 1840, but it also
resulted in the eviction of a large number of cottiers.
The peasantry reacted against evictions by forming
themselves into secret 'ribbon' societies (the nineteenth
century equivalent of the eighteenth century whiteboys),
resulting in a rapid increase in violent agrarian
incidents in the 1820s and 1830s.

The condition of the poor was further exasperated by the
fact that towns in Ireland, in contrast to those in
England, were unable to provide an alternative source of
employment because of industrial decline in the same
period. This industrial decline was an indirect
consequence of the Act of Union, but the effects of the
union were disguised in the first two decades by the
Napoleonic wars. The wars created a high export demand
for certain goods (e.g. textiles for military uniforms),
whereas high agricultural incomes (generated by a war-time
demand for Irish agricultural products) encouraged a high
rural consumption of manufactured goods within Ireland.
However, the demand for most Irish manufactured goods
declined rapidly once the wars ended.

148

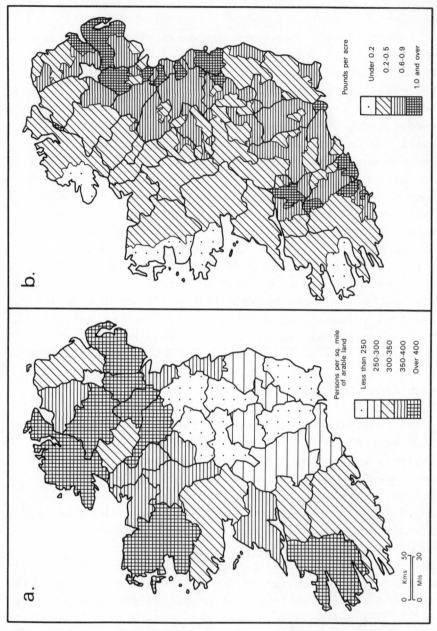

FIG. 13   (a) Population Density, 1841 (b) Valuation Of
          Rural Areas, Circa 1850 (After Jones Hughes, 1965).

Irish industrial decline was further accelerated in the
1820s by increased competition following the elimination
of protective legislation. English industry, by the
beginning of the nineteenth century, had already been
transformed by the industrial revolution into the most
competitive in the world and therefore no longer needed to
be protected from foreign competition by mercantilist
legislation. Indeed, expansion could now be best
accomplished by unbridled free competition, and
laissez-faire consequently replaced mercantilism as
the dominant political economic doctrine. Protective
legislation passed by the Irish parliament was dismantled
by Westminster until, in 1824, Irish industries found
themselves in free competition with those in Britain. The
more advanced British industries generally proved to be
much more more competitive because of economies of scale,
a higher degree of mechanisation, and lower transport
costs to the major urban markets in England. Irish
industrial development was also hampered by a scarcity of
important resources, especially coal, and a shortage of
risk capital: capital accumulated in Ireland tended to be
invested in British industries, government stocks or Irish
land, rather than in Irish industries. Transport
improvements, especially the rapid expansion of railways
in the 1840s, enabled the Irish market to be flooded with
cheaper English goods, resulting in the further eclipse of
Irish industry. With the important exception of east
Ulster (see Chapter 7), Ireland remained generally
unindustrialised.

Given that Irish towns offered few opportunities for
those driven off the land, large numbers began to
emigrate. By the 1840s over 400,000 Irish had flooded
into the major English industrial cities to swell the
ranks of the proletariat; a further 200,000 left for the
United States between 1840 and 1845. However, even mass
emigration proved a hopelessly inadequate safety valve for
the problem of rural over-population. Given the
dependence of a very large section of the population upon

a single crop for their subsistence, disaster was
inevitable. Localised failures of the potato crop in 1817
and 1821 had resulted in partial famines, but widespread
failure in successive years between 1845 and 1848 proved
devastating. It is estimated that at least 800,000 died
of disease and starvation during the Great Famine and a
similar number were forced to emigrate.

DANIEL O'CONNELL

Irish politics in the first half of the nineteenth
century were largely dominated by one man - Daniel
O'Connell, a Catholic landlord and lawyer from Kerry.
O'Connell's political career was closely associated with
two major campaigns, both of which reflected the
aspirations of the Catholic professional and merchant
classes towards an increased share in political power.
The first campaign was for Catholic emancipation; the
other was for a repeal of the Act of Union. Although both
demands were only of direct benefit to the Catholic middle
classes, O'Connell used his personal charisma and
outstanding powers of oratory to mobilise support from the
more disadvantaged sections of the Catholic population.
He therefore played an extremely significant role in the
creation of the Irish nation by uniting Catholics of all
classes in support of a common cause.

Demands for emancipation had been made on behalf of
Catholics in the first two decades of the nineteenth
century by liberal Protestant M.P.s in Westminster without
any success. O'Connell therefore realised that
concessions could only be gained if the demand for
emancipation received mass popular support. However, the
only things denied to Catholics since 1793 were the right
to sit in parliament and the right to hold high state
offices. Both disabilities affected the Catholic middle
classes, but they were totally irrelevant to the vast bulk
of the Catholic population. The probable attitude of most

Catholics towards emancipation was summarised by the
United Irish leader W. J. MacNeven, a Catholic doctor, in
1798:

> 'Catholic emancipation, as it is called, the
> people do not care about; I am sure they ought
> not now; they know, I believe, very generally,
> that it would be attended with no other effect
> than to admit into the house of peers a few
> individuals who profess the Catholic religion,
> and enable some others to speculate in seats in
> the house of commons. No man is so ignorant as
> to think that this would be a national benefit.'
> (Quoted in BICO, 1974, p26).

There therefore appeared to be little likelihood of
gaining mass support for an essentially middle class
demand, but O'Connell and his associates were not easily
deterred and so he began a long campaign to persuade the
peasantry that emancipation would result in an alleviation
of their impoverished conditions. His masterstroke was
the formation of the Catholic Association in 1823. Full
membership of the Association was set at one guinea per
annum, but associate membership was made available for a
penny per month - a fee sufficiently low to enable even
the poor to subscribe. Utilising the Catholic clergy as
local leaders, the Association quickly attracted an
associate membership of hundreds of thousands who paid
their fees, known as the 'Catholic rent', at the churches.
By using the clergy, O'Connell avoided alienating the
Catholic hierarchy who might otherwise have regarded him
as a secular challenge to their authority over the
Catholic people.

Although the Catholic rent was only a penny per month,
it encouraged a very large membership and thereby ensured
a much higher income than an organisation confined to the
more prosperous middle classes would have. More
important, however, was the feeling of common identity
which was generated amongst all those who contributed. As
Dr. Jebb, the Church of Ireland bishop of Limerick, noted:

'There is what we of this generation have never
before witnessed, a complete union of the Roman
Catholic body ... In truth, an Irish revolution
has, in great measure, been effected.' (Quoted
in Whyte, 1967, p251).

However, the significance of the revolution extended far
beyond Dr. Jebb's generation - the Catholic Association
had in fact united Catholics of all classes in all parts
of Ireland in a common cause for the first time ever.

The Catholic Association used its resources to support
Protestant candidates favourable to Catholic emancipation
in the 1826 general election. Although only Protestants
could sit in Westminster, Catholics formed a majority of
the electorate in most constituencies, even though only a
minority of Catholics had the right to vote because the
franchise was confined to freeholders who leased land
worth 40 shillings or more. Fear of eviction had
previously forced most 40 shilling freeholders to vote
according to the wishes of their landlords, but the
Catholic Association countered this by offering to
compensate those who were victimised. They thereby
persuaded freeholders to vote against landlord-nominated
candidates opposed to emancipation in sufficient numbers
to elect pro-emancipation candidates in several
constituencies.

The Catholic Association decided to contest a
by-election in Clare in 1828, but they were unable to find
a suitable Protestant candidate. Although Catholics were
prevented from sitting in Westminster, there was no law to
prevent them from standing for election. It was therefore
decided that O'Connell should contest the election
himself. O'Connell subsequently won by a very large
majority, and thereby created the conditions for
potentially widespread civil disorder unless the
government permitted him to take his seat. The government
decided that it would be more prudent to avoid
confrontation, and it therefore conceded Catholic
emancipation in 1829. O'Connell's personal popularity

subsequently soared higher than ever.

Although the Catholic middle classes gained legal equality with their Protestant counterparts, Catholic emancipation did little to improve the conditions for the vast majority of Catholics. In fact, if anything, their position deteriorated. In order to gain emancipation, O'Connell agreed to disband the Catholic Association and to accept a reduction in the number of Catholic voters by raising the franchise qualification from 40 shilling freeholders to £10 freeholders. The number of voters in Ireland was reduced by five sixths from 100,000 voters to only 16,000 voters. The loss of their voting rights subsequently left the disenfranchised tenants (who were mostly Catholic) more susceptible to rent increases and evictions by their landlords (mostly Protestant). Agrarian unrest, in the form of ribbon activities, increased markedly in the 1830s.

O'Connell immediately began to pursue his second major objective - repeal of the Act of Union. Having gained the right to parliamentary representation for the Catholic middle classes, the logical progression was to campaign for a transfer of power to Ireland so that they could maximise their influence: Catholics would now form a significant, if not the dominant, element in a restored Irish parliament. However, O'Connell found very little support for repeal from either of the two major parties in England.

Realising that there was little possibility of winning a majority in Westminster in favour of repeal, O'Connell decided to support the Whig government throughout the 1830s in the hope of gaining reforms which would strengthen the position of the Catholic middle classes. His support for the government frequently brought him into opposition against other groups demanding more radical reforms, including Sharman Crawford (the liberal M.P. for Down, who proposed radical land reforms), the ribbonmen in Munster, trade unionists who demanded a 10 hour working day, and the Chartists who argued for an extension of the franchise to include working class males. However, despite his social conservatism, O'Connell managed to maintain massive popular support within Ireland, where he was referred to as 'the liberator' because of his success in gaining emancipation.

Anticipating the defeat of the Whigs in the 1841 general election, O'Connell revised his tactics and reverted to the policy which had won Catholic emancipation by forming the Loyal National Repeal Association in 1840. As before, the Catholic clergy were utilised as local leaders and a 'repeal rent' was collected which proved to be even more financially rewarding than the Catholic rent. Two years later the campaign was escalated by the organisation of a series of massive public meetings, some of which were estimated to have been attended by at least 500,000 people, with some estimates as high as one million. Very few of the audience at the larger 'monster' meetings (as they became known) could possibly have heard what O'Connell had to say, but the meetings provided extremely effective demonstrations of solidarity. However, the government refused to be swayed, and when O'Connell announced plans for a meeting to be held at Clontarf in 1843 the government decided to meet the challenge by banning it. This placed O'Connell in a dilemma because he realised that it would be impossible to prevent violence between the large crowd and the military guard which the government had placed on the proposed venue. Given that he wished to avoid a violent confrontation, he therefore had little alternative but to back down by issuing a counter-proclamation to cancel the meeting.

O'Connell's massive support was unaffected by this setback, but the Clontarf incident demonstrated the inherent weakness of his strategy. The monster meetings only disturbed the government because they contained an implicit threat of social revolution, but by cancelling the meeting at Clontarf O'Connell demonstrated that he clearly regarded social stability as more important than repeal. The government could therefore afford in effect

to disregard him. The monster meetings were revived in
1845, following a lull in 1844 during which O'Connell was
imprisoned for three months on a charge of conspiracy, but
the repeal movement was by that time effectively impotent.
Repeal was rapidly eclipsed as a major issue for most
people by the outbreak of the Famine in the autumn of
1845, and two years later the movement effectively
collapsed following O'Connell's death while on his way to
Rome.

Despite the rapid collapse of the repeal movement after
his death, O'Connell can in many respects be regarded as
the father of the Irish nation. The campaign for Catholic
emancipation created a feeling of common identity amongst
Catholics which transcended class divisions; this was
later broadened into a national identity (i.e. a desire
for self-government) by the formation of the Repeal
Asociation. The fact that the Repeal Association used
basically the same organisational structure as the
Catholic Association, including the use of Catholic clergy
as local organisers and leaders, inevitably resulted in a
strong association between the emerging national identity
and Catholicism.

O'Connell consciously developed this fusion between
national and religious identities. His natural support
came from the educated Catholic middle-classes, who had
most to gain from emancipation and repeal; but in order to
mobilise support from the more disadvantaged sections of
the Catholic population, who had little to gain from
either cause, he had to create a sense of solidarity
against a common enemy. He therefore appealed for support
from the Catholic peasantry on the grounds of common
religious and national persecution. In the Clare
by-election, for example, O'Connell warned the tenants of
his opponent, Vesey Fitzgerald, not to heed the

> 'tongues of the tempter and the charmer whose
> confederates have through all the ages joined
> the descendants of the Dane, the Norman and the
> Saxon, in burning your churches, in levelling

your altars, in slaughtering your clergy, in
stamping out your religion. Let every renegade
to God and his country follow Vesey Fitzgerald,
and every true Catholic Irishman follow me.'
(Quoted in Boyce, 1982, p144).

The sense of national identity which O'Connell generated
was more highly developed in some areas than in others
(Figure 14). The major areas of support for repeal were
where the Catholic middle-classes were strongest (i.e. the
urban areas and the large farm areas), and where
communications (and therefore information flows) were more
advanced due to the penetration of commodity production.
Support for repeal was obviously minimal amongst the
Protestants in Ulster due to the close association made by
O'Connell between the nation and the Catholic religion;
but the repeal movement also had a limited impact amongst
the highly marginalised Catholic subsistence peasantry in
the west. The west only became fully integrated into the
Irish nation in the second half of the nineteenth century,
due to the later penetration of commodity production and
the associated improvement in information flows from the
more developed east.

O'Connell was clearly influenced by the growth of
nationalism in Europe (especially Germany and Italy) in
the 1820s and 1830s, but he was neither a separatist nor a
republican. Repeal of the Act of Union would have
resulted in the restoration of the Irish parliament, but
O'Connell never envisaged total separation from Britain or
a break with the British monarchy. On the contrary, he
often made a special point of affirming his undying
loyalty to the crown, and in his earlier days he had even
helped to suppress the republican rebellion of Robert
Emmet while serving with the Dublin Lawyers' Yeomanry
corps (Adamson, 1982). O'Connell's demands for a repeal of
the Act of Union were primarily governed by the pragmatic
material considerations of the Catholic middle classes.

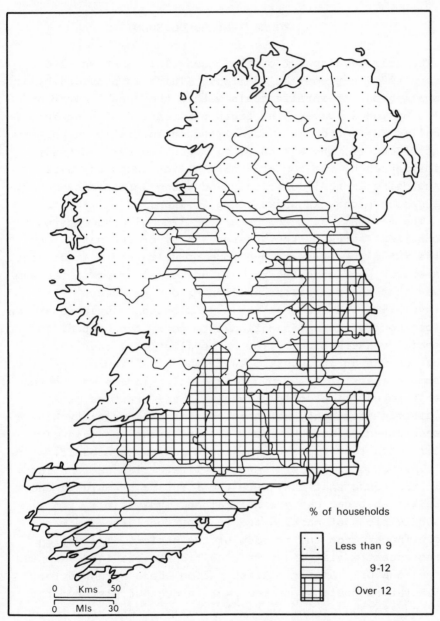

% of households

Less than 9

9-12

Over 12

0   Kms   50

0   Mls   30

FIG. 14   The Percentage Of Households Which Subscribed To
The Repeal Rent, 1843 (After Van Der Wusten,
1980).

THE YOUNG IRELAND MOVEMENT

The full development of the modern Irish nation also required a nationalist ideology. This was provided by a small group of intellectuals within the repeal movement, led by Thomas Davis, who began publication of a newspaper called The Nation in 1842. Although initially supporters of O'Connell, the Nation group were also very strongly influenced by the romantic nationalist ideas of Mazzini and Heine in the Young Italy and Young Germany movements, and soon became known as Young Ireland.

The nationalist ideology of the 'Young' movements on the continent stressed the inherent unity of the nation and the mutual benefits to everyone of self-rule. It did not, however, challenge the prevailing social order in the same way that the radical republicanism of the French revolution had done earlier; so, although revolutionary in some senses, romantic nationalism could even appeal to social conservatives. The nationalist idea that the nation was an indivisible unity had a particular appeal to some members of the Protestant middle classes who feared that repeal might simply result in the creation of a Catholic ascendancy now that the Catholic majority had been emancipated: the Young Ireland group consequently attracted some Protestants, including Davis himself.

The Young Irelanders were the first Irish nationalists, in the sense that they were the first to promulgate the belief that nations are natural and indivisible subdivisions of mankind and that personal freedom was contingent upon the freedom of the nation. The Nation subsequently played a very significant role in developing the idea of a historic Irish nation whose struggle for liberation could be traced back throughout history: the Young Ireland group, especially Davis, wrote articles and poetry which romanticised the struggle of the Irish nation. They were therefore largely responsible for rewriting history to fit into the nationalist mode in which it is still largely found today.

The Young Ireland group supported O'Connell's decision to back down at Clontarf in 1843, but relations with O'Connell became strained in the following year. Realising the futility of peaceful monster meetings, O'Connell began to consider the possibility of a reduced form of autonomy known as federalism in order to broaden his middle class support. The Young Irelanders, however, were opposed to any form of compromise which did not result in legislative independence for the nation. They were also concerned about O'Connell's close identity with the Catholic Church which conflicted with their own ideas of a secular nation. This came to a head in 1845 following a government proposal to create three non-denominational university colleges. The proposal was opposed by the Catholic Church on the grounds that the education offered would not be specifically Catholic; whereas it was supported by Young Ireland on the grounds that Catholics, who were then excluded from scholarships and fellowships at the only existing Irish university, would now have a realistic opportunity of a university education within Ireland. O'Connell supported the Catholic bishops and, despite his assurances to the contrary, he thereby intensified the fears of the Young Irelanders that his real objective was to establish a Catholic ascendancy. However, although relations were strained, the final split did not occur until 1846, following the sudden death of Thomas Davis, aged only 30, in 1845.

The death of Davis left the Young Ireland movement in some disarray, and different strands within the movement tended to go different ways. The ineffectiveness of the government in dealing with the Famine encouraged some to take a much more radical and revolutionary stance. The fact that Ireland was still exporting food, which the poor could not afford to buy, at a time when hundreds of thousands were dying from disease and starvation indicated that the Famine was not simply an ecological disaster, but was a reflection of the nature of the landholding system. Many Young Irelanders were consequently influenced by the ideas of James Fintan Lalor who called for radical land reforms and the establishment of a republic. A wing of the Young Ireland movement, led by John Mitchel, the son of an Ulster Protestant minister, became increasingly militant and separatist in the tradition of the United Irishmen.

Mitchel's advocacy of violent revolutionary methods initially found little support and he left the Nation group early in 1848 to found a rival paper called The United Irishman. However, his ideas gained acceptance following a wave of nationalist revolutions across Europe, after which the Young Irelanders became more militant and began to make plans for an armed rebellion. Although the Young Irelanders had very little grass-roots support, the government took them seriously and arrested most of the leadership in a number of swoops. The subsequent rebellion, later in 1848, was an abysmal failure because the remaining middle class leaders were unable to mobilise any support: the Catholic Church was opposed to secular republicanism, whereas the peasantry were too pre-occupied with simply trying to survive the Famine to be motivated by a romantic nationalist insurrection - even one which promised sweeping reforms. Apart from a pathetic escapade in county Tipperary, in which a handful of rebels were killed, the rebellion was a non-event.

Nevertheless, the 1848 rebellion was an important milestone in the development of Irish nationalism because it repesented a fusion between the romantic nationalist ideas of a historical nation struggling for independence with the republican ideas of radical change. This fusion, however, was not symmetrical: Irish republicanism was subsumed by Irish nationalism; but only a minority of Irish nationalists since 1848 could be described as radical republicans. The Irish national movement has generally been characterised by two wings with different objectives and tactics: one wing has attempted to achieve a higher degree of autonomy for Ireland within the framework of the United Kingdom through parliamentary reforms; whereas the other wing has sought to achieve an independent republic by armed force.

These differences reflect differences in the class composition of the two wings: the leadership of the constitutional wing was generally provided by the large farmer, professional and merchant classes; whereas the leadership of the republican wing was usually provided by the lower ranks of the intelligentsia (i.e. teachers, clerks, journalists, etc.). The leadership of the constitutional wing basically desired a transfer of power from Britain to dominant classes in Ireland with a minimum of social upheaval; whereas the republican wing generally required independence as a pre-condition to poorly specified social reforms within Ireland. However, as we shall see, the fact that radical republicanism was subsumed by the more general nationalist movement has subsequently meant that demands for social reforms have frequently been diverted by constitutional nationalists into socially more conservative demands for national autonomy.

THE FENIANS

The Great Famine, as noted above, resulted in an immediate 20 per cent decline in the Irish population, but it also initiated a series of changes which had a profound economic and demographic impact throughout the rest of the nineteenth century. Many of the landlords were bankrupted by the reduction in rent payments during the Famine and were consequently forced to pay off their creditors by selling their estates. Legislation, known as the Encumbered Estates Act, was passed in 1849 to enable landlords to sell their estates with a minimum of inconvenience. The government had hoped that the estates might be bought by progressive commercial farmers from

Britain, but about 90 per cent of the 3,000 estates sold
under the Act were bought by Irishmen, many of whom were
Catholics.

These changes in ownership were accompanied by
far-reaching structural changes. The new landlords looked
upon their estates as economic investments, rather than as
an inherited source of income, and therefore tended to be
much more economically rational and even less
paternalistic towards their tenants than their
predecessors. Middlemen were increasingly bypassed as the
new landlords rented directly to tenants in order to
maximise their returns, and some smallholders were evicted
to facilitate a further switch from tillage to more
profitable cattle farming. Farm consolidation resulted in
a massive reduction in the number of smallholdings. The
number of holdings of less than one acre dropped from
135,314 in 1841 to 37,728 in 1851, while the number of
holdings between one and five acres dropped from 310,436
to 88,083 (Lee, 1973). The number of farms between five
and fifteen acres declined from 252,799 to 191,854. There
was a corresponding increase in the number of larger
farms, especially farms of more than thirty acres.

Most of this consolidation took place after 1849. The
number of evictions increased from about 3,000 between
1845 and 1847, to 25,700 between 1847 and 1849, to 58,423
between 1849 and 1852. Given that the towns provided few
economic prospects for those evicted, the only alternative
was to emigrate. Emigration remained high throughout the
rest of the century and, coupled with a declining birth
rate because of fewer and later marriages in response to
economic conditions, resulted in a continuous net decline
in population. By 1911 the population of Ireland had
fallen to 4.4 million - little more than half of what it
had been before the Famine. The number of labourers,
cottiers and smallholders as a proportion of the total
population declined even more markedly, partly due to
higher mortality and emigration during the famine, but
mainly due to higher emigration in the post-Famine

period (Table 1).

	Labourers	Cottiers (1-5 acres)	Small Farmers (5-15 acres)	Large Farmers (>15 acres)
1845	700,000	300,000	310,000	277,000
1851	500,000	88,000	192,000	290,000
1910	300,000	62,000	154,000	304,000

Table 1   Changes In Rural Social Structure (Lee, 1973).

The increase in evictions resulted in an upsurge of ribbonism. Charles Gavan Duffy, a survivor of the Young Ireland movement, organised a Tenants' Right League in 1850 to campaign for a set of demands known as the three Fs - fixity of tenure, fair rent and freedom of sale of improvements made by the tenant - in order to protect tenants from the excesses of the new landlords. The demand was basically for the custom which existed in Ulster to be legalised and extended to the rest of Ireland. The League attracted considerable support, not only from Catholic tenants outside Ulster, but also from Protestant tenants in Ulster who found that their landlords were beginning to disregard the Ulster custom.
Almost 50 M.P.s, pledged to support the demands of the tenants, were elected in the 1852 general election and formed an Irish party in Westminster where they held the balance of power. However, this advantage was squandered due to internal dissensions centred on a group who became known as the 'Pope's brass band' because they obediently followed the orders of Cardinal Cullen, the Catholic primate in Ireland (Jackson, 1947). Duffy, branded by Cullen as 'an Irish Mazzini', eventually emigrated to Australia, defeated and disillusioned, in 1855.
Frustration arising from the collapse of attempts to solve the land question by constitutional means created an

environment conducive to an attempt to remedy social injustice by more violent methods: given that radical social reforms were unlikely to be achieved within the context of the United Kingdom, some of the more radical sections of Irish society became increasingly sympathetic to the idea of an independent Irish republic. James Stephens, a Young Irelander, organised a secret oath-bound society known as the Irish Republican Brotherhood (IRB) in 1858 to fight for an independent Irish republic. Meanwhile, Michael Doheny and John O'Mahony, two other Young Irelanders who had emigrated to America after a brief period in Paris, founded the Fenians amongst Irish emigrants in the United States in order to raise money to provide arms for the IRB. Although the leadership was provided by a middle class intelligentsia composed of lawyers, journalists and traders, most of the membership of the IRB (unlike Young Ireland) was drawn from the working classes: farm labourers and small farmers provided support in the rural areas, but the movement was more strongly based in the urban areas where it not only got support from those who had been displaced from the land (e.g. navvies), but also from clerks, shop assistants and artisans (whose livelihood was being undermined by imported goods mass-produced in English factories). Although the membership of the Fenians and IRB was almost entirely Catholic, the fact that they followed Young Ireland in advocating the creation of a secular republic, coupled with their use of violent conspiratorial methods, resulted in intense opposition from the Catholic Church hierarchy.

It was hoped that the Americans, in addition to providing financial support, might be able to send an army at the end of the American Civil War. However, the British government acted promptly and was able to infiltrate the organisation and arrest most of the IRB leadership in 1865, mostly on charges connected with the publication of their newspaper The Irish People which had been established in 1863. The proposed rebellion was doomed to failure, but the IRB decided to rebel anyway in 1867. In the end, they were easily defeated by the government forces with little loss of life.

Although the Fenians failed in their immediate objectives, they established a number of important precedents. The Fenians were the first group to act on what they regarded as the interests of the Irish nation, using violent methods, without first attempting to win mass support from the rest of the Irish people. This secret revolutionary tradition is maintained today by the IRA. They were also the first to mobilise large-scale financial support from Irish emigrants, especially from those in the United States, whose bitter experiences of the Famine and eviction had been distorted by nationalist ideology from being a grievance against landlords and the landholding system (the immediate source of their distress) to a hatred of Britain.

PARNELL

The defeat of the Fenians in 1867 did not result in their total elimination. The IRB continued in existence as a small secret revolutionary organisation supported by funds from emigrants in the United States, but it did not attract mass membership or have a major bearing upon events until it resurfaced as the organising body behind the 1916 rebellion (see below). The national struggle in the half century after the Fenian uprising was conducted almost entirely through the medium of constitutional politics; but the land question, and the associated threat of a peasant rebellion, continued to act as a major underlying factor.

Although defeated in 1867, the fact that the Fenians had been prepared to rebel under such unfavourable circumstances drew government attention to the seriousness of conditions within Ireland. Gladstone, who became the Prime Minister following the Liberals' victory in the 1868 general election, was particularly influenced and he introduced legislation to alleviate the conditions of the Irish tenantry. His first major reform was the Church Act (1869) which disestablished the Church of Ireland. This benefitted Catholics and Nonconformists, who no longer had to pay tithes as part of their rent, but it represented a very serious blow to the Protestant ascendancy. The Land Act passed in the following year represented an attempt to legalise the Ulster custom in the areas where it was already practised and to extend to other parts of Ireland the tenant's right to sell improvements. In practice the Act contained too many loopholes to have any major effect, but it represented the first in a long series of attempts to defuse revolutionary potential in Ireland through land reforms. These reforms, however, clearly threatened the interests of the large landlords, most of whom were still Protestants.

The futility of the Fenian rebellion also had a profound impact upon Isaac Butt, a Protestant barrister who had defended many of the Fenians in trials following their ill-fated rebellion. Butt established the Home Government Association of Ireland in 1870 to campaign for 'home rule'. This called for the creation of an Irish assembly with powers to pass legislation for Ireland, but the control of certain areas (e.g. foreign policy) was to be retained by Westminster, to which Ireland would send a reduced number of M.P.s. The demand for home rule therefore envisaged a lower degree of autonomy than O'Connell's earlier demand for a repeal of the Act of Union.

The Home Government Association initially attracted support from both liberals and conservatives. Liberals saw home rule as a means for implementing reforms, whereas conservatives, especially from the Protestant landed ascendancy who felt their position threatened by Gladstone's church and land reforms, saw home rule as a means for curtailing further reforms. The home rule movement was initially opposed by the Catholic Church, due to its opposition to the Protestant ascendancy, and a counter-organisation known as the Catholic Union was formed by Cardinal Cullen in 1872 to support the British Liberal party. However, relations between the Church and the Liberal government soon became very strained because the Church sought greater control over Irish education than the Liberals were prepared to concede. The Church, realising that the Liberals were not prepared to concede, shifted its support to the Home Government Association; other liberals, realising that they could not hope to compete against the home rule movement without the support of the Church, especially given an upsurge of public interest in the national question following the Fenians' ill-fated rebellion, began to join the Home Government Association in large numbers in 1873. The influx of liberals into the home rule movement in turn alienated the conservatives who realised that there would be little hope of maintaining the landlord ascendancy under home rule: the conservatives therefore turned to unionism as the best means of protecting their interests. The Home Government Association was disbanded in 1873 and replaced by the Home Rule League.

The Home Rule League contested the general election in 1874 as a third party and surpassed even its own expectations by winning 59 seats. This represented a gain of 50 seats, most of which were nominally at the expense of the Liberals - in reality many of the changes were simply due to existing M.P.s changing their allegiances. Part of this success was also due to the fact that the 1874 general election was the first to be contested by secret ballot, following the Ballot Act of 1872: this considerably reduced the influence of the landlords over their tenants' voting behaviour. The League increased its representation further in subsequent elections.

Given that the Conservatives had an absolute majority in Westminster, home rule M.P.s decided that the best way to further their objectives was to obstruct parliamentary business by filibustering. The main proponents of this

tactic were Joseph Biggar, a Catholic wholesale butcher
and Fenian from Belfast, and Charles Stewart Parnell, a
Protestant landlord from Wicklow. Parnell soon rose to
prominence and became the leader of the home rule movement
following Butt's death in 1879.

Parnell, like O'Connell half a century earlier, was an
outstanding politician. Although home rule would have
entailed little more than a transfer of power from
Westminster to the Irish middle classes (i.e.
professionals, traders, large farmers, etc.), Parnell was
able to mobilise widespread popular support by
manipulating agitation for land reforms. Rural
depopulation had reduced the possibility of another crisis
on the scale of the Famine in most parts of Ireland, but
the effects of modernisation had less impact upon the west
than upon the east. The effects of low prices in the late
1870s, followed by crop failures in 1877-9, were
consequently more acutely felt in the west where there was
a much larger number of cottiers and small holders. The
tenants reacted against evictions for rent arrears by
organising large protest meetings. Michael Davitt, who
had only recently been released from imprisonment for
Fenian activities, realised that agitation for land reform
could win popular support for the Fenians' clandestine
separatist movement (although other Fenians feared that
land reforms might have the opposite effect by reducing
the need for separatism) and so he formed an organisation
called the Land League of Mayo in 1879 to campaign for
peasant proprietorship. Parnell, realising that land
agitation could be used to enhance his personal
popularity, became an active participant at meetings and
when Davitt founded a national Land League later in 1879,
Parnell was pleased to accept his invitation to become its
president, although he diluted the demand for peasant
proprietorship to one for rent reductions. Parnell soon
established himself as the undisputed leader of the
movement.

Parnell advised the tenants to oppose eviction by

ostracizing tenants who took up farms from which others had been evicted. This policy became known as 'boycotting' after its most celebrated victim - Captain Boycott, an estate agent for Lord Erne, who was ostracized after evicting tenants for rent arrears. The government attempted to destroy the Land League by coercion, and many of the leaders, including Davitt, were arrested for conspiracy. Parnell meanwhile pressed for land reforms within parliament, resulting in the 1881 Land Act. This legalised the three Fs - fair rent, fixity of tenure and freedom of sale - for the whole of Ireland; but, in order to prevent the Land League collapsing following this success, Parnell attacked the Act as inadequate, using such provocative language that he was jailed in October 1881. As he anticipated, agrarian outrages increased rapidly after his imprisonment as tenants reverted to the more traditional ribbon methods of opposing the landlords (Figure 15). The disorder became so widespread that the government eventually had to release Parnell in May 1882 with the promise of a cessation of coercion and an abolition of outstanding rent arrears in return for the Land League's assistance in curbing ribbonism. Popular opinion gave Parnell credit for rent reductions and the cancellation of arrears, and he now became the 'uncrowned king of Ireland'.

Following his successes on the land question, Parnell turned his attentions back towards the demand for home rule. The Irish National League, based on the Land League, was founded in 1882 to campaign for home rule, but the struggle was mainly conducted within Westminster. Parnell's popular support proved particularly useful following the third Reform Act in 1884. Gladstone, who was prime minister at the time, agreed to extend the electoral franchise to include all adult male householders in an attempt to retain the support of the British trade unions for the Liberal party. The percentage of adult males with the right to vote consequently increased from about 17 per cent to over 55 per cent (Walker, 1973).

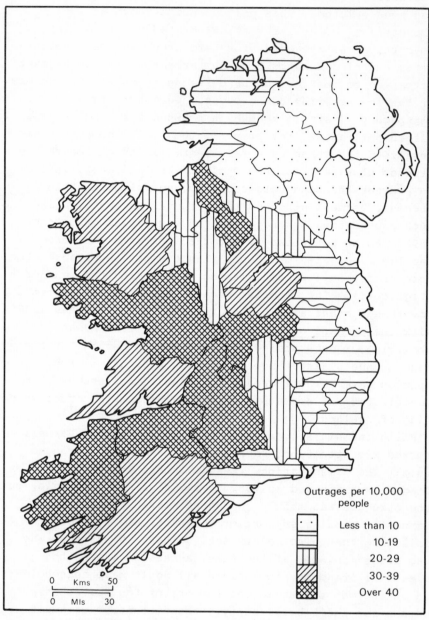

FIG. 15   Agrarian Outrages, 1880-2 (After Rumpf And
           Hepburn, 1976).

This extension of the franchise strengthened the position of the home rule party because of Parnell's widespread support amongst the previously disenfranchised lower classes following the land reforms. It also facilitated further changes in the social composition of the party. The majority of Irish M.P.s when the Home Government Association was first established were Protestant landlords - 68 of the 103 Irish M.P.s in 1868 were Protestants and 73 were landlords. However, by the 1880s home rule M.P.s were more typically drawn from the lower middle classes (i.e. shopkeepers, farmers, solicitors, etc.), reflecting the growing importance of commodity production, and were mostly Catholics: only 5 of the 86 home rule M.P.s elected in 1886 were landlords, and only 11 were Protestants. The Reform Act also strengthened the political influence of the Catholic Church: the Church exerted tremendous control at the grass-roots level; consequently when more of the 'grass-roots' received the right to vote the Church was placed in a stronger position to dictate terms to the politicians. This was reflected by a significant increase in the number of home rule candidates who were proposed and seconded by the clergy after 1884.

The home rule party held the balance of power within Westminster, with the result that they were able to bring down the government in 1885. The Conservatives formed a government for a brief period before a general election could be held in November 1885. This produced an 86 seat majority for the Liberals over the Conservatives, but the home rule party also won 86 seats. Gladstone agreed to introduce a home rule bill in order to gain the support of the home rule party, fearing that the Conservatives would benefit from agreeing to Parnell's demands if the Liberals refused. The bill subsequently came before parliament in 1886, but was defeated due to the defection of a large number of unionist Liberals. These included not only members of the right wing of the party, who were opposed to any disruption to the Empire, but also members of the

left wing, led by Joseph Chamberlain. The defeat of the
government precipitated another general election which
resulted in a comfortable majority for the Conservatives
over all other parties. The hopes for home rule
consequently subsided until the Liberals returned to power
in 1892.

During the interim, the home rule party was thrown into
disarray by a scandal involving Parnell who was cited in a
divorce case in 1890. The puritanical nonconformist wing
of the Liberals threatened to withdraw its support for
home rule if Parnell remained leader of the Irish home
rule party. The majority of the home rule party, faced
with a choice between home rule and loyalty to Parnell,
opted to desert him, resulting in a bitter party split.
The Catholic Church threw its weight behind the
anti-Parnellite faction, with the result that the
Parnellites only managed to win one seat (John Redmond in
Waterford city) in five by-elections against anti-
Parnellite home rulers. Parnell fought his opponents
with great determination, but during one of the election
campaigns in 1891 he contracted an illness and died
suddenly.

The Parnellites continued their struggle against the
Catholic Church supported anti-Parnellite faction in the
1892 general election, but although they managed about one
third of the votes outside of Ulster (where
Protestant-Catholic sectarianism delivered the vote to the
anti-Parnellites) they only won 9 of the 80 home rule
seats. These were in the larger urban areas (including 4
in Dublin) where clerical influence was less marked and in
areas with large percentages of smallholders who remained
loyal to Parnell. Following their return to power, the
Liberals introduced the second home rule bill in 1893.
This was passed by the Commons, but was rejected by the
Lords which had a Conservative majority. The Liberals
were defeated in the 1895 general election, resulting in a
strong Conservative government, and the possibility of
home rule vanished for over a decade until the home rule

party again held the balance of power after the 1910
general elections.

THE GROWTH OF CULTURAL NATIONALISM

The Parnellite split left the home rule party divided
and without an obvious successor for party leadership,
whereas the strong Conservative majority after 1895 left
them impotent within Westminster. With no immediate
possibility of achieving their primary objective, the
party degenerated into a number of factions in competition
for control of the party machine. The national question
faded in prominence within formal politics as rival
factions squabbled and intrigued to gain control at local
level. Patriotism became superseded by patronage, and the
party became increasingly Catholic in outlook as the party
machine became increasingly dominated by the Board of
Erin, an offshoot of the Ancient Order of Hibernians - a
Catholic equivalent of the Orange Order.

Despite the vacuum created by the collapse of a
realistic possibility of home rule, the 1890s and early
1900s became a very important period in the development of
the national movement. Political demands for home rule
had initially been generated by material interests, but
the desire for political autonomy had the effect of
intensifying an awareness of cultural differences between
Ireland and Britain. This awareness took on a momentum of
its own, with the result that the 1890s became a period of
major cultural change, even though the national movement
remained politically stagnant. Intensified national
awarenesss was reflected in the arts and culture,
resulting in the development of a new, specifically Irish,
cultural identity.

The cultural transformation was initiated in the 1880s
in the period leading up to the first home rule bill. One
of the earliest developments was the formation of the
Gaelic Athletic Association (GAA) by Michael Cusack in

1884 under the patronage of Archbishop Croke. The
objective of the GAA was to encourage people to play Irish
games, such as hurling and Gaelic football, rather than
'English' games such as soccer and rugby. The GAA was in
essence a sporting organisation, but its nationalistic
emphasis upon Irish games made it a natural centre of
attraction for political nationalists.

The 1880s and 1890s saw similar types of developments in
the arts. W. B. Yeats and a small handful of talented
writers initiated the Anglo-Irish literary revival.
Although writing in English, Yeats and his associates
broadened the national consciousness by drawing heavily
upon traditional folklore and mythology for inspiration.
Many of the members of the literary revival were
Protestants, drawn from the remnants of the landlord
ascendancy; their writings may therefore have reflected a
subconscious desire to identity with the 'timeless' Irish
nation because of their increasingly threatened social
position. The romanticism of the mythological inspiration
for their writings might also indicate a reaction against
the vulgar commercialism associated with the social
upheavals which were displacing them. However,
irrespective of whatever their psychological motivations
may have been, the effect of their writings was to instil
a feeling of pride in the Gaelic heritage, thereby
reversing the pre-existing association between Gaelic
culture and peasant backwardness.

Probably the most important organisation in the growth
of cultural nationalism was the Gaelic League. This was
founded in 1893 by Douglas Hyde, a Church of Ireland
rector, and Eoin MacNeill, then a Catholic civil servant,
with the objective of preserving the Irish language where
it still existed (mainly in peninsular areas in the west)
and of encouraging its revival in other areas. The
movement was originally urban and middle-class, but it
rapidly gained in popularity as an adult education cum
entertainment organisation. Apart from attempting to
revive the language, the Gaelic League encouraged an

interest in traditional music and dancing and other forms
of Gaelic culture.

The net effect of these various movements was that the
Irish nation became increasingly identified with a
supposedly traditional Gaelic culture. Much valuable work
was done in the 1890s to record what remained of a peasant
culture which was rapidly being destroyed by
modernisation, but the culture espoused by the cultural
nationalists was to a large degree a late nineteenth
century invention. The cultural nationalism of the late
nineteenth century also entailed further elaborations upon
Thomas Davis's rewrite of Irish history to make it conform
with the prevailing nationalist outlook which emphasised
the close links between Irish nationality and the Catholic
Church. One effect of furthering the links between the
Irish nation, the Catholic religion and Gaelic culture was
that Ulster Protestants were further alienated from the
Irish nation by virtue of their religious and cultural
differences. This in turn reinforced the identity between
Irish nationalism and Catholicism. The Catholic-Gaelic
Irish nation, as we know it to-day, came of age in the
1890s.

CONSERVATISM AND SEPARATISM

The Conservatives, who held power from 1886 to 1892 and
from 1895 to 1905, attempted to undermine the Irish
national movement by introducing further reforms to solve
the land question. A series of Land Acts, culminating in
the Wyndham Act of 1903, were introduced to enable tenant
farmers to buy out their holdings using government loans.
Landlord resistance was minimal because the prices of the
estates were fixed at about twice their existing market
price. The scheme, however, was also attractive to
tenants because the loans were to repaid over 68 years at
a very low rate of interest. The annual repayments on a
loan for a peasant proprietor therefore cost about 20 per

cent less than the rent to lease the farm. Ten thousand
estates, comprising a total of 13 million acres, were
consequently sold to over half a million tenants between
1870 and 1910, especially after the Wyndham Act.

These changes had a number of far-reaching implications.
First, they emphasized the final eclipse of the landlords
as the dominant class. The sale of estates reduced the
number of big landlords, whereas the improved system of
agriculture increased output. This in turn resulted in
increased trade and a further strengthening of the
commercial classes. The commercialisation of agriculture
and the security provided by farm ownership also increased
borrowing for investment, thereby strengthening the role
of finance capital. Thus, as the landlords declined as
the dominant class they were replaced by the rapidly
developing middle classes who formed the backbone of the
home rule party. However, probably the most important
effect of the Land Acts was to convert former tenants into
a large class of farmers who owned their own land. This
had the intended effect of deradicalising a major
component of the most radical section of Irish society.
Farmers, because of their numerical strength, became one
of the most influential blocs in Irish politics; but, due
to the fact that their demands had been met, they also
became one of the most conservative. The home rule party
consequently became increasingly conservative, reflecting
the changing material needs of their supporters.

Other groups within Irish society whose needs had not
been met had to look beyond the home rule party. Given
that the satisfaction of these needs was often conditional
upon first achieving a higher degree of political autonomy
for Ireland, a number of new political groupings developed
which began to make more sweeping nationalist demands than
the home rule party. Many of these factions were
urban-based, reflecting the fact that urban areas (with
the exception of mercantile and financial interests) were
being largely bypassed by the rising prosperity due to
their low degree of industrial development.

The interests of the weakly-developed industrial bourgeoisie were articulated by Sinn Féin ('ourselves alone'), a political party founded by Arthur Griffith in 1905 out of a number of factions sympathetic to republicanism (e.g. Cumann na nGael, Inghinidhe na hÉireann, and the Dungannon Clubs in Belfast). Griffith realised that Irish industrial development was undermined by competition from the more highly developed British industries, and he therefore argued, basing his ideas on the German economist Friedrich List, that Irish industry could only develop behind protective tariffs:

'If a manufacturer cannot produce as cheaply as an English or other foreigner, only because his foreign competitor has better resources at his disposal, then it is the first duty of the Irish nation to afford protection for the manufacturer.' (Quoted in ICO, 1966, p6).

However, in order to establish protective tariffs, Ireland first required legislative independence. Griffith originally favoured total separation from Britain, but to win the support of home rulers who still felt an allegiance to the crown, he proposed a dual monarchy similar to that in Austria-Hungary. This proposal, similar in many respects to O'Connell's repeal objectives, was intermediate between home rule and republican separatism.

Griffith also proposed a policy of pacifist abstentionism to achieve these objectives. He argued that the Act of Union was illegal and that elected representatives should therefore ignore Westminster and the British state apparatus, and create an alternative Irish assembly and state apparatus. This was the strategy which had won independence for the Hungarians within the Hapsburg empire. Sinn Féin contested elections against the home rule party, but apart from a few local government victories they made very little impact until after the 1916 rebellion (see below).

The urban proletariat were also represented by

separatist organisations. Unskilled workers were
unionised in the first decade of the twentieth century,
largely due to the efforts of Jim Larkin who formed the
Irish Transport and General Workers' Union. Larkin's
union activities culminated in a showdown in Dublin in
1913 between the ITGWU and the employers who tried to
smash the unions by locking union members out of their
places of work for eight months. During the lock-out,
some of the workers formed the Citizens Army to defend
strikers from police attacks. Larkin left for the United
States in 1914 and was succeeded as union leader by James
Connolly. Connolly was a committed socialist who believed
that socialism could not be established in Ireland under
imperialism: he consequently regarded Irish independence
as an essential pre-requisite to the formation of an Irish
socialist republic.

There was also a degree of revolutionary potential in
some rural areas. Although the Land Acts deradicalised
farmers, they had done little to improve the conditions of
the cottiers and landless labourers. The Congested
Districts Board, set up in 1891, was designed to assist
the poverty-stricken areas of high population in the west,
but it had relatively little impact. Landless labourers,
who were particularly numerous in the northwest,
consequently remained disenchanted and potentially
revolutionary.

The revolutionary wing of the nationalist movement was
represented by the IRB. This remained a small clandestine
organisation dedicated to the establishment of an
independent republic by armed insurrection, but it was
very effectively re-organised by Thomas Clarke after his
return from the United States in 1907 (McCartney, 1967).
The IRB infiltrated other nationalist organisations, both
political (e.g. Sinn Féin) and cultural (e.g. the Gaelic
League and the GAA), to seek out support for a nationalist
revolution: new recruits from the Gaelic League included,
for example, Pádraig Pearse and Éamon de Valera, both of
whom played a very significant role a few years later.

Seán MacDiarmada, manager of the IRB newspaper Irish
Freedom which began publication in 1910, provided a
useful link between the IRB and Sinn Féin for whom he was
a paid organiser.

Although revolutionary, the IRB remained essentially a
nationalist organisation. There was a vague consensus
that widespread social reforms would follow the
establishment of an independent republic, but the nature
of these reforms remained poorly defined: the principal
objective was to secure national independence.

REBELLION AND INDEPENDENCE

The Liberals were returned to power in 1905 with a large
majority, but this majority was reduced to only 2 seats
following the January 1910 general election: the Irish
home rule party, now led by John Redmond, consequently
held the balance of power and were able to insist upon the
introduction of the third Home Rule bill as the price for
their support. The home rule bill was passed by the House
of Commons in 1912. Although the House of Lords no longer
had the power to prevent the bill from becoming law,
following the Parliament Act of 1911, they were able to
delay its implementation by returning it to the House of
Commmons for three readings. In the end, its
implementation was suspended indefinitely due to the
outbreak of World War I in 1914.

The third Home Rule bill produced tremendous opposition
in Ulster, resulting in the formation of the Ulster
Volunteer Force (UVF) in 1912 which threatened to resist
home rule by armed force (see Chapter 7). This in turn
inspired the formation of a nationalist paramilitary
force, led by Eoin MacNeill, called the Irish Volunteers.
MacNeill did not intend to use the Irish Volunteers to
fight the UVF (who were regarded as fellow Irishmen), but
he hoped that the existence of the Irish Volunteers might
prevent the government from being deterred by the threat

of the UVF.

On the outbreak of war, the UVF demonstrated their loyalty by joining the British Army en masse; but so also did the vast majority of the Irish Volunteers, following John Redmond's example (a fact conveniently overlooked in recent times by the propagandists of both nations). At least 100,000 of the 179,000 Irish Volunteers joined the army, where they became known as the National Volunteers, leaving only about 11,000 in MacNeill's IRB-dominated rump.

The leaders of the IRB, Irish Volunteers and Citizens Army decided to join forces in order to take advantage of the war to stage a rebellion with the objective of establishing an Irish republic in 1916. However, the rebels suffered a serious last minute setback when a shipment of arms from Germany was intercepted by the authorities. MacNeill, seeing that the situation was hopeless, withdrew the Irish Volunteers, leaving only a small group from the IRB and Citizens Army, led by Pearse and Connolly, to stage a doomed rebellion beginning on Easter Monday. Apart from a few skirmishes in Galway and Wexford, the 1916 Easter rebellion was largely confined to Dublin. The rebels issued a proclamation declaring an Irish Republic and held out bravely in a number of prominent buildings against superior forces for just over a week.

The rebellion does not appear to have had much public support and it would probably have had little lasting impact if the authorities had not decided to execute the leaders. However, the execution of fifteen of the leaders (including Pearse and Connolly) between the 3rd. and 12th. of May had the effect of transforming them into national martyrs. This, followed by the indiscriminate internment of about 3,000 suspects, swung public opinion very strongly against the government and its allies, including Redmond and the home rule party. Although not directly involved in the 1916 rebellion, Sinn Féin received a massive upsurge in support due to the fact that it was the

political party which came closest to advocating
separatism. The party was consequently swamped by new
members, resulting in a total transformation in its
character: Sinn Féin became more openly identified with
separatist republicanism; and Griffith, a convinced
pacifist, gradually lost control to the new militants.
However, the growth of support for separatism also
resulted in a deradicalisation of the republican wing of
the nationalist movement: the prime objective of the new
republicans, many of whom were converts from the socially
conservative home rule party, was to achieve national
freedom rather than to implement radical reforms.

The changes were symbolised by the displacement of
Griffith as party president by Éamon de Valera (who had
been the commandant in Boland's mill during the rebellion,
but who had avoided execution by virtue of having been
born in the United States) in 1917. De Valera was elected
leader of the Irish Volunteers later in the same year,
thereby bringing the polical and military wings of the
national movement under a common leadership.

Sinn Féin won a number of by-elections in 1917 and
1918, but the major change came in the 1918 general
election when Sinn Féin totally eclipsed the home rule
party, winning 73 seats compared to only 6 by the home
rulers. Following Griffith's abstentionist policy, the
Sinn Féin M.P.s (or, to be more precise, the 27 who were
neither in jail nor on the run) boycotted Westminister and
set up an alternative parliament (Dáil Éireann) in Dublin
in 1919. The Dáil affirmed the 1916 declaration that
Ireland was an independent republic and an alternative
state apparatus was set up, supported by the Volunteers
who became known as the Irish Republican Army (IRA).
Dáil courts, established to administer justice,
demonstrated a willingness to defend the existing social
order by ruling in favour of large landowners threatened
by land-grabbing by their tenants.

The British government, which regarded the activities of
the Dáil as illegal and as a threat to law and order,

tried to re-establish its authority using the army and the Royal Irish Constabulary (RIC). The IRA retaliated by guerilla attacks on the police and army, resulting in the deaths of 14 policemen and soldiers in isolated incidents in 1919. These incidents, which marked the beginning of the Anglo-Irish war, were initially condemned by Irish nationalist public opinion as the work of groups of maverick extremists, but by August 1919 the IRA campaign was co-ordinated by some members of the Dáil, especially Michael Collins, the Dáil Minister of Finance and IRA Director of Intelligence.

The RIC were depleted by resignations due to the attacks, social ostracism on the orders of the Dáil, and the fact that many had sympathies with the republican cause. They therefore had to be supplemented early in 1920 by British ex-servicemen who became known as 'black and tans' and 'auxiliaries'. The black and tans and auxiliaries, however, lacked discipline and they reacted against IRA attacks with indiscriminate retaliations on innocent civilians. Public opinion consequently became even more anti-British, and violence escalated dramatically resulting in the deaths of 232 police and army in 1920. Ireland was rapidly becoming ungovernable.

The Government of Ireland Act, passed by Westminster in 1920, legislated for the creation of two 'home rule' parliaments in Ireland. Elections for both parliaments (i.e. for Northern Ireland and Southern Ireland) were held using proportional representation in May, 1921. Sinn Féin won another massive mandate (124 out of 128 seats) in elections held for the Southern Ireland assembly, but the new assembly was ignored and the elected representatives continued to sit in Dáil Éireann which they continued to regard as the parliament of a sovereign Irish Republic (32 counties).

The British government realised by this stage that the situation was past redemption and it therefore agreed to a truce in the Anglo-Irish war in order to negotiate with representatives of the Dáil. The net outcome was the

Anglo-Irish Treaty, agreed in December 1921. This gave
Southern Ireland (which became known as Saorstát Éireann
or the Irish Free State) virtual independence as a
dominion within the British Empire. However, it also
recognised the right of Northern Ireland to remain within
the United Kingdom. This, as we shall see, was to become
a source of considerable conflict throughout the rest of
the twentieth century.

SUMMARY

It is impossible to pinpoint exactly when the Irish
nation came into existence, but it was sometime during the
period between the Act of Union and the creation of the
Free State: the modern Irish nation, as pointed out in the
previous chapter, did not exist at the end of the
eighteenth century, but by 1920 there was a very strong
sense of common identity amongst Irish Catholics which was
expressed in a nationalist demand for an independent
nation-state.

The Irish nation evolved slowly, unevenly and
discontinuously into its present form during the
nineteenth century. This evolutionary process was
extremely complex and requires a more detailed analysis
than is possible here (e.g. see Garvin, 1981), but the
basic argument is that material aspirations and
frustrations, arising from the penetration of capitalist
relations, created a situation conducive to the acceptance
and advocacy of nationalist ideas which originated in
Europe.

The growth of nationalism mirrored the pentration of
capitalist relations by diffusing from east to west.
After 1916 support for Sinn Féin was widespread, but it
was generally stronger in the western half of the country
(Figure 16). This contrasts strongly with the much
earlier pattern of support for O'Connell's repeal movement
(see Figure 14). The growth of nationalism and a national

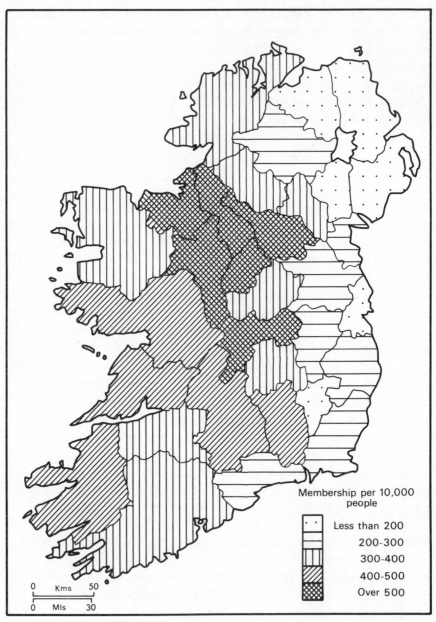

Membership per 10,000
people

Less than 200
200-300
300-400
400-500
Over 500

0   Kms   50
0   Mls   30

FIG. 16   Membership Of Sinn Féin, 1919 (After
Fitzpatrick, 1978).

identity began in the areas of good agricultural land and
large farms in the east and south due to the earlier
penetration of commodity relations. The west only became
mobilised later, especially during the period of the Land
War (cf. Figure 15), but by the post-1916 period it was
the area of greatest support for separatism. The low
level of support for Sinn Féin in Ulster obviously
reflects the growth of unionism amongst Ulster Protestants
(see Chapter 7), but the generally declining level of
support for Sinn Féin from west to east in what is now
the Republic may indicate that the more developed parts of
the country may have been less committed to the idea of
national independence at the beginning of the twentieth
century due to the further extension of its economic links
with Britain. This lack of commitment, however, took the
form of support for home rule rather than for unionism.

The diffusion of nationalism also had a 'vertical'
dimensiom. Nationalist ideas initially had a greater
impact upon the educated middle classes. O'Connell's
campaign for Catholic emancipation was essentially a
demand for a share in political power by the Catholic
middle classes, but O'Connell was able to mobilise mass
support from the more disadvantaged classes, who had
little to gain from emancipation, by an appeal for group
solidarity based upon common religion. Likewise, his
campaign for repeal was essentially an attempt to maximise
the power of the emancipated Catholic middle classes, but
the form which it took (i.e. the demand for a form of
self-government) reflected the influence of the growth of
nationalist movements on the continent. However, the
romantic nationalist ideas of the Germans and Italians
were more explicitly adopted and propagated by the Young
Ireland group. Although the Young Ireland rebellion in
1848 failed to mobilise much support from the more
disadvantaged classes, the fusion of romantic nationalism
and radical republicanism was to have a profound impact
upon the later development of nationalism.

The extent of the 'downward' diffusion of nationalist

ideas was revealed by the growth of Fenianism in the 1850s
and 1860s. The harsh material conditions of the
post-Famine period provided a fertile breeding ground for
the diffusion of the radical nationalist ideology of the
1848 rebels. Material hardships, reflected by evictions
and forced emigration, created a predisposition in favour
of radical social reform, but social reforms could not
apparently be implemented from 'below' within the context
of the United Kingdom: national independence therefore
became regarded a precondition for social reform. The
Fenians, like the United Irishmen in the previous century,
envisaged separatism and republicanism as the means for
achieving social reforms, although the changes desired by
the Fenians were quite different from the bourgeois
reforms sought by the United Irishmen. However, the
Fenians lacked the objective rationality of the United
Irishmen: the espousal of nationalist ideology was
initially stimulated by material conditions, but the
romantic appeal of nationalism was so powerful that
national independence became regarded almost as an end in
itself. There was always a vague notion that things would
get better after independence, but discussion of the form
which the necessary social reforms would take receded into
the background as energies became channelled into the more
immediate objective of achieving national independence.

The subjugation of social grievances to the goal of
national independence, reflected most clearly by the IRB
(although evident to some extent in Connolly's socialism),
facilitated a manipulation of the more deprived sections
of Irish society by the middle classes working towards
their own objectives. The middle classes maintained a
greater degree of materialist rationality. With the
exception of the frustrated small industrial bourgeoisie
(represented by Arthur Griffith's Sinn Féin), the middle
classes did not require sweeping social reforms - they
merely desired a transfer of power from Westminster to
themselves. They were consequently quite content to work
towards home rule, which was a more feasible objective

than total independence, using constitutional methods which minimised the possibility of a social upheaval. Indeed, the mobilisation of support for moderate nationalist objectives provided the middle classes with a very useful means of distracting the attention of urban workers, small farmers and landless labourers away from class exploitation and social injustice.

The hegemony of the middle classes in the Irish national movement was temporarily weakened by the special conditions prevailing during World War I, especially after the 1916 rebellion, resulting in an upsurge of support for separatism; but the middle classes quickly adjusted to the new situation and re-established themselves as the dominant element in the newly independent state, as reflected by the socially conservative position adopted by the Dáil on land appropriation. It should be noted, however, that neither the socially influential middle classes nor the majority of the Irish nation as a whole demanded independence from Britain until after 1916.

The creation of the Irish nation entailed more than simply the mobilisation of support for political autonomy; it also entailed the creation of a specific Irish nationalist ideology to forge a sense of common identity. The groundwork was provided by the reinterpretation of history to fit into a nationalist mould by the Young Irelanders in the 1840s - Brian Boru and Hugh O'Neill, for example, were transformed into patriots fighting on behalf of the Irish nation - but the 1890s, corresponding to a lull to political developments, was the major period of transformation in this respect: it was at this point that the Irish nation became explicitly Catholic and Gaelic.

By the early 1920s the growth of Irish nationalism had resulted in the creation of a new nation-state. However, it had also alienated a large number of Protestants in Ulster who, as we shall see in the following chapter, turned to unionism in response to the perceived threat provided by Irish nationalism to their material well-being. As a result, national independence for part of the Irish nation could only be achieved at the expense of dividing the nation between two states. The reunification of the nation has become the major goal of Irish nationalists ever since.

CHAPTER 7
The Growth of
Ulster Unionism

Irish nationalism, as explained in the previous chapter, developed in the nineteenth century in response to changing material conditions arising from the penetration of commodity relations into rural Ireland: nationalist ideology, although it originated in Europe under quite different conditions, appealed to many sections of Irish society who for different reasons regarded increased political autonomy as a means for solving their own particular material grievances or frustrations. However, capitalist development followed a quite different course in most of Ulster, with the result that a separatist nationalist ideology had a much more restriced appeal due to the different material needs which emerged there. The underlying material needs, reinforced by religious and cultural differences, were reflected by the growth of a quite different ideology - Ulster unionism. The growth of Ulster unionism is examined in the present chapter.

CONTINUITY AND CONVERGENCE

Unionism provides the unifying ideology of what was identified in Chapter 2 as the Ulster nation. Although cultural forerunners of the Ulster nation may be identified prior to the nineteenth century, it would be wrong to assume that Ulster Protestants have always shared a common political identity. Ulster Protestants, as noted

189

in Chapter 5, were on opposite sides in the events culminating in the 1798 rebellion: Presbyterians in Down and Antrim provided the backbone of the United Irishmen, whereas Episcopalians in central and west Ulster, especially those in the Orange Order, supported the Dublin government and were prominent in the Yeomanry. However, by the end of the nineteenth century Protestants of both denominations and in both parts of Ulster were united by their support for Ulster unionism.

Ulster unionism, by the late nineteenth century, was characterised not only by support for the union with Britain, but also by a strong antipathy towards Catholics. Nationalist historians have consequently tried to explain why the Presbyterians in east Ulster 'changed sides' in the nineteenth century: i.e. from being sympathetic to Catholics and republicanism in 1798 to being anti-Catholic and pro-British one hundred years later. This has proved to be one of the most intractable questions in Irish nationalist history.

The main reason why this question has proved to be so intractable is that the Presbyterians in east Ulster did not in fact change sides during the nineteenth century: they only appear to have changed sides when viewed from a nationalist perspective which interprets the whole of Irish history as a conflict between the Irish nation and Britain. Viewed from the perspective of the Presbyterians themselves, the development from republican radicalism in 1798 to Ulster unionism by the late nineteenth century is quite logical and entails no major discontinuities or shifts in allegiance, as illustrated by the following quote from a pamphlet written by unionist Liberals at the time of the first Home Rule Bill:

> 'We were brought up in the district where Ulster disaffection assumed its acutest form. We have talked in our boyhood with aged relatives who remembered the scenes and incidents of the Rebellion, and whose fathers and brothers were deeply involved in the conflict. We were taught

to reverence and respect the memory of those who
took up arms against intolerable oppression, and
struck a blow for freedom. But, at the same
time, we were taught that every object which our
forefathers fought for had long since been
attained. ... Had our forefathers been offered
before the Rebellion a Union such as we now
enjoy with Great Britain, we know on the best
authority that in Ulster at least there would
have been no Rebellion. ... What privilege of
English freedom is it that we do not enjoy?
What legal right is denied us? What career is
open to England's sons that is not open to us?
What place of power or honour is there that any
citizen of the Empire can aspire to which is
denied to the aspirations of any Irishmen? ...
I confess I have in vain striven to find out in
what particular we are oppressed or neglected;
and I think it would puzzle Mr. Gladstone to
tell us plainly why we should revive the
memories of the years preceding 1795, except to
remind us of what Ireland may suffer at the
hands of an Irish parliament.' (Quoted in BICO,
1973, p44-5).

The rebellion of the United Irishmen in 1798, as pointed
out in Chapter 5, was not a nationalist rebellion - it was
primarily designed to secure liberal democratic reforms.
Republicanism was only adopted as a means for achieving
these reforms. When the rebellion was defeated, many of
the United Irishmen welcomed the Union with Britain
because it went a long way towards meeting their demands
by abolishing the Dublin government. Unionism was not
regarded by the United Irishmen as the antithesis of
radical republicanism - they were both merely alternative
approaches to the same objective, namely liberal
democratic reforms. Unionism and radical republicanism
only became diametrically opposed later, following the
growth of nationalism, when radicalism was linked with the

separatist tendency within the Irish nationalist movement by John Mitchel and other members of Young Ireland in the late 1840s.

The fact that there is a high degree of continuity between radical republicanism in the late eighteenth century and Ulster unionism one hundred years later does not mean that the Presbyterians' collective outlook remained totally stable throughout the nineteenth century. On the contrary, their outlook changed in two important respects. First, their attitude towards Catholics changed from one of tolerance to one of animosity. Second, they changed from being one of the most progressive and radical groups in Ireland to being amongst the most conservative.

Protestants (especially Episcopalians) in central and west Ulster, on the other hand, have always tended to be more conservative and less fraternal towards Catholics; however, they were originally opposed to the Act of Union. Their fervent espousal of unionism by the late nineteenth century therefore represents a notable shift in attitude. The consolidation of the Ulster nation, characterised by a feeling of common identity between all Ulster Protestants and by a loyalty to the Union, did not simply entail the conversion of Presbyterians from republicanism: it also entailed the conversion of Episcopalians to unionism. Protestant unity in Ulster was therefore the product of a convergence between Presbyterians and Episcopalians, rather than being due to the Presbyterians changing sides as supposed by Irish nationalists.

In order to explain this convergence, which culminated in the emergence of a united unionist opposition to the home rule movement in the 1880s, this chapter examines the reasons why the Episcopalians turned to unionism, and why the Presbyterians became less ecumenical and more conservative. The remainder of the chapter is divided into eight sections. These are organised thematically rather than sequentially although, except for the first section (which examines the economic background to the events discussed in the other sections) and the concluding

summary section, they are arranged in approximate
historical sequence.

ECONOMIC BACKGROUND

Ulster developed in a totally different manner from the
rest of Ireland in the nineteenth century. The reasons
why Ulster's regional economy should have diverged so
markedly are the subject of considerable debate, but the
nineteenth century was a period of tremendous economic
growth, especially in east Ulster, whereas it was a period
of industrial decline and rural dislocation in the rest of
the island.
Ulster avoided the worst excesses of rural poverty which
affected most of the rest of Ireland. This was partly due
to the existence of the Ulster custom which protected
tenants from rack renting by landlords. However,
structural differences in agriculture were probably a more
important factor. Ulster was characterised by fairly
small tenant farms with the result that there were
relatively few landless labourers and cottiers compared
with the big farm areas in the south and east. However,
the farms were generally sufficient, especially if
supplemented by incomes from linen weaving, to provide a
reasonably secure standard of living, in contrast to the
small peasant holdings in the west. Most of Ulster
consequently escaped the worst effects of the Famine
(Figure 17). However, the major difference between Ulster
and the rest of Ireland was the rapid growth of Belfast as
a major industrial city at a time when other urban areas
were economically stagnant.
The early growth of Belfast was associated with the
growth of the domestic linen industry. Belfast was
initially only one of a number of local market centres for
brown (i.e. unbleached) linen until the last quarter of
the eighteenth century; but, following the completion of
the White Linen Hall in 1783, Belfast replaced Dublin as

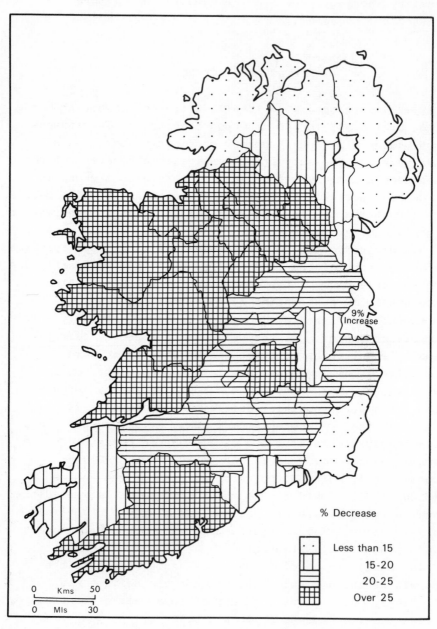

FIG. 17   Population Decrease, 1841-1851.

the major market centre and port for white (i.e. bleached) linen.

Belfast's major growth phase, however, did not occur until the nineteenth century and it was founded upon factory-based industry rather than trade, although the linen trade provided the initial risk capital for industrial investment. The first factory-based industry was cotton spinning, introduced in 1777 using technology imported from Glasgow. Water power (introduced in 1784) and later steam power (introduced in the first decade of the nineteenth century) were used to drive machines. Weaving, however, was done by hand looms. By 1810 over 2,000 people were employed in cotton production in Belfast, mostly in mills which employed up to 300 people. The city meanwhile consolidated its position as the major port and market centre for agriculture and linen through improvements in transport links with the rural hinterland.

As elsewhere, the Belfast cotton industry was adversely affected by the end of the Napoleonic wars and the introduction of free trade, resulting in its virtual collapse in the depression of 1825. The late 1820s were a period of high unemployment and very low wages in the city. By 1838 only 5 cotton mills survived, most of which were finally killed off during the 1860s when the American Civil War interrupted the supply of cotton. However, the collapse of the cotton industry in the 1820s initiated a chain reaction of industrial innovations which transformed Belfast from a medium sized town into one of the largest cities in the British Isles within a few decades.

Following a fire in 1828, Mulholland's cotton mill was converted into a mechanised flax mill using a wet spinning process developed in England. The venture proved so successful that by 1835 there was a total of 10 flax mills; by 1852 the number had increased to 28. Flax spinning became a major employer: Mulholland's mill alone employed over 600 by the 1860s (Jones, 1960). The demand for machinery in the rapidly growing linen spinning industry provided the stimulus for an engineering

industry. This in turn encouraged the development of a
ship building industry on land reclaimed by the Harbour
Commissioners. William Hickson, the owner of the Belfast
Iron Works, took over a small iron-shipyard in 1853 to
provide an outlet for surplus iron plates, but within a
few years he sold it to his manager, Edward Harland.
Harland, in turn, formed a partnership with Gustavus
Wolff, following which the yard grew rapidly in the
subsequent decades due to local technological innovations
and business contacts with several major shipping lines
(e.g. the Bibby Line). Employment increased from 500 in
1861, to 2,400 in 1870, to over 9,000 in 1900, by which
time Harland and Wolff had become the largest shipyard in
the world. The growth of the shipbuilding industry
naturally resulted in a further expansion of the
engineering industry.

Meanwhile the textile industry expanded following the
introduction of factory-based linen weaving in the 1850s
to complement the existing spinning industry. Linen
exports received a major boost in the early 1860s when the
American Civil War cut supplies to the cotton industry,
and by the 1870s the industry employed 60,000 factory
workers. By the 1890s the Ulster Spinning Company had
achieved a world monopoly in thread spinning, and had a
total workforce of 70,000 including its branches in New
Jersey and Germany (Gibbon, 1975).

The Belfast economy in the late nineteenth century was
based upon the linen, shipbuilding and engineering
industries, but expansion of the port resulted in the
development of a large number of port-related industries.
Apart from flour and corn mills, the city claimed the
world's largest tobacco factory and the world's largest
ropeworks (owned jointly by Mulholland and the shipyard
owners).

Belfast grew at a phenomenal rate, especially in the
second half of the century, as a result of this rapid
industrial expansion. The population in 1800 was about
20,000. This increased to 50,000 by 1830, and to 100,000

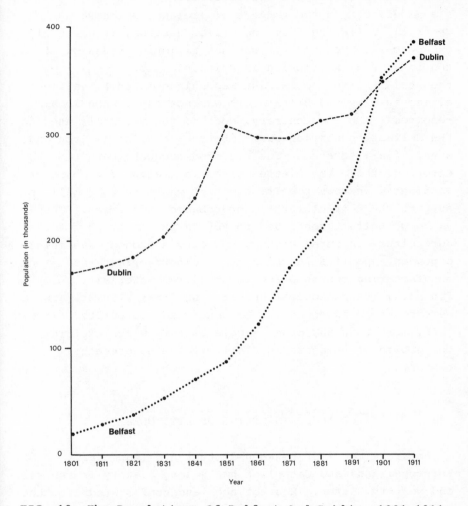

FIG. 18   The Populations Of Belfast And Dublin, 1801-1911.

by 1850; but it mushroomed in the second half of the
century to 350,000 by 1900. Belfast briefly overtook
Dublin as the largest city in Ireland around the turn of
the century (Figure 18). Most of the population increase
was due to inmigration from rural Ulster, especially from
counties Antrim and Down: there was very little migration
from other parts of Ireland.

The growth of Belfast was fast, even by British standards; but in the context of Ireland, which was generally suffering from industrial decline, it was truly exceptional. However, it was not a simple extension of the industrial revolution in Britain. Rapid industrialisation in Belfast was unique in that, unlike cities in mainland Britain, it was not based upon local resources. On the contrary, most of the materials used in the Belfast industries were imported: e.g. coal, iron and steel, flax, tobacco. The finished products were exported: there was little demand in Ireland for ships or machinery, whereas the Irish market was much too small to support the Belfast textile or tobacco industries. Thus, although Belfast continued to act as the major port for agriculture in rural Ulster, the city's economy was mainly dependent upon its function as an export-orientated manufacturing centre using imported raw materials. Financial, technological and trading links with Britain were regarded as essential to continued prosperity. It is this, more than any other single factor, which explains the growth of unionism in Ulster in the nineteenth century.

CHANGES IN RELIGIOUS ATTITUDES

Sectarian conflict between Protestants (especially Episcopalians) and Catholics has a long history in central and western Ulster. Most of the land confiscated from the Catholic Gaelic aristocracy at the time of the Ulster plantation was allocated to Protestant English and Scottish undertakers and servitors. Although the leadership of the Gaelic aristocracy fled in 1607, the other members of the clans (who under brehon law held the land communally) remained, harbouring grievances of dispossession. Meanwhile, Protestant tenants, brought in by the new landlords, believed that they had a right to the land by virtue of the labour which they had expended

in clearing and improving it; they consequently did not
take kindly to the idea of being displaced by new tenants
prepared to bid higher rents. Given that the distinction
between the original inhabitants and the new landowners
(and their tenants) was reflected and preserved by
religious differences, and given that the Protestants had
not settled in sufficient numbers to establish a decisive
majority, relations between Catholics and Protestants
remained strained. This was reflected by the growth of
Defenderism and Orangeism in the late eighteenth century
(see Chapter 5). Little happened in the nineteenth
century to remedy the situation: competition for a scarce
resource (i.e. land) in times of extreme hardship, coupled
with the growth of an Irish nationalist ideology which
eulogized the heroic struggle of the historic Irish nation
against oppression by foreign invaders, only served to
perpetuate and deepen divisions along sectarian lines.

Sectarian conflict was less pronounced in east Ulster,
probably because the Protestant majority (mostly
Presbyterian) was much larger and therefore felt less
threatened (Figure 19). This was the core area of the
United Irishmen in the late eighteenth century, and
relations between Presbyterians and Catholics appear to
have remained very good for the first two and a half
decades of the nineteenth century. The synod of the
Presbyterian Church, for example, passed a unanimous
resolution in favour of Catholic emancipation in 1814, and
would appear to have been generally in favour of
O'Connell's campaign for emancipation in the following
decade. However, there would appear to have been a marked
deterioration in Protestant-Catholic relations, especially
in Belfast, in the late 1820s and early 1830s.

Sectarian conflict in Belfast was originally imported
into the city by rural immigrants from central Ulster.
The first outbreak of sectarian rioting between
Protestants and Catholics - a recurring feature of Belfast
ever since - occurred in 1813 following an Orange parade
through a Catholic sector of the city. Most of the

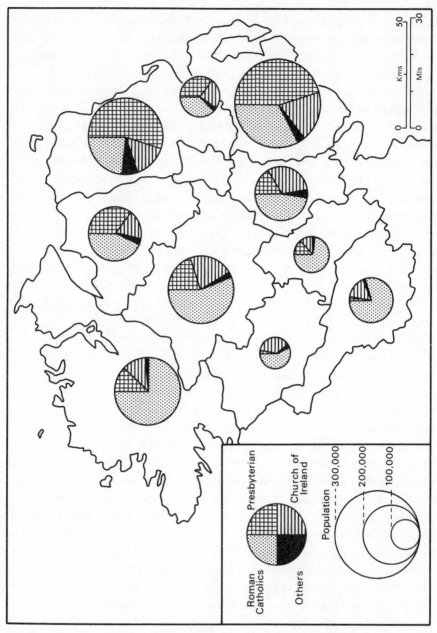

FIG. 19   Religious Affiliation In Ulster, 1861.

Orangemen were poor Protestants (mostly Episcopalians) who had been forced off the land; most of the Catholics were also poor rural immigrants. The riots were primarily a continuation of rural feuds between Orangeism and Defenderism.

Sectarian conflict between Catholics and Episcopalians increased noticeably in the 1830s. The 1832 elections in Belfast were marked by riots between Protestant supporters of the victorious Tory candidates and Catholic supporters of the Liberal candidates (both of whom were Protestants). Further riots occurred in 1835, 1841, 1843, 1852 and 1857. These were sparked off either by elections or Orange marches, but they were probably a reflection of the intense competition for survival which developed between the rural poor of both religions who flooded into the city. The fact that the immigrants contained a higher percentage of Catholics than Protestants, reflecting the more disadvantaged position of Catholics in the rural areas, was perceived as a threat by Protestants: the percentage of Catholics in Belfast increased rapidly during the 1840s, reaching an estimated 43 per cent at the peak of the Famine in 1848 (Baker, 1973), although it declined again in the second half of the century to about 25 per cent.

The introduction of sectarian strife into Belfast by immigrant Catholics and Protestants was paralleled by a hardening of attitudes towards Catholics by the formerly moderate Presbyterians. Although the Presbyterians generally supported O'Connell's campaign for Catholic emancipation, many of them became increasingly apprehensive about the possibility of a Catholic ascendancy being substituted for the existing Protestant ascendancy. Presbyterian fears intensified following O'Connell's campaign for repeal: the United Irishmen had opposed a Dublin parliament controlled by the Protestant ascendancy - it now appeared as if O'Connell wished to restore the Dublin parliament under the control of a Catholic ascendancy. Repeal of the Act of Union therefore appeared to Presbyterians as a threat to their religious freedom. This threat may not have been as great as they imagined, but even some members of the Young Ireland movement who advocated repeal expressed reservations about O'Connell's real motivations: Thomas Davis, for example, wrote in a letter to a friend 'I am determined not to be the tool of a Catholic ascendancy, while apparently the enemy of British domination.'

The growing Presbyterian distrust of Catholicism also reflected changes in the nature of Catholicism itself. Under the Penal laws in the eighteenth century, the Catholic clergy in Ireland had to go to the continent for training. Many of the Catholic bishops in the early nineteenth century had therefore been trained in France where they had been influenced by a French form of Catholicism known as Gallicanism. Gallicanism recognised the authority of the state over secular affairs, and denied the right of the Pope to interfere in the affairs of the Church in each country. It also tended to be liberal in outlook. However, the British government was concerned that priests trained on the continent might act as a source of radical ideas in Ireland following the French Revolution, and therefore the Royal College of Saint Patrick was established as a Catholic seminary in Maynooth in 1795. Catholic priests were subsequently trained in Ireland, and began to look to Rome, rather than to France, for inspiration with the result that Gallicanism was gradually replaced by Ultramontanism as the dominant outlook in the Irish Catholic Church. Ultramontanism recognised the supreme authority of the Pope, and it claimed the authority of the Church over areas which had previously been regarded as the domain of the state (e.g. education). It also tended to be socially conservative.

The Presbyterians' formerly sympathetic attitude towards Catholics had been based on the premise that a person's religious beliefs were a matter of personal conscience. However, when the Catholic Church began to demand control

over areas which the Presbyterians regarded as secular,
the Presbyterians began to fear that the Catholic Church
would not be prepared to tolerate religious freedom in
others, especially given the increase in Catholic social
power following emancipation. Presbyterian distrust
eventually turned into open hostility, and in the second
half of the century Presbyterians became as anti-Catholic
as Episcopalians, especially after a fundamentalist
revival in the late 1850s. Presbyterians began to join
the Orange Order in Belfast in greater numbers from the
1850s onwards.

Sectarian riots continued in Belfast throughout the
second half of the century, although they increasingly
came to take on a political as well as a sectarian
dimension. Twelve people were killed, and over one
hundred injured, in serious riots between Protestants and
Catholics in west Belfast sparked off by the unveiling of
a monument to Daniel O'Connell in Dublin. Further riots
occurred in 1872, 1880, 1884, 1886 and 1898. The Belfast
riots, especially in the second half of the century,
indicate the strength of Protestant opposition to the
possibility of a Dublin parliament which they believed
would be under the control of the Catholic Church. As
noted by Lee (1973, p132): 'These were no petty squabbles
... Belfast riots alone accounted for more fatalities than
all the nationalist risings of the nineteenth century.'

URBAN UNIONISM

The United Irishmen, representing the interests of the
emerging bourgeoisie in Belfast in the late eighteenth
century, were strongly opposed to the landlord-dominated
Dublin parliament; but, as noted in Chapter 5, they
exhibited no major objections against the union with
Britain. As the local Belfast economy continued to expand
at an increasing rate throughout the nineteenth century
based upon industrial growth, the bourgeoisie became

204

increasingly apprehensive about the effects of a possible
return of the Dublin parliament. Repeal of the Act of
Union, or the introduction of home rule, would have
resulted in the creation of a Dublin assembly dominated by
landlords or farmers with little understanding of, or
sympathy towards, the needs of industry in Ulster. A
continuation of the union, on the other hand, ensured the
continuation of government by a parliament sympathetic to
the needs of the industrial bourgeoisie. Material
considerations consequently reduced the romantic appeal of
Irish nationalism for the Belfast bourgeoisie. One of
their major fears was that the prosperous industries in
Ulster would be expected to provide the bulk of the
taxation required to support the Dublin administration,
due to the generally poor state of agriculture in the rest
of the island. This would obviously have reduced profit
levels, and possibly even have threatened the viability of
Belfast industry in the face of overseas competition.

The Belfast industrial bourgeoisie also feared that a
Dublin government would introduce import tariffs. These
would have enabled underdeveloped Irish industries to
develop local markets while protected against competition
from Britain, but they would have undermined the already
developed industries in Belfast. As noted above, most of
the major industries in Belfast depended upon imports of
cheap raw materials and easy access to the British markets
for exports: protective tariffs could have interfered with
the movement of raw materials and commodities, and
possibly even with the flows of capital and technology.
The material interests of the Belfast bourgeoisie not only
required them to oppose the creation of a Dublin
parliament, but also required them to support actively the
maintenance of their close connections with Britain. Many
industrialists consequently threatened to withdraw their
investments from Ulster if the first Home Rule Bill was
passed. Share prices plummeted in 1886 but recovered
strongly once the bill was defeated.

The industrial bourgeoisie would be expected to have a

very clear understanding of the implications of a
devolution of power to Dublin for Belfast business
interests, but it is important to note that the Belfast
proletariat also had a very clear idea of the implications
of home rule for themselves. The Irish nationalist
literature often depicts the Belfast proletariat as being
duped by the landlords and factory owners into support for
the union with Britain against their own material
interests, but the proletariat clearly realised the
implications of a business collapse upon their jobs and
living standards. They also realised that the trade
unions could expect much less protection in an Irish
parliament which was dominated by the interests of
landowners, than in Westminster where the voice of the
industrial proletariat became increasingly powerful after
the extension of the franchise in 1884. The attitudes of
the Belfast proletariat are clearly indicated in the
following excerpt from a manifesto addressed to the
British labour movement and signed by 2,000 trade
unionists in 1914:

'You have been told by the radical and socialist
press ... that Ulster's resistance to Home Rule
is an aristocratic plot engineered by the
aristocracy for its own ends and for the
suppression of the people. This is false. We,
your fellow trade unionists in the North of
Ireland, the only part of Ireland where labour
is fully organised and articulate, as in your
own country, tell you this is false. ... We are
working men and trade unionists and have at
heart the interests of trade unionism no less
than you have. The Irish Parliament under the
Home Rule Bill can pass labour laws for Ireland
... Under an Irish Parliament, controlled by
small farmers, the Factory Acts and the factory
regulations would remain a dead letter ... We
know that the privileges won for the workers by
trade unionism are in danger, and that the loss

of these privileges means the degradation of
labour in Ireland.' (Quoted in BICO, 1972, p65).

The Belfast proletariat were not a pliable mass under
the control of the bourgeoisie: trade unionism was well
established by the last quarter of the century and class
conflict was as acute in Belfast as in any other British
city. However, class differences were less important than
the common threat posed to the material well-being of both
the bourgeoisie and the proletariat by the Irish national
movement. The growth of a unified opposition to Irish
nationalism, which transcended class divisions, by the
1880s should therefore be regarded as the product of a
convergence of interests between different classes, rather
than the product of one class being manipulated by the
other.

It should of course be stressed that the Belfast
proletariat were divided on the national question along
religious lines: Belfast Catholics were strongly
nationalist rather than unionist. The fact that most were
rural immigrants, or only one generation removed from the
land, probably predisposed them in favour of land reform,
and therefore to nationalism. Sectarian conflict with the
Orange Order, which became stridently unionist (see
below), would also have predisposed Catholics in favour of
Irish nationalism, especially given the possibility that a
Dublin parliament would be under Catholic control.
However, possibly the major reason why the Catholic
proletariat did not become unionist was that Catholics
were in general poorly represented in the industries which
benefitted most from the union with Britain, and therefore
generally occupied an inferior position in the labour
market.

The reasons for the generally inferior social position
of Catholics are complex. The fact that the city was
initially strongly Presbyterian meant that most of the
bourgeoisie and skilled workers would have been
Presbyterians in the early decades of the century. New
immigrants fleeing the land, both Catholic and Protestant,

would not have had the capital to become part of the
bourgeoisie. However, a higher percentage of Protestants
would have had experience of domestic weaving in rural
Ulster and would therefore have been better able to
establish themselves in skilled jobs. These initial
distinctions were subsequently defended by skilled workers
from one generation to the next by a variety of mechanisms
designed to exclude entry by outsiders (e.g. informal
contact systems, trade unions, the Orange Order, etc.).
These mechanisms took on a more overtly sectarian
dimension as relations between Protestants and Catholics
polarised, although the first recorded complaint of
discrimination against Catholics by Protestant employers
(according to Budge and O'Leary, 1973) did not occur until
1886. Nevertheless, whatever the reasons for the
generally inferior social status of Catholics in Belfast,
the net effect was to reduce the extent of their material
interests in preserving the union.

RURAL UNIONISM

   The material motivations in rural Ulster were quite
different. Many of the big landlords, who were mostly
Episcopalian, initially resented the union with Britain
because the abolition of the Dublin parliament undermined
the political power of the Protestant ascendancy in
Ireland. Most, however, quickly adapted to the new
situation and some even established themselves as major
figures in British politics (e.g. Lord Castlereagh). As
the century progressed, the landed ascendancy increasingly
looked towards the union to protect their interests as the
Catholic middle classes, especially after emancipation,
increasingly began to demand the return of an Irish
parliament. An Irish parliament, under Catholic control,
would not only have threatened the dominant social
position of the Protestant ascendancy, but might also have
eventually threatened the landlords' property rights.

208

Landlord support for the union, however, remained
somewhat ambivalent until quite late in the century
because of the growth of bourgeois power in Britain. The
traditional social power of the landed aristocracy in
Britain became increasingly undermined by the emergence of
the bourgeoisie as the new dominant class following the
industrial revolution. The British bourgeoisie,
especially as represented by the Liberals, had little
interest in maintaining the Irish landlord ascendancy;
consequently, Irish landlord support for the union was to
some extent contingent upon the implications of government
policy for Irish landowners. The Irish landlords
generally regarded their interests as being best
represented by the Conservatives at Westminster; but even
as late as the early 1870s, following the disestablishment
of the Church of Ireland and the introduction of land
legislation by the Liberals, a substantial section of the
Protestant ascendancy favoured home rule on the assumption
that they could come to some agreement with the Catholic
middle classes.

Landlord support for home rule faded throughout the
1870s as the home rule movement was taken over by the
Catholic lower middle classes, and it all but vanished
following the close association established between the
home rule movement and the Land League by Parnell in the
late 1870s. The landlords were increasingly forced into
the Conservative camp, especially after the Liberals sided
with the home rule movement in 1885. The landlords
declined, both numerically and as a distinctive social
force, following the Land Acts passed by the Conservatives
towards the end of the century: apart from enabling tenant
farmers to buy their farms at favourable rates, the Land
Acts also benefitted the landlords by enabling them to
sell their estates at very generous prices. Nevertheless,
the remnants of the landed ascendancy played a significant
role in the leadership of the unionist movement, although
hegemony by the end of the nineteenth century had
generally passed to the industrial bourgeoisie.

The motivations of the landlords' Protestant tenants were obviously different. Although many of the tenants, especially in central and western Ulster, were Episcopalians, they were not part of the Protestant ascendancy. Their material needs, in fact, were not too different from those of Catholic tenants. Protestant tenants, like their Catholic counterparts, benefitted from the legalisation of the Ulster custom and the tenant purchase of farms under the Land Acts, both of which were an indirect outcome of the home rule movement. It therefore appears paradoxical that they should have rallied behind their landlords in support of the union and the Conservatives. However, the land question entailed more than a straightforward struggle between landlords and tenants: it also entailed conflict between different classes and groups of tenants.

In the case of central and west Ulster these conflicts often took on a sectarian dimension. Protestant tenants initially enjoyed a privileged position relative to Catholics because the landlords originally had to offer them favourable conditions to entice them to colonise the area in sufficient numbers to defend it against the native Irish. However, once the threat had passed, the landlords became willing to accept Catholic tenants who, because of their greater need, were prepared to pay higher rents. The Protestant tenants consequently came to regard Catholics as either a real or potential threat to their livelihood. Although the Protestant tenants were being exploited by their landlords, there was little that they could do about it so long as Catholics were prepared to bid higher rents to displace them. The Protestants formed themselves into societies such as the Orange Order to defend what they regarded as their rightful privileges. The Orange Order became stridently pro-union in the early decades of the nineteenth century, especially following O'Connell's campaign for repeal, because the union was regarded as the best defence against Catholicism.

The situation was somewhat different in east Ulster.

Protestants formed a substantial majority in east Ulster,
consequently the land question was not confused by
sectarian conflict to the same extent; grievances on the
land question more often tended to take the form of
demands for agrarian reform. However, by the second half
of the century, Presbyterian attitudes towards Catholics
had hardened (see above). East Ulster was also
increasingly being brought into the sphere of influence of
Belfast due to the development of industrial linkages.
The city also became the major market for local
agriculture. Rural Protestants in east Ulster
consequently became increasingly influenced by ideas
emanating from Belfast, including concerns about the
possible effects of home rule.

THE CONSERVATIVE ALLIANCE

By the end of the nineteenth century unionism was
closely associated with the Conservative party. This did
not represent a fundamental shift in allegiance for the
majority of the large landowners, or for their Orange
tenants whose modest but relatively privileged position
created a predisposition against social change. However,
it apparently represented a major shift in outlook in east
Ulster - the centre of radicalism 100 years previously.
In reality the change in outlook was not as great as it
might appear. Radicalism in the 1790s was governed by the
desire of the emerging bourgeoisie to establish a
bourgeois conception of democracy in opposition to the
existing control of society by the landed oligarchy, but
by the 1890s bourgeois democracy had been established, and
therefore there was nothing inconsistent about not
desiring further radical reforms. The major source of
demands for social reforms in the 1890s was no longer the
bourgeoisie but the proletariat.

Conservatism became the dominant element within Belfast
politics in the 1830s, due to the fact that the Liberals

were regarded as suspect because of their association with O'Connell. Opposition to repeal therefore drove a considerable number of erstwhile liberals into the Conservative camp. The Conservatives continued to dominate politics in the city in most of the subsequent elections, partly due to the fact that they were much better organised, although liberalism remained a significant component in Belfast politics until the 1880s. Indeed, the Liberals won one of the two Belfast seats in Westminster as late as 1868 (the other was won by an Orange candidate standing in opposition to the Conservatives). However, the situation changed dramatically at the time of the first home rule bill.

The Conservatives and Liberals in Ulster both opposed home rule in the 1885 general election. When Gladstone agreed to introduce home rule legislation in order to secure the support of Parnell's Irish party who held the balance of power in Westminster, the Liberals in Ulster consequently had to chose whether to support Gladstone's Liberal government or the union. Most chose to support the union, and along with Liberal unionists in Britain they defected to the Conservative camp.

The Liberal party in Ulster never recovered. Most of the gains of the home rule party in Ulster were at the expense of the Liberals, due to the fact that Catholics who previously voted for the Liberals in preference to the Conservatives now voted for the home rule candidates. Many of the Protestants who previously voted for the Liberals supported the Ulster Liberal Unionist Committee, set up in parallel to the Conservative-dominated Ulster Loyalist Anti-Repeal Union in 1886. However, after the two bodies merged to form a unified unionist movement, to fend off the perceived common threat posed by the home rule movement, the Liberal component became overshadowed by the Conservative component.

The Labour party, which was beginning to emerge in Britain, was strangled at birth in Ulster by the national question. The labour movement in Britain, partly because

of its associations with the Liberal party, tended to
support the home rule movement; whereas the labour
movement in Ulster tried to avoid taking sides on the
national question in order to maximise the possibility of
working class unity on class issues. Labour issues
consequently came to be regarded as 'non-political': the
major political issue was the national question and people
voted unionist or nationalist as appropriate. The labour
movement therefore found it very difficult to make an
electoral impression because the national question
appeared to have a more direct bearing on people's
material well-being than class issues. However, the fact
that there was a very strong support for conservative
unionist candidates from the Protestant proletariat should
not be interpreted as indicating a lack of interest in the
labour movement. The labour movement was in fact highly
developed in Belfast, but politics assumed a different
form to those in Britain because of the urgency of the
national question.

UNIONIST IDEOLOGY

By the 1880s Ulster Protestants of different
denominations and class backgrounds were united in
opposition to the Irish national movement. However,
unionist unity disguised a large number of internal
conflicts: the unionists in the west distrusted the
industrialists in Belfast because they believed the latter
would jettison them in order to safeguard the Belfast
industries; there was class conflict between the
industrial bourgeoisie and the labour movement in Belfast;
and there was a conflict of interests between the
landlords and their tenants which hindered unionist unity,
especially in Fermanagh (Buckland, 1975). The need for
internal unity, in the face of a perceived external
threat, was reflected by the growth of a unionist ideology
which emphasised the similarities between Ulster

Protestants of different backgrounds, and also the
differences between unionists and Irish nationalists.

Irish nationalism, as noted in the previous chapter, was
further mysticised in the 1880s and 1890s by the growth of
cultural nationalism. Unionist opposition to Irish
nationalism was consequently reflected by the growth of an
ideology which emphasised the differences between Ulster
Protestants and the traditional peasant nation
romanticised by Irish nationalists. Thus, whereas Irish
nationalists looked back to a mythical Gaelic golden age
of pastoral tranquility which could only be restored
through national liberation, unionists looked to a future
of progress and prosperity based upon industrial
urbanisation. Nationalists blamed their economic
backwardness on external factors and the lack of local
control, whereas unionists attributed their proserity to
internal factors such as self effort, hard work and
thriftiness, and the link with Britain - then the most
industrialised and urbanised country in the world.
Nationalist historians reinterpreted history in terms of
the heroic struggle of the Irish people against foreign
invaders, whereas unionist historians interpreted history
in terms of the beneficial effects of British
civilisation. Protestant values of personal freedom were
counterposed to the alleged dogmatic authoritarianism and
political manoeuvrings of the Catholic Church.

The need for a distinctive unionist ideology to unify
Ulster Protestants from different backgrounds was reduced
to some extent by the fact that many of the features
espoused by Irish cultural nationalism were alien to
Ulster Protestants. The emphasis placed by Irish
nationalists upon Gaelic culture and the Irish language in
the 1880s and 1890s only served to alienate Ulster
Protestants due to the fact that they had no tradition of
speaking Irish or of playing Gaelic games. The fact that
Gaelic games espoused a rural ethos further alienated
urban Ulster. Ulster Protestants were therefore unified
to some extent by their mutual cultural exclusion from the

Irish nation.

The unionist ideology was more pragmatic and less romantic than that of Irish nationalism which depicted the Irish nation as a downtrodden people struggling against enormous odds throughout history to maintain its distinctive cultural identity. The differences are graphically captured by a reviewer of Robert Kee's book The Green Flag who refers to:

> 'the superior attraction for the cultivated mind of the winding caravans of Irish nationalism with its poets, assassins, scholars, crackpots, parlour revolutionaries, windbags, mythopoeic essayists, traitors, orators from the scaffold, men of action, emerging from so long and so great suffering of the people to impart an almost mystic quality to their often futile and often brutal deeds - the superior attraction of that to the hard assertive, obsessive, successful self-reliance of the Ulster Protestant which has about it as much poetical imagination as is contained in a bowler hat.'
> (Quoted in Nairn, 1977, p230).

These differences to a large extent reflect the different objectives of Irish nationalists and Ulster unionists. Irish nationalists sought a greater degree of autonomy on the grounds that they constituted a distinctive nation; emphasis was consequently placed on the ways in which they differed from the British. Unionists, on the other hand, wished to retain the existing constitutional arrangement; they therefore appear more mundane because it was not in their interests to draw attention to their regional cultural distinctiveness or to behave flamboyantly, but to appear as British (i.e. as 'ordinary') as possible.

THE HOME RULE CRISIS

Ulster unionism may lack the romantic appeal of Irish

nationalism, but it is important not to underestimate the determination of the Ulster nation to defend itself against the perceived threat of the Irish nation, even if this entails armed conflict with the British government. This was well illustrated at the time of the third home rule bill.

The first home rule bill in 1886 was marked by serious rioting in Belfast over a period of four months during which 32 people were killed and 371 were injured (Budge and O'Leary, 1973). Tension increased again at the time of the second home rule bill in 1893; but things generally remained calm for almost two decades, apart from riots in 1898, 1907 and 1909. However, unionist concern increased rapidly when the Liberal government was left dependent upon the support of Irish nationalist M.P.s after the second of the two 1910 general elections. The second home rule bill had been passed by the Commons, but the unionists had been saved on that occasion by the Lords. Now, however, following the Parliament Act in 1911 which eliminated the power of the House of Lords to reject bills passed by the Commons, the unionists had to consider other forms of defence.

When the Liberals introduced the third home rule bill in 1912, it was met by concerted unionist opposition in Ulster, led by Edward Carson and James Craig. A pledge, known as the Ulster Solemn League and Covenant, was drawn up beginning:

> 'Being convinced in our consciences that Home
> Rule would be disastrous to the material
> well-being of Ulster as well as the whole of
> Ireland, subversive of our civil and religious
> freedom, destructive of our citizenship and
> perilous to the unity of the Empire, we, whose
> names are undersigned ... do hereby pledge
> ourselves ... to defeat the present conspiracy
> ...'

This was signed on September 28th. by 237,368 men and 234,046 women (i.e. almost the entire adult Protestant population) in an impressive show of solidarity (Buckland, 1973).

Meanwhile unionists had begun to form paramilitary organisations. These were organised into a single body known as the Ulster Volunteer Force by the Ulster Unionist Council early in 1913. Membership of the UVF was limited to 100,000 men who were organised into county divisions, regiments and battalions under Lieutenant-General Sir George Richardson. Despite the availability of recruits, the UVF provided a poor deterrent to home rule throughout 1913 because they lacked arms and were forced to drill with wooden guns. However, the government was forced to take the UVF more seriously when 35,000 rifles and five million rounds of ammunition bought in Germany were smuggled into Larne in April 1914. The unionists meanwhile, fearing the worst, established a provisional government for Ulster which met in July 1914.

The third home rule bill was passed by the House of Commons for the third time in May 1914, having been rejected on the previous two occasions by the House of Lords, and it therefore became law in September 1914. However, enforcement of the act was suspended due to the outbreak of World War I, thereby deferring the problem of what to do about militant unionist opposition. By the end of the War, the situation had changed dramatically following the 1916 rebellion and the subsequent shift of public opinion in the south towards Sinn Féin. Home rule was unacceptable to both sides: the majority of Irish nationalists wanted the establishment of an independent republic, whereas the unionists wished to remain within the United Kingdom. However, unionists had argued for the retention of the whole of Ireland in the United Kingdom before 1914; now they were prepared to abandon the small percentage of unionists in counties outside what is today Northern Ireland. This enabled the government to seek a compromise by dividing Ireland into two: Northern Ireland (comprising 6 counties) and Southern Ireland (comprising the other 26). Both were to be

granted 'home rule' within the United Kingdom under the
Government of Ireland Act. The unionists had originally
opposed any form of home rule or partition, but they
agreed to the creation of a unionist-controlled Northern
Ireland parliament because they felt that it provided
stronger safeguards than direct rule from a hostile
Liberal government in Westminster.

Elections were duly held for both parliaments in May
1921 using proportional representation. The Southern
Ireland elections, as noted in Chapter 6, only served to
demonstrate the massive degree of support for Sinn Féin,
thereby forcing the government to agree to the creation of
the Irish Free State. The Northern Ireland elections were
regarded as a plebiscite on the national question,
resulting in the Unionist party winning 40 of the 52
seats. A boundary commission was established to redraw
the boundary between Northern Ireland and the Free State
so as to minimise the minorities in both states, but the
commission's recommendations were never enforced. The
border was consequently left to correspond with the
existing county boundaries. This gave Northern Ireland
more territory than could be justified by reference to the
national allegiances of the majority of people living in
border regions, but it also left Northern Ireland with a
substantial minority who did not recognise the legitimacy
of the state. This, as we shall see in the following
chapter, had far-reaching implications for the way in
which the Northern Ireland state subsequently developed.

SUMMARY

Irish nationalists tend to regard Ulster unionism as an
aberration, whereas the nationalist desire for an
independent Irish nation state tends to be regarded as
natural and unexceptional. The problem, from this
perspective, is to explain why the Ulster Protestants
defected from the Irish nation. However, some form of

political union between Britain and Ireland was regarded
as natural and unexceptional (if maybe not desirable) even
by nationalists throughout most of the nineteenth century:
separatism only became the dominant tendency in the Irish
national movement after 1916. The real problem,
therefore, is not to explain why Ulster Protestants became
unionists, but to explain why Irish Catholics became
nationalists and separatists. Unionism did not require a
conscious decision to defect from the Irish nation: it
merely reflected the absence of the material conditions
which fostered the growth of nationalism elsewhere in
Ireland. Unionism, to some extent, emerged by default.

The reasons for Irish nationalism were outlined in
Chapter 6. Irish nationalism developed in response to
rural poverty and industrial decline, both of which became
attributed to domination by Britain. Ulster, however, as
noted above, escaped the worst effects of rural poverty,
whereas the nineteenth century was a period of
unprecedented industrial growth. The material conditions
which underlay the growth of Irish nationalism did not
apply to most of Ulster. The Protestant tenantry were by
and large protected by the Ulster custom, and consequently
did not have the same degree of vested interest in land
reforms or an extension of the three Fs to the rest of
Ireland. The possibility of protective trade tariffs
likewise had little appeal for the industrial bourgeoisie
and Protestant proletariat in Belfast. The lack of
Protestant support for the Irish nationalist movement can
therefore in large measure be attributed to a lack of
motivation to deviate from their acceptance of the
status quo (i.e. union with Britain).

Unionism, however, extended beyond a neutral absence of
support for Irish nationalism: it entailed both a
conscious opposition towards Irish nationalism, and a
positive support for the union with Britain. The
emergence of Ulster unionism as a unified movement in the
1880s was the culmination of a process of convergence
between Protestants of different classes and denominations

in both urban and rural Ulster. The growth of unionism was reactionary in the sense that different groups came together as a defensive response to the perceived common threat posed by the growth of Irish nationalism. The perceived threat varied from one group to another (e.g. landlords had a different set of concerns from the industrial bourgeoisie), but the nationalist threat was sufficiently strong to overcome internal divisions along class and denominational lines. Unionism also tended to be conservative in the sense that various groups either wished to maintain their existing social position (e.g. the landlords) or else wished to maintain the current course of development and change (e.g. the bourgeoisie). Irish nationalism, although also for the most part socially conservative, contained at least a potential threat to the existing social order, especially given that the political centre of power would have been both spatially and socially remote from industrial Ulster.

Unionism, despite the impression created by the aggressive sectarianism of many Ulster Protestants, was essentially defensive. The defensive nature of unionism, as we shall see in the following chapter, is important to an understanding of the later development of the Northern Ireland state.

CHAPTER 8
Partition
and Polarisation

The previous two chapters considered the growth of Irish
nationalism and Ulster unionism respectively, culminating
in the political partition of Ireland. The creation of
Northern Ireland and the Irish Free State, however, did
not solve the national question for either side. The Free
State gained its independence, but only at the expense of
the loss of part of what most Irish nationalists regard as
the national territory. The unionists in Northern
Ireland, on the other hand, have always felt threatened by
the territorial claims of what they regard as a foreign
state supported by a substantial irredentist minority
within Northern Ireland. Relations between the two states,
and between the majority and the minority within Northern
Ireland, have consequently remained strained since the
1920s. Indeed, the fact that the national question has
tended to dominate politics in both parts of Ireland has
resulted in further polarisation between the two
nationalities. Polarisation and conflict, in turn, have
ensured that the national question retains a central
position within Irish politics.

The pre-eminence of the national question has inhibited
the development of other forms of politics, and has
therefore acted as a major barrier to social progress in
both parts of Ireland. This problem is unfortunately
compounded because the relative lack of social progress is
often attributed to a failure to resolve the national
question, thereby increasing the apparent urgency of the

national question and diverting attention further away
from other important political issues.

This chapter examines the effects of the national
question upon the internal development of both states
since partition. The chapter is divided into three
sections, followed by a short summary. The first section
examines the effects of the national question upon the
Free State (later the Republic of Ireland), while the
second examines its effects upon Northern Ireland. The
third section traces the evolution of the present troubles
in Northern Ireland since the early 1960s.

THE SOUTHERN STATE

The Anglo-Irish war (1919-1921) was terminated by
negotiations betweeen the British government and a
delegation from the Dáil, headed by Michael Collins and
Arthur Griffith. These negotiations culminated in the
Anglo-Irish Treaty which in effect gave 'Southern Ireland'
independence, but which also recognised the right of
Northern Ireland to remain within the United Kingdom. The
Dáil delegates were reluctant to accept partition as the
price for independence, but they signed the Treaty because
it made provision for the creation of a boundary
commission to review the position of the border which,
they believed, would reduce the spatial extent of Northern
Ireland to such an extent that it would not be able to
survive.

The Dáil accepted the Treaty early in 1922 by 66 votes
to 56. However, a minority republican faction, led by
Éamon de Valera, argued that the Treaty was a repudiation
of the ideals of the 1916 rebels due to the fact that it
accepted the partition of Ireland and also required an
oath of loyalty to the British crown. They consequently
boycotted the Dáil, leaving it in the control of the
pro-Treaty faction led by Collins and Griffith.

Elections held in the summer of 1922 indicated fairly

strong popular support for acceptance of the Treaty: the
pro-Treaty government won 58 seats, whereas anti-Treaty
republicans only won 35 seats. The remaining seats were
divided between Labour 17, Farmers 7, and independents 11
- most of whom were prepared to accept the Treaty. The
IRA, however, was more evenly divided and the republican
faction was unwilling to concede so easily. The net
result was the outbreak of civil war between the
pro-Treaty free staters and anti-Treaty republicans. The
civil war, which lasted from June 1922 until May 1923,
divided erstwhile colleagues and even families, and was
very bitter: more people were executed than in the
previous six-year struggle against the British. The
government, led by William T. Cosgrave following the
assassination of Collins by republicans and the death of
Griffith from natural causes, eventually emerged
victorious following a ceasefire called by de Valera.

The civil war was by no means a straightforward class
conflict, but in general the pro-Treaty forces were
supported by those sections of society which had most to
gain from a return to stable conditions with minimum
disruption (i.e. the urban bourgeoisie, state
functionaries, landowners and the large farmers), whereas
the republicans generally tended to be those who hoped to
change the nature of Irish society - land-hungry peasants,
republican intellectuals and urban revolutionaries (e.g.
the remnants of Connolly's Citizens Army). These
tendencies were reflected by a higher percentage vote for
anti-Treaty candidates in the small-farm and less-
urbanised west in the August 1923 general election
(Figure 20).

The fact that the free staters emerged as the dominant
faction from the civil war ensured that the southern Irish
state remained socially and politically conservative
throughout the 1920s, whereas partition ensured that it
would be Catholic and rural in outlook. The exclusion of
Northern Ireland, which was the most Protestant and
urbanised part of the island, left the southern state

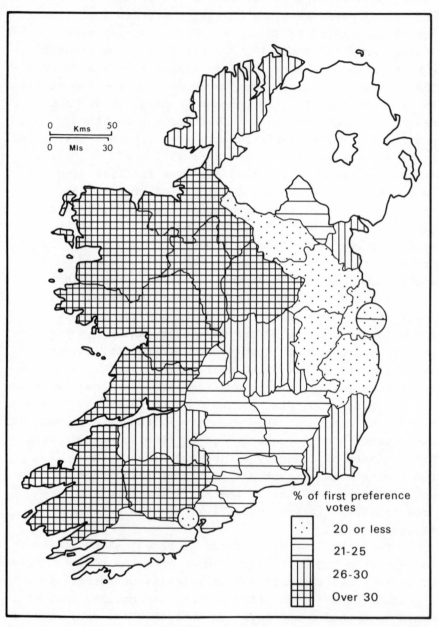

FIG. 20   Percentage Of First Preference Votes For Anti-
Treaty Candidates (After Rumpf and Hepburn, 1976).

predominantly rural and overwhelmingly Catholic: 67.7 per cent of the population lived in rural areas or in towns with fewer than 2,000 people; 92.6 per cent were Catholics (1926 figures). Only 80,000 skilled workers, out of a total of 300,000 in Ireland as a whole, lived in the southern state.

Given the high degree of religious homogeneity in the southern state, and given the lack of resources for implementing fundamental changes, many of the functions provided by the state in other countries were left under the control of the Catholic Church. Primary school education was provided by national schools generally managed by Catholic clergy, whereas secondary school education was mainly available in fee-paying schools run by Catholic religious orders. Most of the major hospitals were likewise run by religious orders. The system seems to have been quite acceptable to southern Protestants, who ran their own secondary schools and hospitals, but the continuation of Catholic control over areas often regarded elsewhere as secular has had a profound influence on the later development of the southern state. It has also tended to reinforce northern Protestant fears that a united Ireland would be directly controlled by the Catholic Church.

Following the loss of the northern industries because of partition, the southern state became heavily dependent upon agricultural exports, mostly from the large commercial farm areas in the east and south, to pay for imports of manufactured goods. The government considered the possibility of establishing trade tariffs, but opted for a policy strongly in favour of free trade to maximise exports. Although policy decisions were rationalised in terms of the 'national interest', they in fact largely reflected the interests of large farmers as the dominant element in the new state.

Agricultural output failed to expand during the 1920s, whereas prices in Britain for Irish agricultural produce fell markedly because of overseas competition. Irish

industry meanwhile was severely affected by the Wall
Street crash in October 1929: worldwide overproduction
resulted in the Irish market being flooded by cheap
foreign-produced goods, resulting in a rapid rise in
unemployment as uncompetitive Irish industries which
depended upon the home market were forced to close. The
adoption of protective economic policies by other west
European governments in response to the world recession
eventually forced the Irish government to impose tariffs
and quotas to prevent dumping on the Irish market in 1931.

The economic crisis of the late 1920s and early 1930s
was instrumental in the growth of the Fianna Fáil party,
founded in 1926 by de Valera and supported by most of the
republican faction defeated in the civil war. A minority
of republicans, represented by the remnants of Sinn Féin
and the IRA, remained committed to the idea of an
all-Ireland republic and refused to acknowledge the
legitimacy of either the Free State or Northern Ireland.
Fianna Fáil, described by one of its leading members,
Seán Lemass, as 'a slightly constitutional party',
remained somewhat ambivalent: it accepted the de facto
existence of partition and Northern Ireland, but not their
de jure existence. Fianna Fáil also compromised the
traditional republican commitment to a secular state by
recognising the effective social power of the Catholic
Church.

This was illustrated in several Dáil debates in the
late 1920s and early 1930s which discussed alleged
discrimination against Protestants. In one particular
case, a Protestant woman was appointed Mayo County
Librarian, but the Mayo Library Committee, supported by
Mayo County Council, refused to ratify the position
because, in the words of the Catholic Dean of Tuam: 'We
are not appointing a washerwoman, but an educated girl who
ought to know what books to put into the hands of the
Catholic boys and girls of the country ... Is it safe to
entrust a girl who is not in sympathy with Catholic views
with their handling?' (Quoted in BICO, 1972, p13). The

government (formed by the pro-Treaty Cumann na nGaedheal
party) dissolved Mayo County Council, but it was attacked
by Fianna Fáil in the Dáil. During the debate, de
Valera declared that 'if I had a vote on a local body, and
if there were two qualified people who had to deal with a
Catholic community, and if one was a Catholic and the
other was a Protestant, I would unhesitatingly vote for
the Catholic.' (Quoted in Hepburn, 1980, p136).

Discrimination against Protestants in public
appointments in the Free State was not widespread, and was
probably a reaction to discrimination against Catholics in
Northern Ireland (see below). But, the fact that southern
political leaders were prepared (or perhaps even felt
obliged) to publicly concede authority to the Catholic
Church on matters which northern Protestants regarded as
secular only served to reinforce unionist opposition
against the possibility of a united Ireland.

Having made their peace with the Catholic Church, Fianna
Fáil swept into power in the 1932 general election. The
major area of support for Fianna Fáil, similar to that
for anti-Treaty candidates in the previous decade, was in
the west; but they also gained widespread support from
most other parts of the country (Figure 21). Cumann na
nGaedheal had introduced protective economic policies in
response to tariffs imposed by other governments; but
Fianna Fáil, drawing its support from the more radical
sections of Irish society, enthusiastically espoused
protectionism as the means for establishing economic
self-sufficiency along the lines originally outlined by
Sinn Féin. Commercial agriculture suffered, especially
as the British government imposed levies on imports of
Irish cattle to recover the value of land annuities which
the Fianna Fáil government decided to withhold; but this
was compensated by a growth in protected industries
orientated towards the home market. The construction
industry also received a major boost as Fianna Fáil
attempted to tackle the massive problem of slum housing,
especially in Dublin, which had been largely neglected by

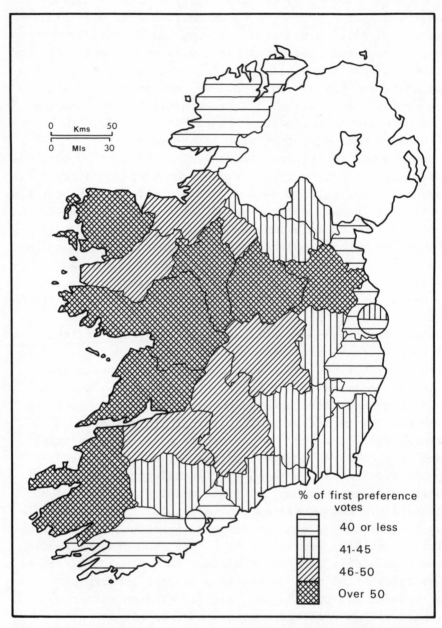

FIG. 21   Percentage Of First Preference Votes For Fianna
Fáil Candidates, 1932 (After Rumpf and Hepburn)

Cumann na nGaedheal. The government also attempted to re-orientate Irish agriculture towards tillage and national self-sufficiency by a complex set of pricing policies.

The first Fianna Fáil government was actively interventionist, in contrast to its almost laissez-faire Cumann na nGaedheal predecessor. The Irish civil service consequently expanded by over 30 per cent in the decade after 1932, despite having failed to expand at all in the previous decade since independence. A large number of semi-state bodies were also created in an effort to maximise self-sufficiency: the Irish Sugar Company, for example, was set up in 1933 - 80 per cent of sugar was home produced by 1938; the Turf Board, a forerunner of the highly innovative Bord na Móna, was set up in 1934 to reduce energy imports; and Aer Lingus (the state airline) was set up in 1936 (Daly, 1981).

The first Fianna Fáil government was possibly the most radical in the history of the state. However, its major impact was not so much a radical solution to the country's social and economic problems as the creation of a new élite class to rival that of the large commercial farmers (represented after 1933 by Fine Gael - the successors of Cumann na nGaedheal). The new élite was typically comprised of self-made small-town businessmen, solicitors and building contractors; but the Fianna Fáil party maintained a very large popular support amongst small farmers and the urban working classes, partly because of its perceived ability to solve problems. (This was partly facilitated by the power of central and local government to allocate new state jobs and public sector housing). Fianna Fáil has consequently been able to consolidate its position as the 'natural' party of government and it has rarely been out of office since 1932. It has consistently won more seats than any other party and was prevented from forming the government on only 5 occasions in the next half century, in each instance necessitating a rather unnatural coalition between Fine Gael and other groups

230

(including the Labour party) who were united only by their opposition to Fianna Fáil (Table 2).

Election	Fianna Fáil	Fine Gael	Labour	Others	Gov
1922	35 (27.3)	58 (45.3)	17 (13.2)	18 (14.1)	PT
1923	44 (28.8)	63 (41.2)	14 (9.2)	32 (20.9)	CG
1927(Jun)	44 (28.8)	47 (30.7)	22 (14.4)	40 (26.1)	CG
1927(Sep)	57 (37.2)	62 (40.5)	13 (8.5)	21 (13.7)	CG
1932	72 (47.1)	57 (37.3)	7 (4.6)	17 (11.1)	FF
1933	77 (50.3)	48 (31.4)	8 (5.2)	20 (13.1)	FF
1937	69 (50.0)	48 (34.8)	13 (9.4)	8 (5.8)	FF
1938	77 (55.8)	45 (32.6)	9 (6.5)	7 (5.1)	FF
1943	67 (48.6)	32 (23.2)	17 (12.3)	22 (15.9)	FF
1944	76 (55.1)	30 (21.7)	8 (5.8)	24 (17.4)	FF
1948	68 (46.3)	31 (21.1)	19 (12.9)	29 (19.7)	C
1951	69 (46.9)	40 (27.2)	16 (10.9)	22 (15.0)	FF
1954	65 (44.2)	50 (34.0)	19 (12.9)	13 (8.8)	C
1957	78 (53.1)	40 (27.2)	13 (8.8)	16 (10.9)	FF
1961	70 (48.6)	47 (32.6)	16 (11.1)	11 (7.6)	FF
1965	72 (50.0)	47 (32.6)	22 (15.3)	3 (2.1)	FF
1969	75 (52.1)	50 (34.7)	18 (12.5)	1 (0.7)	FF
1973	69 (47.9)	54 (37.5)	19 (13.2)	2 (1.4)	C
1977	78 (53.4)	47 (32.2)	17 (11.6)	4 (2.7)	FF
1981	78 (47.0)	65 (39.2)	15 (9.0)	8 (4.8)	C
1982(Feb)	81 (48.8)	63 (38.0)	15 (9.0)	7 (4.2)	FF
1982(Nov)	75 (45.2)	70 (42.2)	16 (9.6)	5 (3.0)	C

(The final column indicates Government: PT=Pro-Treaty, CG=Cumann na nGaedheal, FF=Fianna Fáil, C=Coalition)

Table 2. Number And Percentage Of Seats Won By Each Party In Each Election.

Southern politics have been dominated by Fianna Fáil since the 1930s, with Fine Gael (the second largest party) providing the major opposition. Both parties, however,

are basically conservative and tend to reflect the needs
of the middle classes. Although each tends to appeal to
different sections of the middle classes, the differences
in terms of social composition are not clearly defined.
Given that the two parties tend to share a broadly similar
stance on most issues, the national question has
consequently assumed a very important role by acting as
the major point of difference between the two parties.
Fianna Fáil, given its anti-Treaty origins, has generally
maintained a more intransigent position (in theory, if
maybe not in practice) on the national question; Fine
Gael, although in favour of a united Ireland, has tended
to be more willing to accept the reality of northern
unionist opposition to such a proposal. It was Fianna
Fáil, for example, that drafted the 1937 Constitution
which makes the territorial claim to the whole of Northern
Ireland (see Chapter 1), thereby refusing recognition to
the 1921 Treaty signed by the Sinn Féin delegates and a
tripartite agreement signed by the Cumann na nGaedheal
government in 1925. By keeping the national question to
the fore in southern Irish politics (to produce what is
sometimes referred to as 'civil war politics'), the two
major conservative parties have effectively prevented
serious political opposition along class lines.

Fianna Fáil generally try to appeal to anti-Treaty
republican sympathies for electoral purposes, but despite
their dominance in southern Irish politics they have
rarely shown any more commitment to the traditional
republican ideal of a secular republic while in power than
they did when in opposition. The 1937 constitution, for
example, recognised the 'special position of the Holy
Catholic Apostolic and Roman Church', whereas article
41.3.2 enshrined Catholic teaching on family law: 'No law
shall be enacted providing for the grant of a dissolution
of marriage.' (The article recognising the special
position of the Catholic Church was deleted by referendum
introduced by the Coalition government in 1974).
Censorship, introduced by the Cumann na nGaedheal

Censorship Act in 1929, was carried to extremes under
Fianna Fáil. Banned books, for example, included
Sigismund Freud's <u>Collected</u> <u>Papers</u> (Volume 2), <u>The</u>
<u>Grapes</u> <u>Of</u> <u>Wrath</u>, and <u>Catch</u> <u>22</u>. The decision to ban
<u>The</u> <u>Laws</u> <u>of</u> <u>Life</u>, a family planning guide written by a
Catholic gynaecologist and published with the <u>permissu</u>
<u>superiorum</u> of the Catholic Archbishop of Westminster,
resulted in a motion of no confidence in the Censorship
Board being discussed in the Seanad (i.e. the upper house
in the Irish parliament) in 1942. The Chairman of the
Censorship Board defended his decision on the grounds
that:

> 'Engaged couples, under ... economic pressure
> who cannot afford to marry, and yet unable to
> resist the carnal urge, might be tempted to use
> this. The first edition, providing a
> calculation as to how to determine the infertile
> periods becomes what I called it at the time we
> were reporting to the Minister - the
> fornicator's vade mecum or, if you like, the
> harlot's handbook. This is what it would become
> if circulated indiscriminately published, with
> those words - that "the Catholic Church permits
> the use of the safe period".' (Quoted in
> Hepburn, 1980, p148).

The motion of no confidence was defeated by 34 votes to 2.

Fine Gael, on the few occasions when they came to power,
proved themselves as unwilling as Fianna Fáil to
challenge the Catholic Church. Dr. Noel Browne, a very
popular Minister of Health, following a highly successful
tuberculosis eradication programme, and a member of one of
Fine Gael's coalition partners Clann na Poblachta, was
very concerned that the infant mortality rate in the
Republic of Ireland (as the Free State became officially
known after the Republic of Ireland Act, passed in 1949)
was 55 per cent higher than that in England and Wales. He
therefore proposed a scheme in 1951 to provide free
maternity care to every mother, plus child care to the age

of sixteen. Although Dr. Browne's mother and child
proposal was very modest compared with the National Health
system which had been recently introduced in Britain, it
was regarded by the Catholic Church as a direct challenge
to its authority due to the fact that the scheme would
have allowed local medical officers to give sex education
to Catholic women (Murphy, 1975). The Catholic bishops
protested to the Taoiseach, John A. Costello, and when
Browne refused to yield on what he saw as the central
issue - free health care for mothers - he was forced to
resign by his party leader Seán MacBride (Fanning, 1983).
Church pressure, in this instance, actually brought about
a change in government: Browne's forced resignation,
coupled with the defection of a few loyal supporters,
eroded the inter-party government's narrow majority and
forced a general election which resulted in a victory for
Fianna Fáil.

Fianna Fáil formed the government from 1951 to 1954,
before being replaced by the second inter-party
government. However, rapid economic decline resulted in
the return of Fianna Fáil in 1957. The economic decline
was initiated by British post-war food rationing and
world-wide overproduction of food which resulted in low
prices for Irish agricultural exports. This in turn
reduced the home demand for Irish industrial goods,
resulting in the collapse of many of the protected
industries. Economic decline resulted in a rapid increase
in emigration which reached a peak of 40,000 per annum
during the 1950s.

Realising that their protective economic policies had
failed, the new Fianna Fáil government announced a
totally different strategy in the First Programme For
Economic Expansion published in 1958. This concentrated
upon improving exports. The emphasis was initially placed
upon beef production and agricultural exports, but
industry assumed an increasingly important role in the
overall development strategy. The Industrial Development
Authority (IDA), originally established in 1949, was

empowered in 1956 to give grants to foreign companies investing in Ireland (Daly, 1981). The Second Programme For Industrial Expansion, introduced in 1963, placed even more emphasis upon attracting foreign industries in order to boost exports.

The Republic of Ireland has been dramatically transformed by urbanisation and industrial expansion in the past two decades as a result of this shift in economic policy, but prior to the early 1960s it could justifiably be described as rural, Catholic and conservative.

THE NORTHERN STATE

If the southern state became a Catholic state for a Catholic people, the northern state became a Protestant state for a Protestant people. However, the two developments were not mirror images: the Free State became a Catholic state because the overwhelming majority of its citizens were Catholics, whereas Northern Ireland became a Protestant state despite the fact that more than one third of its citizens were not Protestants. The two states also differed in the ways in which they were non-secular: the Free State became institutionalised as a Catholic state because of the influence of Catholic doctrine and Church influence upon southern legislation; Northern Ireland, on the other hand, is de jure a secular state - there is little, if any, anti-Catholic legislation - but the state has de facto operated in an explicitly anti-Catholic manner.

The anti-Catholic nature of the northern state was not the product of religious zeal, but rather reflected the conservative and defensive nature of unionism. Unionists, under the hegemony of the industrial bourgeoisie, opposed Irish nationalism because it threatened industrial prosperity in east Ulster. Their basic objective was to preserve this prosperity. Although they had never actually campaigned for increased local autonomy, Ulster

unionists regarded partition and the creation of the
Northern Ireland state as an acceptable compromise.
However, partition was unacceptable to Northern Ireland
Catholics, most of whom were Irish nationalists. Most
Catholics consequently refused to recognise the legitimacy
of the new state and refused to co-operate with it in the
belief that it was only an interim solution. Many
teachers in Catholic schools, for example, initially
refused to recognise the Northern Ireland Ministry of
Education by following the Dublin syllabus and by drawing
their salaries from the Dáil. State power in Northern
Ireland therefore became almost exclusively Protestant
because of the withdrawal of co-operation by the Catholic
minority.

The non co-operation of the Catholic minority was
regarded by the Protestant majority as an indication that
they intended to overthrow the new state and thereby force
northern Protestants into a Catholic-dominated and
predominantly rural united Ireland. Northern Catholics
therefore came to be regarded with suspicion; not because
they were Catholics as such but because, in the eyes of
unionists, they were potential, if not actual, fifth
columnists dedicated to the overthrow of the state. This
suspicion became self-fulfilling: Northern Ireland
Catholics, no matter how willing to come to terms with the
new situation, found themselves persecuted by the state
and treated as second class citizens. This only served to
reinforce a belief that the only solution to the problem
of social inequality was an end to partition.

Relations between the Protestant majority (represented
by the Unionist party) and the Catholic minority
(represented by the Nationalist party and Sinn Féin),
already poor to begin with, became increasingly polarised
in the first few years of the new state. Some aspects of
this process are now examined in more detail.

The Anglo-Irish war had a limited impact in the north
before 1920: the major function of the IRA was to defend
Catholic areas against possible Protestant attacks.

Nevertheless, operating out of Catholic areas, they took
the offensive against the RIC on a few occasions.
Although the IRA attacks were directed against the British
security forces, they were regarded by Protestants as
attacks on the unionist community. Protestant mobs
therefore retaliated with attacks on Catholic areas, but
the Protestant backlash was not very discriminating: the
IRA did not wear uniforms and were not readily
identifiable, therefore Protestant anger tended to be
directed at Catholics in general, most of whom were
innocent. Catholics were driven out of predominantly
Protestant places of employment, including the shipyards
and many of the larger engineering works; and Catholics
living in predominantly Protestant areas were driven out
of their homes and forced to seek refuge in Catholic
areas. The pogroms were mainly confined to Belfast, but
particularly bad incidents occured in Lisburn and
Banbridge following the killing of policemen from those
towns. The Lisburn incident resulted in the destruction
of 273 houses. Between 1920 and 1922, the pogroms
resulted in 455 deaths (267 Catholics and 185
Protestants), over 2,000 injuries and considerable damage
to property. Thousands of Catholics lost their jobs.

Given the rise in violence in Ulster, coupled with the
fact that most of the British security forces were already
engaged in a guerilla war in the south, a special reserve
constabulary known as the Ulster Special Constabulary
(USC) was created in the north in 1920. This was
initially intended to be divided into three categories: A,
B, and C. The A category were to work with the RIC on a
full-time basis, the B category were to act as
part-timers, and the C category were to serve as a reserve
force which could be called in times of emergency. In
practice only the B category was fully operationalised. A
very large proportion of the B Specials, as they became
known, were recruited from the UVF. The B Specials, who
came under the control of the Northern Ireland government
after 1921, were consequently regarded as a partisan force

by the Catholic minority.

Protestants also became dominant in other branches of the state apparatus. Although the government did not discriminate against Catholics on the basis of their religious beliefs - indeed one third of the places in the Royal Ulster Constabulary (RUC) were supposedly reserved for Catholics - its insistence that all members of the public service should be loyal to the state amounted to near enough the same thing. The very fact that a civil servant was a Catholic was sufficient to raise suspicions of sinister intent, and the onus was consequently placed upon Catholic civil servants, even those with many years of impeccable service, to prove their loyalty. Catholics, for their part, do not appear to have applied in great numbers for public service positions: apart from a reluctance to accept the legitimacy of the Northern Ireland state, long-term career prospects could not have appeared very promising in a climate of religio-nationalistic hostility. Consequently, although Catholics comprised about one third of the total Northern Ireland population, by 1943 there were only 37 Catholics (less than 6 per cent) in the administrative class and analogous technical grades of the civil service; the 55 most senior positions were all held by Protestants. Likewise, by 1936 the RUC was comprised of 488 Catholics and 2,361 Protestants; and only 9 of the 55 officers who held the rank of district inspector or above were Catholics (Buckland, 1979). The exclusion of Catholics from the new state apparatus only served to intensify Catholic suspicions of the Northern Ireland government and to reinforce their reluctance to recognise the existence of the new state.

Polarisation between northern Protestants and northern Catholics was further aggravated by uncertainty arising from the boundary commission in the Anglo-Irish Treaty. Many northern Catholics, especially those living in the peripheral parts of Northern Ireland where there was a Catholic majority, believed that they would be transferred

238

to the Free State. Catholics living in predominently
Protestant areas hoped that, if the transfer of territory
to the Free State was sufficiently large, unionists might
even be forced to compromise on partition. This reduced
their willingness to accept the existence of the Northern
Ireland state. Protestants, on the other hand, were
determined that the authority of the state should apply to
all parts of Northern Ireland.

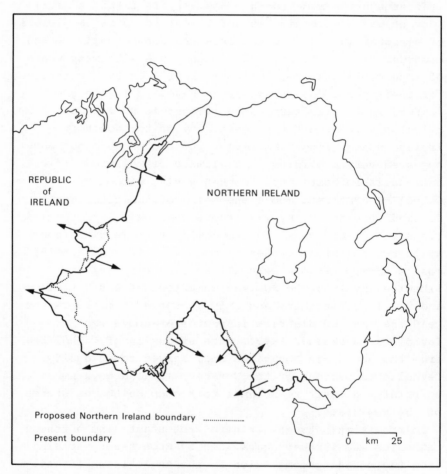

FIG. 22   Principal Changes Recommended By The Boundary
           Commission, 1925.

As it turned out, the boundary commission, when it was established in 1924, recommended only relatively minor changes (Figure 22). These would have resulted in the net transfer of 25,000 Catholics to the Free State, but the recommendations were not actually implemented because they were prematurely released in an inaccurate form by the Morning Post newspaper and resulted in so much controversy that the British, Northern Ireland and Free State governments decided that it would be more prudent to sign a tripartite agreement in 1925 ratifying the existing border. Nevertheless, the uncertainty created by the delay in finalising the location of the boundary had by that time left an indelible impact upon the structure of Protestant-Catholic relations within Northern Ireland.

This is most clearly seen in the case of local government. Although the Unionists had a very decisive majority in the Northern Ireland parliament - 40 out of 52 seats following the 1921 elections contested using proportional representation - many of the local authorities, especially in the west of the province and including Fermanagh and Tyrone county councils, were under nationalist control following the 1919 local government elections which had also been contested using proportional representation. These nationalist-controlled councils refused to co-operate with the Northern Ireland government. The government retaliated by dissolving Fermanagh County Council in December 1921 after it passed a resolution that 'we do not recognise the partition parliament and pledge our allegiance to Dáil Éireann'. A further twelve local authorities were dismissed in March and April 1922 for failing to return information requested by the government.

The government, realising that it was necessary to re-establish the local authorities under Unionist control, introduced legislation to abolish proportional representation in local government elections. It also decided to revise electoral boundaries, supposedly because population movements from rural to urban areas had resulted in problems of malapportionment. A commission, under Judge John Leech, was established to hold public enquiries at which all interested parties could make proposals regarding possible boundary changes. Nationalists, as anticipated, refused to co-operate, partly because they were afraid that to do so might prejudice their demand to be transferred to the Free State. Most of the proposals received by the Leech commission consequently came from local Unionist branches and were in most instances quite blatant attempts to gerrymander the boundaries so as to maximise Unionist representation. The absence of nationalist proposals (except in Ballycastle and Irvinestown) was 'interpreted' by the government as an indication that they had no major objections to the Unionist proposals which, with the exception of those for Enniskillen, were implemented with very few modifications.

The local government system was also biased towards the Unionists by restricting the local government franchise to rate-payers. In 1967, for example, only 694,483 people out of 933,723 entitled to vote in Stormont elections were entitled to vote in local government elections (Probert, 1978). This created a bias in favour of property owners; but given that a higher percentage of Protestants than Catholics owned property, it also created a bias in favour of the Unionists.

The Unionists were further assisted by a nationalist boycott of most of the local government elections held in 1923 and 1924, with the result that the number of nationalist-controlled local authorities declined from 25 to 2 - the sole surviving nationalist councils being those for Omagh and Strabane urban districts (Farrell, 1976). Nevertheless, the Leech gerrymanders, reinforced by later modifications, ensured permanent Unionist control even when the elections were contested by nationalists in many areas where Protestants were clearly the minority.

This is illustrated by the local government boundaries for Derry, Northern Ireland's second city. The Unionists

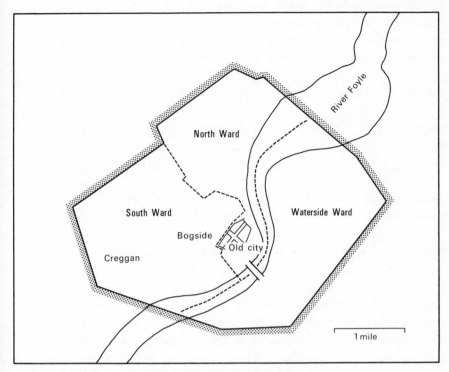

FIG. 23   Ward Boundaries In Londonderry.

had regained control after the abolition of proportional
representation, but by the 1930s they were worried that
they would not be able to maintain control. The city
wards were therefore redefined in 1936 (Figure 23). The
South ward, which returned 8 seats, was defined so as to
have a very large nationalist majority; whereas the other
two wards were defined to have much smaller, yet safe,
unionist majorities. Apart from the obvious gerrymander,
the Derry wards also provide a clear example of
malapportionment: by 1967 the nationalist South ward had
almost twice as many voters as the unionist North ward,
yet each returned the same number of represenatives (Table
3). These malpractices were regarded as legitimate by the
Northern Ireland government due to the fact that
Protestants, despite their smaller population, were

estimated to contribute about two thirds of the city
finances: the boundaries were therefore justified on the
grounds that they represented a compromise between the
principles of people and property.

Ward	Total Votes	Nationalist	Unionist	Elected
North	6,467	2,530 (39%)	3,946 (61%)	8 Un.
Waterside	5,549	1,852 (33%)	3,697 (67%)	4 Un.
South	11,185	10,047 (90%)	1,138 (10%)	8 Nat.
Total Votes	23,210	14,429 (62%)	8,781 (38%)	
Total Seats		8 (40%)	12 (60%)	

Table 3.   Results of Londonderry Corporation Elections,
1967 (Busteed, 1972).

Irish nationalists provided an obvious and direct
challenge to the maintenance of the status quo, but
the unionist bourgeoisie also faced an equally serious, if
less obvious, threat from the Protestant proletariat. The
Northern Ireland economy, partly because of its export
orientation, was severely affected by the world recession
in the 1920s and 1930s and by the development of more
competitive overseas industries (e.g. by German, Swedish
and Japanese ships, Indian cotton, and later by synthetic
fibres). Unemployment by 1931 was 28 per cent, and even
by 1939 it was still over 20 per cent. Although the
unemployment rate was higher for Catholics than
Protestants, the Protestant bourgeoisie found themselves
facing increased opposition from the Protestant
proletariat.
    The Unionist response to this threat was to play down
class issues by emphasising the national question and the
common threat posed by Irish nationalism. The shipyards,
for example, were severely disrupted in 1919 by strikes
for a 40 hour week. These spread to the power stations

and factories throughout the city by 1920. Meanwhile, the Belfast Labour Party won 13 seats against Unionist opposition in the 1920 municipal elections. Carson, the Unionist leader, retaliated against the trade unions by accusing them of forming a Bolshevik-Sinn Féin alliance in order to divide Protestant unity on the national question along class lines to enable Sinn Féin to take over. Protestant workers consequently reacted by expelling Catholic workers and Protestant trade union leaders from the shipyards.

Similar tactics were used in the 1930s when protests against the inadequate level of unemployment relief resulted in a violent confrontation between the police and protesters in the Catholic Falls Road area of Belfast, causing Protestant workers in the nearby Shankill Road area to riot in sympathy with their Catholic fellow workers. The implications for the government were enormous. The threat of a united working class opposition however was swiftly dealt with by depicting the whole episode as a nationalist conspiracy. Three years later things were back to normal: a sniper attack on an Orange parade resulted in a Protestant backlash in which 514 Catholic families were driven from their homes, 13 people were killed (5 Catholics and 8 Protestants), and 2,241 were injured (Harkness, 1983).

Protestant working class disenchantment with the government was also reflected by electoral setbacks for the Unionists in elections for the Northern Ireland parliament in the 1920s. The Unionists won 40 of the 52 seats in the Northern Ireland assembly in the 1921 general election, due to the fact that the national question was by far the most important issue. However, the Unionists lost 8 seats to candidates who opposed them on class issues in the 1925 general election. Seven of the lost seats were in Belfast where the Unionists' share of the 16 seats dropped from 15 to only 8. The Unionist government was in little immediate danger of falling, but the Unionists could not afford to lose the support of the

Protestant proletariat because of class grievances. Their
solution was to change the electoral system from multiple
seat proportional representation, as used in Northern
Ireland in 1921 and 1925, to single seat plurality, as
used in Westminster elections. This had the effect of
reducing the number of important election issues to one
and the Unionists ensured that the single most important
issue would remain the national question. Their motto for
the 1929 general election, in which they regained most of
their lost seats despite a decline in their percentage of
the vote, was 'Safety First - Vote Unionist' - the
implication being that a Protestant vote for anyone other
than a Unionist party candidate would be equivalent to
voting for the Nationalists.

The threat posed by Irish nationalism enabled the
Protestant bourgeoisie to rally the Protestant proletariat
behind them in support of unionism, and thereby helped to
circumvent the possibility of class opposition. The
Nationalist party, representing the interests of the
Catholic middle classes and the Catholic Church, fulfilled
a very similar function in the Catholic community.

Because they were in opposition to the Unionists, the
Nationalists were able to appear radical in their attacks
on the government. However, in practice the Nationalist
party were very closely linked with the Catholic Church
(most Nationalist M.P.s were nominated by parish priests)
and were strongly anti-trade union. Class politics were
regarded as something that would have to be deferred until
the national question had been resolved. To quote the
Nationalist leader Eddie McAteer:

> 'When we get our country back then and only then
> will there be scope for ordinary political
> representation. As matters stand at present you
> are either pro- or anti-Partition. It will be
> so until Partition is removed.'

However, the very fact that the Nationalists put so much
emphasis upon the national question simply played into the
hands of the Unionists by providing them with a supposed

threat which could be used to maintain inter-class unity between Protestants.

The strategy of the Nationalist party did little to alleviate the conditions of Catholics within Northern Ireland. Nationalist intransigence gave the Unionists sufficient grounds to maintain discrimination against the Catholic working classes. The policy was also futile because the nationalists were destined to remain a 2:1 minority unless the unionist majority could be split, but by closely identifying with the Catholic Church, and by ignoring class issues, the Nationalists virtually eliminated any possibility of winning Protestant support.

The Protestant bourgeoisie could only retain the electoral support of the Protestant proletariat providing Protestant working class disenchantment did not become too strong. This was achieved by ensuring that the Protestant proletariat did not suffer any more than could be avoided: they therefore received preferential treatment in the allocation of resources. The principal objective was probably to undermine potential Protestant working class opposition rather than to deprive Catholics; but, given that resorces were scarce because of the poor economic climate, the allocation of resources to Protestants necessarily entailed discrimination against Catholics.

Control over local government proved to be particularly important in this respect. The local authorities occupied a very important position in the overall state apparatus because of their control over the allocation of jobs, houses and local government contracts. Given the relatively low degree of industrialisation outside of Belfast and the major towns, the local authorities had a major say in deciding, both directly (through their control over council jobs) and indirectly (through the allocation of contracts), who would and who would not get a job, especially in the more rural (and religiously more evenly divided) west of the province. Given the chronic housing shortage, they also had a major say in who would or would not get a house, especially among the less affluent sections of society.

These powers were politically very important in two respects. First, the power to allocate jobs and houses to Protestants provided Unionists with a useful means for rewarding loyal supporters, thereby minimising the potential threat of disunity within the ranks. Second, the power not to allocate jobs and houses to Catholics provided Unionists with a means to force Catholics to emigrate, and thereby help maintain Unionist control of the local authority. This was important given the higher birthrate amongst Catholics which would otherwise have eroded the Protestant majority. Nationalist-controlled councils do not appear to have behaved more fairly: it was alleged that no Protestants were employed by Newry Urban District Council as clerical or outdoor workers in 1958, and that 480 of 497 houses built at Newry were occupied by Catholics (Barritt and Carter, 1962). Nevertheless, given the disproportionate Unionist domination of local government, because of gerrymandering and other electoral malpractices, the bulk of the discrimination at local government level was directed against the Catholic minority. Enforced emigration was probably one of the most important reasons why the percentage of Catholics in Northern Ireland remained fairly constant between 1926 and 1971 (33.5 and 31.4 per cent respectively), despite the higher birthrate for Catholics.

Local government discrimination was reinforced by discrimination in the private sector. Sir Basil Brooke (later Viscount Brookeborough), Prime Minister of Northern Ireland from 1943 to 1963 and a large landowner in Fermanagh, boasted in 1933:

'There are a great number of Protestants and Orangemen who employ Roman Catholics. I feel I can speak freely on the subject as I have not a Roman Catholic about my own place ... I would appeal to loyalists, therefore, wherever possible, to employ good Protestant lads and lassies.' (Quoted in Probert, 1978, p62).

Few employers were as candid as this, but there can be
little doubt that Catholics were often discriminated
against by Protestant employers, very often at the
insistence of Protestant employees. The converse also
occurred but, given that more employment was controlled by
Protestants than Catholics, the net effect of the private
sector was to reinforce discrimination against Catholics
in the public sector.

THE CIVIL RIGHTS MOVEMENT AND THE TROUBLES

The situation began to change in the 1960s when the
Catholic minority within Northern Ireland began to demand
civil rights rather than simply the overthrow of the
Northern Ireland state. The reasons for this shift in
attitude are open to question, but the growth of the
welfare state must have been an important factor.
Northern Ireland followed the rest of the United Kingdom
by introducing free medical services, free education,
comprehensive pension schemes and improved welfare
benefits in the late 1940s. These benefits applied to all
citizens, including the Catholic minority. Life for the
poorer sections of society consequently became
considerably easier in Northern Ireland than in the
Republic where, as noted above, attempts to introduce a
limited health scheme were opposed by the Catholic Church
and where poverty in the 1950s was a major cause of
outmigration. The rate of emigration from Northern
Ireland during the 1950s was less than half of that from
the Republic, and although Northern Ireland Catholics
fared worse than Northern Ireland Protestants they still
fared much better than Catholics in the Republic (Simpson,
1983). Northern Catholics did not abandon the goal of a
united Ireland, but the national question began to assume
a less prominent position as many northern Catholics began
to consider alternative methods of improving their
material conditions within the context of the Northern

Ireland state.

Conciliation was also encouraged by an improvement in the relations between the Northern Ireland and Republic of Ireland governments. The two governments co-operated in a number of schemes in the early 1950s, including the Foyle fisheries, the Erne drainage/hydroelectric scheme, and the joint nationalisation of the Great Northern Railway. By the late 1950s the Republic's government began to hint at a de facto recognition of Northern Ireland in return for further economic co-operation. This trend towards rapprochement culminated in a historic meeting between premiers O'Neill and Lemass in January 1965. The Nationalist party agreed to form the official opposition in Stormont one month later.

The introduction of free education at all levels in Northern Ireland under the Education Act (1947) was also a significant factor. University education became available on academic merit rather than according to economic circumstances. This facilitated the growth of a group of articulate university-educated spokespersons for the Catholic working classes by the 1960s. (Approximately 22 per cent of university students in Northern Ireland in the 1960s were Catholics). Improvements in access to education, however, were not matched by similar improvements in job opportunities, and frustrations eventually resulted in protests about discrimination against the Catholic community as a whole.

The situation was also changing on the unionist side. The traditional Northern Ireland industries went through a crisis in the 1950s, resulting in the loss of 120,000 jobs in linen, shipbuilding and agriculture between 1949 and 1960. The government response was to try to encourage outside investment, using a strategy very similar to that adopted in the Republic from about 1958 onwards. The Industries Development Acts (1945-53) enabled the government to lease factories and to provide grants to overseas companies. The scheme was extended by the Capital Grants to Industry Acts (1954-62). A total of

69,000 jobs were created at a cost of £123 million between 1945 and 1969. Local capital, as a result, became less important vis-a-vis outside capital as an employer: 22.5 per cent of manufacturing jobs in Northern Ireland were provided by outside companies in 1961; by 1972 this had increased to 44.9 per cent.

This had two important effects. First, it destroyed the hegemony of the traditional unionist bourgeoisie over Protestant workers. Second, it increased Catholic hopes for equal employment opportunities. These hopes, however, were frustrated when many foreign-owned companies began to locate in predominantly Protestant areas in the east of Northern Ireland, thereby reinforcing Catholic suspicions of government manipulation. The Unionists, on the other hand, claimed that the foreign companies preferred the east because of better communications, a larger industrial workforce and other such factors (Hoare, 1981), and pointed to the fact that Michelin refused an extra £1 million grant by locating in Ballymena in the east rather than Derry in the west.

The new Unionism was epitomised by Terence O'Neill, who suceeded Lord Brookborough as Northern Ireland Prime Minister in 1963. Under O'Neill the state played a much more active role in the economy by attempting to create conditions which would prove attractive to overseas investors. Consultants were employed to draw up plans for the built environment (Matthew, 1964) and economic development (Wilson, 1965), and capital was invested on developing a motorway system, building a new city and establishing a second university. The new initiative also entailed adopting a more enlightened attitude towards the Catholic community as part of the drive towards further modernisation.

O'Neill, however, met with opposition from the more traditional elements within the Unionist party. These represented the interests of small businessmen and farmers, especially in the west of the province where the centralising and interventionist tendencies of the

250

government were undermining the traditional basis of local
Unionist control. O'Neill also faced strong opposition
from elements within the Protestant proletariat in the
east, led by Ian Paisley, who felt threatened by O'Neill's
conciliatory moves towards the traditional 'enemies of
Ulster'. Nevertheless, the major area of support for
O'Neill was in the east where the Protestant majority was
largest and where Protestants therefore felt less
threatened by the possibility of a Catholic/nationalist
takeover (Figure 24).

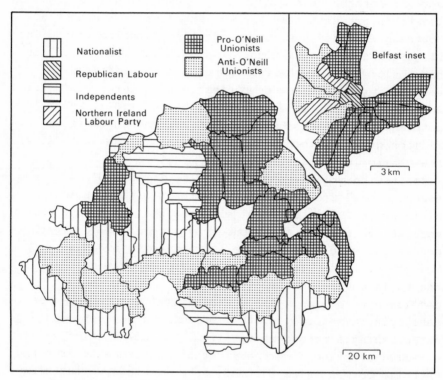

FIG. 24   Distribution Of Seats Won By Pro- And Anti-
           O'Neill Unionists, 1969.

Because of the opposition from within the Protestant
ranks, O'Neill was obliged to reform more slowly than was
necessary to satisfy Catholic aspirations. Promises of

reforms were not sufficient, and attempts by the
government to placate the opposition from conservative
unionists, for example by naming the new city Craigavon
after the first Unionist Prime Minister and by locating
the new university in Protestant Coleraine rather than in
Catholic Derry (the second largest city in Northern
Ireland), only served to antagonise Catholic opinion.

Frustrated by the apparent lack of progress and inspired
by the civil rights movement of Martin Luther King in the
United States, advocates of democratic reforms formed the
Northern Ireland Civil Rights Association (NICRA) in 1967.
A series of peaceful protest marches were organised,
beginning in June 1968. These were initially supported by
liberal Protestants, especially students in Queen's
University Belfast, but they were opposed by conservative
Protestants led by Paisley.

William Craig, the Minister of Home Affairs and a
representative of the traditional wing of the Unionist
party, banned some of the NICRA marches because they
threatened to result in a public disturbance between
marchers and Paisleyites. The NICRA initially complied
with the banning orders, but it soon became apparent that
the NICRA would be unable to hold any further peaceful
demonstrations because all the Paisleyites had to do to
prevent them was to announce plans to hold a
counter-demonstration. The NICRA were consequently
obliged to ignore the bans, which immediately brought them
into conflict with the police. After this, it was a
relatively simple matter for their opponents to resort to
traditional tactics by depicting the NICRA as an enemy of
the state and a front for the IRA.

The conflict consequently polarised along familiar
nationalistic/sectarian lines. O'Neill, the voice of
liberal reform, was increasingly deserted by both sides,
especially after a package of reforms announced by the
government in November 1968, including local government
reforms and the introduction of a points scheme for the
allocation of council housing, was rejected by the NICRA

as inadequate. Catholics viewed O'Neill as offering too little too late; Protestants regarded him as a traitor who was prepared to risk the security of the state.

The blow by blow details of the escalation of violence need not concern us here. It suffices to note a few of the more important events.

1) The British army was introduced in August 1969 when the RUC were unable to control a Protestant backlash in Belfast which resulted in 6 deaths and the destruction of 130 houses, following an attack on a Protestant parade in Derry. The army was initially welcomed by Catholics, who had very serious misgivings about the impartiality of the RUC, but relations between the army and the Catholic community degenerated rapidly following house to house searches by the army for armaments.

2) Contrary to the anti-NICRA propaganda of the conservative unionists, the IRA had declined as a significant force by 1969, as illustrated by its inability to defend Catholic areas against Protestant attack. The events in August 1969, however, highlighted the need for a local defence force in Catholic areas, and thereby facilitated the re-emergence of the IRA, allegedly armed using money provided by 'friendly sources in Dublin' (Flackes, 1980). By 1970 the IRA had taken the offensive, initially through a bombing campaign but followed by attacks on the army in 1971. Since then the violence has mainly been between the IRA (and other nationalist groups such as the INLA) and the British security forces (i.e. British army and the RUC). Protestant paramilitary groups (e.g. UDA) formed about the same time to defend Protestant areas from IRA attacks, have for the most part remained on the sidelines, intervening only when they felt that the official security forces were not doing enough to curb the threat posed by the IRA. However, given that the nationalist paramilitaries do not wear uniforms, attacks by Protestant paramilitaries have often proved much less discriminating than those by the IRA who have for the most part confined themselves to 'legitimate' targets (i.e.

members of the official security forces).

3) Due to the deepening crisis, the Stormont government
was abolished and replaced by direct rule from Westminster
in 1972. Several attempts have since been made to create
the conditions for a return of some form of localised
parliament for Northern Ireland based upon a degree of
consensus between the two communities. The first attempt
was the Northern Ireland Assembly elected in 1973. This
formed a 'power-sharing' Executive comprised of
representatives of the Official Unionist Party, the Social
Democratic and Labour Party (which had eclipsed the
Nationalists as the main Catholic party since its
formation by civil rights activists in 1970) and the
Alliance Party (also formed in 1970, and the only major
party to get support from both communities). The
Executive, however, was opposed by some Official Unionists
and members of a number of other newer unionist parties
(including Paisley's Democratic Unionist Party) who
favoured 'majority rule'. Unionist members of the
Executive were eventually forced to resign, resulting in
the collapse of the whole power sharing experiment,
following a general strike by Protestant workers organised
by an ad hoc body known as the Ulster Workers Council
(UWC) in May 1974.

The present conflict, it should be noted, is no longer
centred on the issue of civil rights. Most of the demands
made by the NICRA in 1968 (viz. one man one vote in local
government elections; an end to gerrymandering; laws to
prevent discrimination by local authorities; allocation of
houses using a points system; repeal of the Special Powers
Act; and disbandment of the B Specials) were conceded by
the early 1970s. Local government boundaries, for
example, were completely revised in 1973 to create 26
District Councils with very limited powers to be elected
using the single transferable vote method of proportional
representation. Most of the more important powers, often
subject to abuse by local politicians, have been
centralised (e.g. all public sector housing is now under

the control of the Northern Ireland Housing Executive).
It would be incorrect to say that Catholics enjoy perfect
equality - allegations of disrimination in employment,
especially in the private sector, still abound - but civil
rights are no longer the major issue in the present
troubles. The major issue is the national question.

SUMMARY

The partition of Ireland was a logical outcome of the
emergence of two distinct and mutually antagonistic
national identities in the nineteenth and early twentieth
centuries. These national identities, as argued in the
previous two chapters, reflected the different material
requirements of the industrialised northeast and the
largely rural remainder of the island. However, although
partition enabled the dominant groups in both parts of
Ireland to shape government policies to suit their own
material needs, national conflict since partition has
increased rather than subsided. The major reason is that
partition does not satisfy the nationalist objectives of
independence from Britain for the Catholic minority within
Northern Ireland nor of national unity for Irish
nationalists in both parts of Ireland. The unionists, in
consequence, although content with the present
constitutional arrangements feel persistently threatened
by the irredentist aspirations of the Northern Ireland
minority, supported, as they see it, by the aggressive
territorial claims enshrined in the Constitution of the
Republic of Ireland.

Although introduced because of the existence of national
conflict, partition has in fact resulted in further
polarisation and a reinforcement of attitudes. The fact
that the Republic became dominated by a narrow
conservative Catholic ethos until the 1960s, and in some
respects even to the present, only served to reinforce
unionist apprehensions about what the future would hold in

store for them in a united Ireland. These fears were reflected within Northern Ireland by a paranoiac fear of the nationalist minority, resulting in the exclusion of the latter from meaningful participation in public life and the denial of basic civil rights. This, in turn, only served to reinforce the belief of northern Catholics that social justice could not be achieved as long as partition remained. The present troubles are the end-product of this process of polarisation.

Nevertheless, the process of polarisation was not continuous. It was interupted by a period of rapprochement during the early and mid 1960s when it appeared as if the divisions caused by the national question were beginning to recede into the background. Rapprochement, however, was followed by renewed animosity, and eventually violence, between the traditionalists on both sides, resulting in a return to polarised attitudes on the national question. Nevertheless, although the trend towards rapprochement has been overshadowed by the violence associated with the troubles, it has continued in a number of subtle forms throughout the 1970s and 1980s. The implications of this tendency are discussed in the next chapter.

CHAPTER 9
Synopsis
and Discussion

The present conflict in Northern Ireland is complex and multifaceted, but it is centred on the national question. Irish nationalists argue that Northern Ireland is by rights part of the Irish national territory and should therefore be politically united with the Republic of Ireland; Ulster unionists argue that the majority of people in Northern Ireland regard themselves as British and that Northern Ireland should therefore remain within the United Kingdom. These two outlooks are clearly incompatible and provide little scope for compromise: either Northern Ireland is united with the Republic or else it remains separate - there is no compromise which would be fully acceptable to both sides.

Viewed from a nationalistic perspective as one nation against another, there appears to be little hope for a solution to the conflict other than for one side to surrender to the other. However, given that this is unlikely under present conditions, it is essential to try to transcend the nationalistic interpretation of the problem in the quest for an alternative solution. This is the objective of the present work.

Five theses were outlined at the end of Chapter 1. Taken together these theses comprise the basic argument of the book. The first four theses were discussed in more detail in subsequent chapters; the fifth thesis, however, was only briefly touched upon in Chapter 8. The arguments relating to each of the five theses are summarised in the

first five sections of the present chapter. Some
implications of the analysis presented in this book are
then discussed in the sixth and final section.

HOW MANY NATIONS?

Irish nationalists and Ulster unionists disagree about
whether or not they form part of the same nation. Irish
nationalists generally argue that everyone in Ireland,
including northern Protestants, belongs to a single Irish
nation, and that a minority of this nation (i.e. the
Ulster unionists) do not have a right to secede from the
rest of the Irish nation. Ulster unionists, on the other
hand, argue that they are British rather than Irish, and
that they therefore constitute part of a second nation in
Ireland. Being British, they argue, they have a right to
remain within the United Kingdom or, failing that, at
least to remain separate from the Republic of Ireland.

The question of the number of nations in Ireland is
contentious because most people in Ireland, on both sides,
adopt a nationalistic perspective which assumes the right
of nations to self-determination. The principle of
self-determination is accepted by both sides; consequently
the major issue of contention is whether this principle is
applicable to one nation or two. Arguments about the
number of nations are therefore used by propagandists on
both sides to legitimise their respective claims to the
territory which at present constitutes Northern Ireland.

The question of the number of nations is viewed as
important in this book for a different reason. It is
argued that if we are to transcend traditional
nationalistic interpretations of the conflict, which as we
have seen offer little hope of a solution, then it is
necessary to analyse the emergence of national identities
in Ireland from a historical perspective. It is essential
to establish the number of nations in Ireland as a
necessary prerequisite to an analysis of the origins of

national identities.

Although the question of the number of nations in Ireland has proved contentious, there have been surprisingly few attempts to define what a nation is. Two approaches to defining a nation were identified in Chapter 2, namely the checklist and self-definition approaches. The checklist approach entails identifying a list of objective criteria which a group of people should satisfy in order to be regarded as a nation. It is argued that, using this approach, it is impossible to identify a set of criteria which would enable one to make a distinction between the Irish and the British nations without at the same time excluding Ulster Protestants from the Irish nation. Ulster Protestants are more similar in every respect to people in Britain than they are to Irish Catholics, except for the fact that they happen to live on the same island. Using a checklist approach, one would be forced to conclude that either there are two nations in Ireland or else only one in Britain and Ireland taken together.

The self-definition approach is more useful, and comes much closer to the essence of nationality. Under this approach a group of people may be regarded as a nation if they regard themselves to be a nation. Using this approach, one is again forced to conclude that there are two nations in Ireland. Irish Catholics quite clearly regard themselves as different from the British, but by the same token Ulster Protestants quite clearly regard themselves as different from Irish Catholics. The self-definition approach, however, reveals a few anomalies. Ulster Protestants, for example, regard themselves as British, but it is not too clear whether people in Britain also regard Ulster Protestants as British. The important point in the present context, however, is that Ulster Protestants do not regard themselves as 'Irish' (as defined by Irish nationalists) and are prepared to resort to force of arms to avoid being absorbed by the Irish nation. In practice the right to self-determination is generally only 'granted' to groups who are strong enough and determined enough to take it, if need be, by force. The Irish nation won its right to self-determination during the War of Independence; Ulster unionists have shown themselves to be no less determined and believe themselves to be strong enough to defend their national identity.

The conclusion that there are two nations in Ireland should not be interpreted as a moral vindication of the unionist position. This would only follow if one accepts as an absolute right the nationalistic principle of national self-determination. However, the whole objective of this study is to produce an analysis which transcends traditional nationalistic interpretations. This requires one to question all nationalistic assumptions, including that of the right of nations to self-determination. The conclusion that there are two nations in Ireland should therefore be regarded merely as a statement of fact; it should not be interpreted as a statement of support for one side in what is in many respects an historically irrelevant conflict (see below).

THE TEMPORAL DIMENSION

The present two nations in Ireland cannot be traced back for thousands of years in the case of the Irish nation, or even to the time of the Ulster plantation in the case of the Ulster nation. This becomes evident if one examines the events culminating in the 1798 rebellion (see Chapter 5). Northern Protestants fought on both sides in the 1798 rebellion: Presbyterians in east Ulster were prominent in the United Irishmen - the forefathers of the modern republican movement - whereas Episcopalians, especially those in the recently formed Orange Order, dominated the government-organised Yeomanry. The present Ulster nation was therefore bitterly divided on constitutional issues less than 200 years ago.

Irish nationalist propagandists have tended to ignore
the role played by pro-ascendancy Protestants in the 1798
rebellion and have sometimes emphasised the republicanism
of the Presbyterians as evidence that northern Protestants
were sympathetic to the historic struggle of the Irish
nation until they were in some way manipulated into a
position of support for unionism. This argument, however,
is based on the fallacious premise that all republicans
must be nationalists, whereas the major issue for most
United Irishmen was democratic reform rather than
independence from Britain. The argument also ignores the
fact that Irish Catholics also fought on both sides in the
1798 rebellion. Many Irish Catholics, especially those
who were members of Defender organisations, fought on the
republican side in the 1798 rebellion, but many others
were in the government-organised Militia. The Irish
Catholics were therefore as divided in the 1798 rebellion
as Ulster Protestants.

The events culminating in the 1798 rebellion could be
interpreted as a case of civil war within each nation.
The argument here, however, goes much further. It is
argued that the events leading up to the 1798 rebellion
indicate that neither nation, as defined in Chapter 2, had
come into existence by the end of the eighteenth century.

Following the self-definition approach, a group of
people constitute a nation if they believe themselves to
be a nation. However, a group of people cannot regard
themselves as a nation unless they have some awareness of
what a nation is. They must, in other words, subscribe to
the general nationalist world outlook (or national ideal)
which emerged in France and Germany in the late eighteenth
and early nineteenth centuries. Nations, as we now know
them, post-date rather than pre-date the emergence of
nationalism and nationalist ideologies.

This is not to say that groups resembling nations did
not exist in earlier periods. People have tended to
identify with in-groups and recognise others as outsiders
throughout history, but it was not until the nineteenth

century that political loyalties began to consciously
focus on cultural groups. Gaelic Ireland, for example,
was characterised by a high degree of cultural uniformity,
but the political system, as in many other parts of
Europe, was highly fragmented. Political loyalties in
Gaelic Ireland tended to be fluid and cut across cultural
divisions. Cultural differences, for example, did not
prevent alliances between Gaelic and Viking leaders in
their wars against other Gaelic and Viking leaders, nor
did cultural differences prevent alliances later between
Gaelic and Anglo-Norman lords.

Cultural attributes were sometimes used as a rallying
cry by leaders trying to muster support for wars in the
late medieval period. Hugh O'Neill, for example,
attempted to rally support from the other Gaelic lords in
his struggle against Elizabeth I through an appeal based
on common religion and Gaelic culture. However, the Tudor
wars were a continuation of the struggle between the
centralising monarchy of the Tudors and the more powerful
lords in peripheral regions (i.e. the élites on either
side), rather than a war between the English and Irish
nations (i.e. the common people). The concept of a nation
did not assume its modern form until people began to
become citizens, rather than merely subjects, following
the growth of democracy.

The American War of Independence played a major part in
the struggle for democracy, but it was the French
Revolution which established the nation (i.e. the people),
rather than the king, as the basis of legitimate political
power. Both events had a major impact upon the growth of
a 'national' consciousness in Ireland: the American War of
Independence inspired demands for free trade and
democratic reforms by the Irish Volunteers, whereas the
French Revolution inspired a resurgence of demands for
democratic reforms in the following decade by the United
Irishmen. However, 'national' consciousness was still
largely confined to the Protestant middle classes.

It was not until the period of Daniel O'Connell that the

vast bulk of the Catholic population became politically mobilised. O'Connell, more than anyone, mobilised the Irish Catholic population in support of a common political objective. However, the Irish people did not gel into a nation until after the introduction of the general nationalist ideology by the Young Ireland movement in the 1840s. Meanwhile, northern Protestants increasingly began to identify with the British nation and British state.

THE HISTORICAL SPECIFICITY OF NATIONALISM

The comparatively recent advent of nationalism in Ireland is by no means peculiar to Ireland: other groups of people only became nationalistic elsewhere around the same time. This raises questions as to why nationalism became such a pervasive ideology at this particular point in history. Was it simply a new outlook, invented for no particular reason, which became fashionable because of its inherent attractive qualities, or was it a reflection of other changes occurring around the same time? The argument here is that nationalism emerged at this particular point in history because it satisfied psychological needs arising out of changes (sometimes referred to as 'modernisation') associated with the growth and penetration of industrial capitalism. The growth of nationalism consequently tended to mirror the spatial penetration of capitalist relations. In the case of Ireland, the growth of nationalism in the nineteenth century reflected the spatial diffusion of modernisation from east to west.

The French Revolution established the concept of the nation (i.e. the citizens of a state) as the basis of legitimate political power, but the full nationalist ideology, stressing the supposedly natural and inviolable nature of nations (recognised by their cultural attributes), only emerged in Germany and Italy in the early nineteenth century. In both areas political fragmentation hindered the development of market conditions suitable for the growth of competitive capitalism. Nationalism, stressing the importance of cultural groups as the natural basis for state delimitation (as opposed to relict feudal territories), consequently emerged as a powerful ideology for mobilising support from all sections of society for 'national unity'.

The nationalist outlook quickly diffused to other parts of Europe where it had an appeal because of aspirations or fears generated by the changes associated with the growth of industrial capitalism. However, modernisation, and the associated growth of nationalism, took different forms in different places. In some areas, and for some groups of people, nationalism had an appeal because it challenged the old order and offered hopes of radical progressive change. In other areas, and for other groups of people, nationalism had an appeal for those who felt threatened by the changes associated with modernisation because it emphasised continuity with the past. In each instance the intelligentsia (i.e. the educated middle classes) were the first, because of their education, to be aware of the new ideas coming in from outside. The intelligentsia were consequently important as early propagators of nationalist ideas and were also frequently prominent in the initial leaderships of national independence movements. The other classes only became mobilised at a later date. In many areas the intelligentsia were drawn from, and represented the interests of, the emerging industrial bourgeoisie; but this was not always the case. Eastern Europe, for example, was generally less industrialised than western Europe; consequently the intelligentsia in many parts of eastern Europe were more often drawn from the landed classes.

Nationalism developed differently in each area depending upon the specific combination of local conditions, but a broad distinction may be made between the growth of nationalism in eastern and western Europe. Apart from being less industrialised, eastern Europe differed from

western Europe with respect to its existing political
structures. Eastern Europe was politically divided
between four large multicultural empires (i.e. the
Prussian, Russian, Austrian and Ottoman), whereas western
Europe was divided into a much larger number of
long-established but smaller states. National identities
in western Europe generally tended to focus upon the
existing states which, with the growth of industrial
capitalism, increasingly came into conflict with one
another as the nineteenth century progressed in the quest
for overseas colonies as a source of cheap raw materials
and as a market for manufactured goods. Nationalism in
western Europe consequently intensified with the growth of
imperialism.

Nationalism in eastern Europe, on the other hand, tended
to follow the German and Italian models more closely by
emphasising cultural characteristics rather than
identifying with the existing political units (i.e.
empires). However, whereas the objective of the German
and Italian nationalists was to create a larger political
unit by unifying smaller political units, the objective of
most east European nationalists was to create smaller
political units by establishing independence from the
existing empires.

Ireland is perhaps peculiar by providing examples of
both the east European and west European models. Irish
nationalism in many respects represents an example of the
east European model in western Europe - i.e. it arose out
of a desire to separate from an existing empire. Ulster
unionism, in contrast, fits into the west European model -
i.e. unionists identified with the state in which they
lived and sought to preserve its integrity.

THE MATERIAL BASIS OF NATIONALISM AND UNIONISM

The growth of nationalism in the nineteenth century, it
is argued, tended to reflect local conditions. Local

conditions in Ireland, however, varied to such an extent
that they were reflected by the growth of two quite
distinct national identities. The nineteenth century was
a period of economic prosperity and rapid urban industrial
growth based on textiles, engineering and shipbuilding in
the greater Belfast region. Northern Protestants,
benefitting from the growth in economic prosperity, had
little reason to oppose the constitutional status quo
and consequently developed a sense of British national
identity in much the same way as people in England,
Scotland or Wales did around the same time.

Elsewhere in Ireland the nineteenth century was a period
of decline, or at best stagnation, characterised by crises
in the predominantly rural economy (reaching an apex in
the Great Famine of the 1840s). The response to these
crises was a massive restructuring of the agricultural
economy which in turn resulted in the forced migration of
the poorest sections of the rural population to Britain
and, increasingly as the century progressed, to North
America. Economic decline and social change generated
feelings of intense deprivation amongst the impoverished,
feelings of frustration amongst the upwardly socially
mobile Catholic middle classes, and feelings of anxiety
amongst the downwardly socially mobile Protestant
ascendancy classes. Nationalism, with its glorification
of the past and its promise of a brighter future, held an
appeal for each of these groups, although for different
reasons. The Catholic middle classes saw increased
national autonomy as a means of circumventing the
remaining social and economic barriers to further
progress; the impoverished sections of society were led to
believe that national independence would in some way solve
the problems of social inequality; whilst some members of
the ascendancy classes, feeling their position being
undermined by the British parliament and feeling
themselves being peripheralised by the growing importance
of the Catholic middle classes, saw secular nationalism
and increased autonomy as a means of reversing the trends

towards downward social mobility and peripheralisation.
In the later parts of the century, however, following the
further growth in power of the Catholic middle classes and
the development of a specifically Catholic form of Irish
nationalism, most members of the ascendancy classes
believed their interests would be better safeguarded by
unionism.

Northern Protestants identified with the British state
because they had little reason not to, but unionism (an
intense form of British nationalism) entailed much more
than an identification with the British state - it also
entailed an intense distrust of, and antagonism towards,
Irish nationalism, especially when the latter became very
closely identified with Catholicism and a stereotyped
image of Gaelic culture in the last two decades of the
nineteenth century. Northern Protestants, conscious of
the threat posed by Irish nationalism to the economic
prosperity of industry in the north-east, and fearful of
the growing social power of the Catholic Church, espoused
values opposite to those espoused by Irish nationalism:
viz. Protestant notions of religious freedom, progress
through urban industrialisation, and of course opposition
to the possibility of political domination by an Irish
nationalist dominated Dublin parliament. Ulster unionism,
like Irish nationalism, appealed to different groups of
people for different reasons, resulting in a convergence
of interests on the national question between different
religious denominations, between town and country, and
between different social classes. Unionism can in many
respects be regarded as a reaction to the growth of Irish
nationalism.

Many Irish nationalists tend to regard unionism as
ephemeral compared with Irish nationalism. Northern
Protestants are consequently regarded as members of the
Irish nation who were duped by unionist propaganda into
frustrating the historic destiny of the nation.
Unionists, in other words, are regarded as traitors who
deserted the rest of the nation in its historic struggle

for independence. However, this interpretation fails to
recognise the equally modern origins of Irish nationalism.
The 'historic' struggle for national independence,
depicted by Irish nationalists as the principal objective
in Irish politics since at least the time of Brian Boru,
in fact only gained the full support of the Irish nation
after the 1916 rebellion. Before 1916 the majority of
Irish people favoured some form of autonomy (e.g. home
rule) within the context of the United Kingdom rather than
total independence. Had history taken a slightly
different course, the Anglo-Irish War of Independence
might have been avoided and the national identity in
Ireland today might not have been too different from that
in other parts of the United Kingdom - i.e. Irish in terms
of culture, but British in terms of political allegiance.
Viewed in this way, it was not the Ulster unionists who
broke from the Irish nation; rather it was the Irish
nation which broke away from the British state - the
unionists simply refused to reverse the modernising trends
of the nineteenth century towards further integration with
Britain.

TWENTIETH CENTURY CONVERGENCE

   The growth of Irish nationalism and Ulster unionism in
the nineteenth century resulted in partition and the
creation of an independent Irish state in the 1920s.
Partition and independence subsequently served to polarise
attitudes on the national question to an even greater
extent than hitherto.
   Nationalism is a political ideology based on the desire
for self-government. If self-government does not already
exist, then the group for which self-government is sought
must be defined in cultural terms, and must be seen to be
clearly different from the culture of the people from whom
self-government is sought in order to mobilise support.
National independence is consequently often followed by a

period of 'Ayatollahism' during which the perceived unique
cultural traits of the nation are vigorously propagated
and foreign traits are zealously expunged. This is what
happened in the Free State in the first few decades of
independence (e.g. see Brown, 1981), but in so doing Irish
nationalists drove the wedge further between themselves
and the unionists.

The reluctance of the Irish nationalist minority within
Northern Ireland to accept partition reinforced unionist
fears that the minority were set upon the overthrow of the
Northern Ireland state. This in turn resulted in the
exclusion of Catholics from an equal participation in
public life, thereby reinforcing a belief amongst
Catholics that Northern Ireland was inherently sectarian
and that social equality could only be achieved in the
context of a united Ireland.

The present troubles can be regarded as the logical
outcome of this process of polarisation, but it is
important to note that the material conditions which
originally gave rise to the two sets of conflicting
national identities have now largely disappeared. The
difference in living standards which previously existed
between Northern Ireland and the Republic has been eroded
by the recent more rapid rate of economic growth in the
Republic: indeed a recent report published in the Irish
Banking Review suggests that living standards in the
Republic had overtaken those in Northern Ireland by 1981
(Irish Times, 7th. July, 1984). More important,
however, is the fact that the economic policies in both
parts of Ireland have converged in response to changing
economic conditions (Walsh, 1979). A high level of
unemployment caused by a decline in the traditional
industries forced the Northern Ireland government to adopt
a policy of providing incentives to attract industrial
investment from overseas in the 1950s. Meanwhile, the
government in the Republic, recognising that little
further could be gained from protective economic policies,
adopted a similar strategy. Economic convergence has

270

subsequently been reinforced by the entry of both the
Republic and the United Kingdom into the E.E.C.

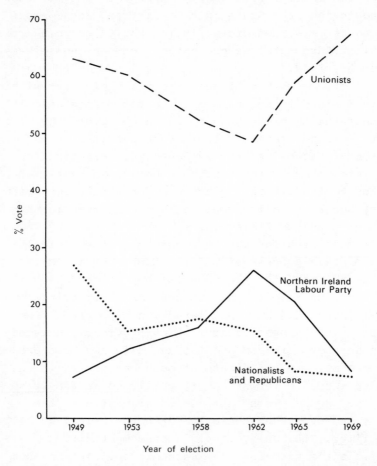

FIG. 25   Percentage Of Votes For Each Of The Major Parties
          In Northern Ireland General Elections, 1949-69.

The net effect of these economic changes is that the
material considerations which originally underlay the
growth of Irish nationalism and Ulster unionism have now
been rendered historically obsolete. Industrialisation in
the Republic has undermined the need for protective
economic policies (one of the motivating forces underlying

separatism); whereas the decline of the traditional
industries in Northern Ireland, which depended upon free
access to the resources and markets of the British Empire,
has undermined the necessity of the British link. The
national question in Ireland, in short, no longer has any
real material basis.

The indications are that the national question was in
fact beginning to recede as a major political issue in the
late 1950s and early 1960s. Economic convergence, as
reported in Chapter 8, resulted in a rapprochement between
the northern and southern governments in the 1960s. This
in turn signalled the beginning of a brief period of
improved relations between the two communities within
Northern Ireland. The changing political climate was
reflected in Northern Ireland by a decline in electoral
support for both Unionists and Nationalists, and an
upsurge in support for the Northern Ireland Labour Party,
which achieved its highest percentage of the votes ever
(26 per cent) in the 1962 general elections (Figure 25).
Meanwhile the IRA was forced to terminate an offensive
which it had been conducting in the border areas since
1956 because of public apathy. The IRA leadership, in
winding up the campaign in February 1962, bitterly
complained about the decline of interest in the national
question:

> 'Foremost among the factors responsible for the
> ending of the campaign has been the attitude of
> the general public whose minds have been
> deliberately distracted from the supreme issue
> facing Irish people - the unity and freedom of
> Ireland.' (Quoted in Harkness, 1983, p131).

Although the material conditions were conducive to the
relegation of the national question from the political
limelight, thereby permitting the possibility of greater
emphasis being given to other issues (such as economic
development and social equality), the national question
was manipulated as a distractive ploy by conservative
elements whose relatively privileged positions might have

been undermined by any departure from the traditional form of politics. Thus, for example, the civil rights movement in Northern Ireland was depicted by conservative Unionists as a front for the IRA, with the result that the civil rights issue became inextricably entwined with the national question. The net effect was a return to nationalistic politics, reflected for example by the decline in electoral support for the Northern Ireland Labour Party in the late 1960s (see Figure 25). The emphasis placed upon the national question generated renewed sectarian tension, eventually culminating in the outbreak of widespread violence. Violence, in turn, has resulted in further polarisation and reinforced the central position of the national question in Irish politics.

However, although the national question has been re-established as the major issue in Irish politics since the late 1960s, it is important to note that many of the modernising trends apparent in the early 1960s have continued, both north and south, throughout the 1970s in response to changes in the underlying material conditions.

The Roman Catholic Church, for example, still occupies a very powerful position in the Republic, but all the signs point to a continuation of the present trend towards a more secular and liberal society, to the extent that it is now very difficult to imagine a confrontation between church and state taking a similar course to the one which resulted in the collapse of the government in 1951 over the proposed mother and child scheme. Likewise, censorship is now much more relaxed than it was, while formerly taboo subjects such as contraception and divorce are now discussed openly and will probably be the subject of more liberal legislation in the not too distant future.

There would also appear to be a shift in public opinion in the Republic on the national question. People in the Republic now appear to be much better informed about the true nature of the conflict in Northern Ireland. When the troubles began in the late 1960s, many people in the south

seemed to believe that the British government represented
the major (or even the only) barrier to unification. Now,
most people in the Republic (despite the impression
created by the politicians) realise that the major barrier
to a united Ireland is the opposition of the unionist
majority in Northern Ireland.

Perhaps of even more importance is the fact that a
substantial number of people in the Republic now appear to
be indifferent about the goal of a united Ireland.
According to a recent opinion poll carried out by MORI for
London Weekend Television, 75 per cent of the people
interviewed in the Republic would like to see a united
Ireland - the other 25 per cent are presumably opposed to
the idea (Irish Times, 22nd. August, 1984). 42 per
cent of those interviewed said that they would accept
Northern Ireland remaining part of the United Kingdom. 18
per cent even said that they would be prepared to accept
majority rule (i.e. unionist rule) in Northern Ireland.
The degree of commitment to the sacred goal of a united
Ireland would seem to be much less than one might imagine
from listening to southern politicians. However, these
results probably disguise the true extent of southern
indifference to the national question. An opinion poll
conducted by the Market Research Bureau of Ireland before
the November 1982 general election in the Republic found
that only 5 per cent of those interviewed perceived the
Northern Ireland problem as a major issue (Irish
Times, 23rd. November, 1982). Issues perceived as more
important included unemployment (75 per cent), inflation
(31 per cent), social welfare (15 per cent), government
finances (14 per cent), inequitable taxation (12 per cent)
and crime and vandalism (11 per cent).

Evidence of changing attitudes in Northern Ireland is
less obvious. This is hardly surprising given that one of
the major effects of the continuing violence is to
polarise the two communities and to reinforce mutual
bigotry based upon ignorance. Nevertheless, there are
some indications of positive change. Many Protestants, I

believe, have a better understanding of the problems faced
by the Catholic minority and would now make a much clearer
distinction between the national question and issues
relating to civil rights. Many would also make a much
clearer distinction between Catholics prepared to work
with the state (e.g. High Court Judges - regarded as
legitimate targets by the IRA) and nationalists, and
between nationalists seeking to achieve their objectives
by peaceful means and those who resort to violence.

It should also be remembered that a significant minority
of Northern Ireland voters of both religions (about 10 per
cent) still vote for parties (such as the Alliance Party)
which attempt to bridge the sectarian divide, despite the
polarising effects of violence. Further, although most
Catholics vote for parties which favour a united Ireland,
a survey of opinion polls in Northern Ireland between 1974
and 1982 by a group of Belfast academics, calling
themselves the Integration Group, found that the
percentage of Catholics favouring a united Ireland as
their first choice for a solution to the Northern Ireland
problem was never higher than 41 per cent (Irish
Times, 22nd. August, 1984). Indeed, the highest
percentage of Catholics in Northern Ireland who saw a
united Ireland as even an 'acceptable' solution was only
66 per cent; whereas 45 per cent said that they would
regard total integration into the United Kingdom as
acceptable. The results of opinion polls must always be
treated with caution, but the evidence would seem to
suggest that even the group which would appear to have
most to gain from a united Ireland do not regard the goal
of national independence as having overriding importance.

DISCUSSION

Having summarised the major points of the argument, it
only remains to consider some of its implications. The
question which we must consider now is whether the

analysis presented in this book provides any basis for a
solution to the national problem.

The solution to any problem very much depends upon what
one thinks the problem is. In this instance most people
tend to think simply of the problem in terms of the
continuing conflict over the constitutional position of
Northern Ireland. However, it is argued here that the
major problems facing the people of Ireland, both north
and south, are the ones affecting their material
well-being - i.e. unemployment, inadequate housing,
emigration, etc. Although the national question formerly
had a considerable direct bearing upon these problems, the
convergence of the two economies in the last few decades
has rendered the national question increasingly irrelevant
to the material well-being of people in both parts of the
island. The national conflict, in short, no longer has a
real material basis - it is simply a conflict between two
competing ideologies which reflect the material conditions
of a now bygone age.

This is not to say, however, that the national conflict
does not have a bearing upon the material well-being of
the people in both parts of Ireland. On the contrary, it
has a considerable bearing upon their material well-being,
but its impact is almost entirely destructive. This
impact has been more pronounced in Northern Ireland, where
it is estimated that 39,000 jobs were lost in the 1970s
because of the violence (Rowthorn, 1981), but it has also
had a damaging effect upon the economy in the Republic
(New Ireland Forum, 1984).

The economic costs of the violence provide an obvious
example of the negative impact of the national question.
However, its impact upon the nature of Irish politics is
possibly of even greater concern. Politics in both parts
of Ireland have traditionally been dominated by
conservative groups with a strong vested interest in
maintaining the status quo. Politics in Northern
Ireland before the troubles were dominated by the Unionist
party, representing the interests of landowners and the

industrial bourgeoisie, although for the most part
enjoying widespread support from the rest of the
Protestant community. Whenever this support appeared
threatened, as for example during the 1920s, the Unionists
were always able to re-establish their authority by
accusing their opponents of being in league with the
nationalists. The Nationalist party, by intransigently
insisting upon the overriding importance of the national
question, assisted the Unionists in maintaining their
hegemony over the Protestant working classes by providing
the illusion of a nationalist threat to their material
well-being. By maintaining the centrality of the national
question, the Unionists and Nationalists between them
successfully managed to block any possible development of
a strong working class opposition.

The situation began to change to some extent in the
early 1960s when economic convergence began to undermine
the material basis of the national question. However, the
conservative elements on both sides, fearing the potential
implications of any digression from the traditional form
of politics, manipulated the situation by reinterpreting
developments in nationalistic terms. Catholic frustration
caused by the slow rate of reforms, coupled with
Protestant fears of a nationalist conspiracy worked up by
conservative Unionist politicians, eventually culminated
in violence and polarisation, thereby ensuring the
survival of nationalistic politics (and the exclusion of
any form of progressive politics) for as long as the
violence and polarisation continue. However, it is
perhaps significant that even the renewed emphasis placed
upon the national question could not prevent the
disintegration of both the traditional Unionist and
Nationalist parties. Although no less unionist or
nationalist than their predecessors, the emergence of new
parties such as the Democratic Unionist Party, Social
Democratic and Labour Party, and (Provisional) Sinn Féin
represents a significant shift towards a less élitist form
of public representation.

The national question has also helped to prevent the development of class-based politics in the Republic. Southern politics are dominated by two basically conservative parties which are now virtually indistinguishable except for their attitudes on the national question. Fianna Fáil and Fine Gael each favours a united Ireland, but Fianna Fáil (following the tradition of the anti-Treaty forces in the 1922-3 civil war) adopts, at least in theory, a less compromising stance. Despite the recent changes in Irish society generated by industrial urbanisation, the major cleavage in southern Irish party politics is still largely centred on the national question, although many other issues, as noted above, are regarded by Irish voters as much more important. However, it is very unlikely that either of the major parties, representing the interests of the more affluent sections of Irish society, will adopt the radical policies required to tackle these problems in any meaningful way. In the meantime, relatively minor differences on the national question (which I have argued is historically irrelevant anyway) are magnified and publicised to distract attention away from the more fundamental problems in Irish society.

Nationalism in the early nineteenth century was a revolutionary doctrine; it still is today in many Third World countries. In Ireland, however, the national question is used by socially-conservative vested-interest groups to help maintain their hegemony by diverting the energies of more radical groups into a conflict which no longer has any real material basis. The national question consequently represents a major barrier to social progress, both north and south. This creates a dilemma, for those who would like to see the development of a more equitable society, about what should be done about the national question.

There are two possible strategies in this respect. The first is to resolve the national question before turning one's attention to questions of social reform. This would

appear to be the strategy of the more progressive elements
within the INLA and IRA. However, this strategy has a
number of drawbacks, the most serious of which is the fact
that there is little likelihood of achieving a united
Ireland in the foreseeable future given the vehement
opposition of one million unionists. In the meantime,
meaningful social progress is hampered because the
solidarity required to bring about such changes is divided
by national conflict. Also, even if the national question
could be resolved, there is no guarantee that social
reforms would necessarily follow: national independence in
the Republic does not appear to have eliminated social
inequalities - it simply facilitated the emergence of a
new conservative national élite.

The second strategy is to recognise the divisive and
counter-productive nature of the national question and to
work towards social reforms within the existing
constitutional framework. Progress, following this
strategy, is likely to prove difficult, especially within
Northern Ireland, given the polarising effects of the
violence reinforced by a communications gap compounded by
segregated education and ghettoisation. Nevertheless,
given the unlikelihood of one side either defeating or
surrendering to the other, it might be better to ignore
the national question whilst working towards the creation
of a more just society in both parts of Ireland, rather
than deferring all efforts in this regard until the
national question is eventually resolved (if ever).

Although there are no simple solutions to the national
problem, there are a number of steps which could be taken
at this stage to defuse the conflict and thereby
facilitate the development towards long-term progress. An
essential prerequisite, so long as the conflict is viewed
within a nationalistic perspective, is for each side to
recognise the national rights of the other. This would
require the Republic, for example, to drop its claims to
the territory of Northern Ireland as enshrined in articles
2 and 3 of the Constitution of Ireland. This, it should

be noted, would not require Irish nationalists to relinquish their aspirations of a united Ireland: it would simply require the existing aggressive (and rather meaningless) articles to be replaced by articles expressing a desire for a united Ireland with the consent of the Northern Ireland majority.

An acceptance of the existence of two nations in Ireland, and of each nation's rights to self-determination, by the Republic would go a long way towards eliminating unionist fears of annexation. However, acceptance of the two nations theory also requires unionists to recognise the existence of two nations within Northern Ireland. Catholics within Northern Ireland are not simply a religious minority, they are a national minority whose national rights should be recognised and safeguarded, providing that they do not interfere with the national rights of the majority nation. Laws which prohibit the flying of the Irish flag and the use of the Irish language for street names (even in nationalist areas) could, for example, be repealed. Also, in return for a guarantee that they would not be coerced into a united Ireland against their will, unionists could perhaps be persuaded to accept that the Irish government has a legitimate interest in the welfare of its co-nationals living within Northern Ireland.

The mutual recognition by each nation of the rights of the other would help to defuse the present conflict, but the only hope for peace and social progress in the long-term would seem to be to work towards building a post-nationalist (and post-unionist) society in which the national question would be seen as having no real significance. This, paradoxically, could actually create the conditions for a united Ireland. At present unionists are not even prepared to consider the possibility of a united Ireland because it would be seen as a defeat by Irish nationalists. But, if the national question was no longer regarded as important, and if the Republic continued along its present course of secularisation and modernisation to become more acceptable (and perhaps even attractive) to northern Protestants, the pragmatic advantages of unification might eventually be sufficient to give rise to a united Ireland. However, by that time it is unlikely that very many will care either one way or the other.

It is difficult to imagine any dramatic shifts in peoples' attitudes within the immediate future as long as the violence continues, or indeed for a long time after. Nevertheless, given the convergence in the northern and southern economies, the national question no longer has any real material basis; consequently a post-nationalist society must emerge sooner or later. The objective of progressive forces within Ireland, both north and south, should be to try to make it sooner. The construction of a post-nationalist society will take time and will require a gradual process of education about the evolution of nationalism and the national conflict. It is hoped that this book may in some way help to further such a process.

References

Adamson, I. (1982). The Identity Of Ulster. Belfast.

Baker, S. (1973). 'Orange and Green. Belfast, 1832-1912', in Dyos, H.J. and Wolff, M. (eds.), The Victorian City - Images And Realities. Routledge and Kegan Paul, London.

Barritt, D.P. and Carter, C.F. (1962). The Northern Ireland Problem. Oxford University Press, London.

Beckitt, J.C. (1966). The Making Of Modern Ireland, 1603-1923. Faber and Faber, London.

BICO (1971). The Home Rule Crisis, 1912-14. BICO, Belfast.

BICO (1972). Aspects Of Nationalism. BICO, Belfast.

BICO (1973). Ulster As It Is. BICO, Belfast.

BICO (1974). The Origin And Progress Of The Irish Union. Athol Books, Belfast.

BICO (1975). The Two Irish Nations. BICO, Belfast.

Boyce, D.G. (1982). Nationalism In Ireland. Gill and Macmillan, Dublin.

Brown, T. (1981). Ireland. A Social And Cultural History, 1922-79. Fontana, London.

Buchanan, R. (1982). 'The Planter and the Gael: Cultural Dimensions of the Northern Ireland Problem', in Boal, F.W. and Douglas, J.N.H. (eds.), Integration And Division: Geographical Perspectives On The Northern Ireland Problem. Academic Press, London.

Buckland, P. (1973). Irish Unionism, 1885-1922. General Pamphlet 81, The Historical Association, London.

Buckland, P. (1975). 'The Unity Of Ulster Unionism, 1886-1939'. History, 60, 211-223.

Buckland, P. (1979). The Factory Of Grievances: Devolved Government In Northern Ireland, 1921-39. Gill and Macmillan, Dublin.

Budge, I. and O'Leary, C. (1973). Belfast: Approach To Crisis. Macmillan, London.

282

Busteed, M.A. (1972). Northern Ireland: Geographical
Aspects Of A Crisis. Research Paper 3, Department of
Geography, Oxford University.

Byrne, F.J. (1967). 'Early Irish Society (1st.-9th.
Century)', in Moody, T.W. and Martin, F.X. (eds.), The
Course Of Irish History. Mercier, Cork.

Coakley, J. (1980). 'Self-Government for Gaelic Ireland:
The Development of State Language Policy'. Europa
Ethnica, 37(3), 114-124.

Collins, M.E. (1980). Ireland, 1478-1610.
Educational Company, Dublin.

Cosgrove, A. (1981). Late Medieval Ireland,
1370-1541. Helicon, Dublin.

Curtis, T.C. and McDowell, R.B. (1977). Irish
Historical Documents, 1172-1922, 3rd. edition.
Methuen, London.

Daly, M.E. (1981). Social And Economic History Of
Ireland Since 1800. Educational Company, Dublin.

Dolley, M. (1972). Anglo-Norman Ireland. Gill and
Macmillan, Dublin.

Fanning, R. (1983). Independent Ireland. Helicon,
Dublin.

Farrell, M. (1976). Northern Ireland: The Orange
State. Pluto Press, London.

Fitzpatrick, D. (1978). 'The Geography of Irish
Nationalism'. Past And Present, 78, 113-144.

Flackes, W.D. (1980). Northern Ireland: A Political
Directory, 1968-79. Gill and Macmillan, Dublin.

Garvin, T. (1981). The Evolution Of Irish Nationalist
Politics. Gill and Macmillan, Dublin.

Gellner, E. (1964). 'Nationalism', in Thought And
Change. Weidenfeld and Nicholson, London.

Gibbon, P. (1975). The Origins Of Ulster Unionism.
Manchester University Press, Manchester.

Harkness, D. (1983). Northern Ireland Since 1920.
Helicon, Dublin.

Hepburn, A.C. (1980). The Conflict Of Nationality In
Modern Ireland. Edward Arnold, London.

Heslinga, M.W. (1962). The Irish Border As A Cultural
Divide. Van Gorcum, Assen.

Hoare, A.G. (1981). 'Why They Go Where They Go: The
Political Imagery of Industrial Location'.
Transactions, Institute of British Geographers,
6(2), 152-175.

ICO (1966). The Working Class In The Irish National
Revolution, 1916-23. ICO, London.

Jackson, T.A. (1947). Ireland Her Own: An Outline
History Of The Irish Struggle. Cobbett Press, London.

Jones, E. (1960). A Social Geography Of Belfast.
Oxford University Press, London.

Jones Hughes, T. (1965). 'Society and Settlement in
Nineteenth Century Ireland'. Irish Geography, 5(2),
79-96.

Kamenka, E. (1973). Nationalism: The Nature And
Evolution Of An Idea. Edward Arnold, London.

Kee, R. (1972). The Green Flag: A History Of Irish
Nationalism. Quartet, London.

Lee, J. (1973). The Modernisation Of Irish Society,
1848-1918. Gill and Macmillan, Dublin.

McCartney, D. (1967). 'From Parnell To Pearse
(1891-1921)', in Moody, T.W. and Martin, F.X. (eds.),
The Course Of Irish History. Mercier, Cork.

McDowell, R.B. (1967). 'The Protestant Nation
(1775-1800)', in Moody, T.W. and Martin, F.X. (eds.),
The Course Of Irish History. Mercier, Cork.

Mac Niocaill, G. (1973). Ireland Before The Vikings.
Gill and Macmillan, Dublin.

Mackie, J.D. (1964). A History Of Scotland. Penguin,
Harmondsworth.

Martin, F.X. (1967). 'The Anglo-Norman Invasion
(1169-c.1300)', in Moody, T.W. and Martin, F.X. (eds.),
The Course Of Irish History. Mercier, Cork.

Matthew, R. (1963). Belfast Regional Survey And Plan.
Cmd. 451, HMSO, Belfast.

284

Mitchell, G.F. (1967). 'Prehistoric Ireland', in Moody, T.W. and Martin, F.X. (eds.), The Course Of Irish History. Mercier, Cork.

Murphy, J.A. (1975). Ireland In The Twentieth Century. Gill and Macmillan, Dublin.

Nairn, T. (1977). The Breakup Of Britain. New Left Books, London.

New Ireland Forum (1984). New Ireland Forum Report. Government Stationary Office, Dublin.

Nicholls, K. (1972). Gaelic And Gaelicised Ireland In The Middle Ages. Gill and Macmillan, Dublin.

Nicholls, K. (1976). Map 1 in Moody, T.W., Martin, F.X., and Byrne, F.J. (eds), A New History Of Ireland. Oxford University Press, London.

Ó Corráin, D. (1972). Ireland Before The Normans. Gill and Macmillan, Dublin.

Ó Corráin, D. (1977). 'Nationality and Kingship in Pre-Norman Ireland', in Moody, T.W. (ed.), Nationality And The Pursuit Of Irish Independence. Appletree, Belfast.

Ó Tuathaigh, G. (1972). Ireland Before The Famine, 1798-1848. Gill and Macmillan, Dublin.

Orme, A.R. (1970). Ireland. Longman, London.

Probert, B. (1978). Beyond Orange And Green. Academy Press, London.

Robinson, P. (1982). 'Plantation and Colonisation: The Historical Background' in Boal, F.W. and Douglas, J.N.H. (eds.), Integration And Division: Geographical Perspectives On The Northern Ireland Problem. Academic Press, London.

Rowthorn, W. (1981). 'Northern Ireland: An Economy in Crisis'. Cambridge Review of Economics, 5.

Rumpf, E. and Hepburn, A.C. (1976). Nationalism And Socialism In Twentieth Century Ireland. Liverpool University Press, Liverpool.

Seton-Watson, H. (1977). Nations And States: An Enquiry Into The Origins Of Nations And The Politics Of Nationalism. Methuen, London.

285

Shafer, B.C. (1972). Faces Of Nationalism. Harcourt, New York.

Simms, J.G. (1958). The Williamite Confiscation In Ireland, 1690-1703. Faber and Faber, London.

Simpson, J. (1983). 'Economic Development: Cause or Effect in the Northern Ireland Conflict', in Darby, J. (ed.), Northern Ireland: The Background To The Conflict. Appletree, Belfast.

Smith, A.D. (1971). Theories Of Nationalism. Duckworth, London.

Stalin, J. (1913). Marxism And The National Question. Reprinted by BICO, Belfast, 1971.

Stewart, A.T.Q. (1977). The Narrow Ground: Aspects Of Ulster, 1609-1969. Faber and Faber, London.

Van Der Wusten, H. (1980). 'The United Kingdom and its Contenders, 1800-1922'. Netherlands Journal of Sociology, 16, 171-184.

Walker, B. (1973). 'The Irish Electorate, 1868-1915'. Irish Historical Studies, 18, 359-406.

Walsh, F. (1979). 'The Changing Industrial Structures of Northern and Southern Ireland'. Maynooth Review, 5(2), 3-14.

Whyte, J.H. (1967). 'The Age of Daniel O'Connell (1800-47)', in Moody, T.W. and Martin, F.X. (eds.), The Course Of Irish History. Mercier, Cork.

Wilson, T. (1965). Economic Development in Northern Ireland. Cmd. 479, HMSO, Belfast.

Author Index

General Index

290

291